*The*
*Author*

William Strawson, a Methodist minister, was born in Lincolnshire, England, and was educated at Cambridge and London Universities. During World War II, he was a chaplain in the Royal Air Force, and from 1946 to 1955 was a circuit minister. In 1955, Mr. Strawson was appointed Tutor in Systematic Theology and Philosophy of Religion at the University of Birmingham. In 1959, he presented *Jesus and the Future Life* as the Fernley-Hartley Lecture at Bristol. He is a contributor to British religious journals.

# JESUS AND
# THE FUTURE LIFE

*The Fernley-Hartley Lecture 1959*
*A Synopsis of which was delivered at*
*The New Room, Broadmead, Bristol,*
*on 7th July 1959*

# JESUS AND
# THE FUTURE LIFE

## A STUDY IN THE SYNOPTIC GOSPELS

by

### WILLIAM STRAWSON

THE WESTMINSTER PRESS : PHILADELPHIA

© *The Epworth Press 1959*

*Library of Congress Catalog Card No. 60-5617*

TYPESET IN GREAT BRITAIN

PRINTED IN THE U.S.A.

TO

ENA AND JAMES

IN LOVE

# CONTENTS

PREFACE . . . . . . . ix

1 INTRODUCTION . . . . . . 1

2 HEAVEN . . . . . . . 16

3 HEAVENLY FATHER . . . . . 40

4 KINGDOM OF HEAVEN AND KINGDOM OF GOD . 56

5 DEATH . . . . . . . 69

6 JUDGEMENT . . . . . . 107

7 THE FATE OF THE LOST . . . . 137

8 THE DESTINY OF THE SAVED . . . . 156

9 TWO SPECIALLY SIGNIFICANT PASSAGES . . 203

10 CONCLUSION . . . . . . 221

BIBLIOGRAPHY . . . . . . 237

INDEX OF SUBJECTS AND NAMES . . . 240

SCRIPTURAL INDEX . . . . . 244

INDEX OF GREEK WORDS . . . . 250

# PREFACE

THE Doctrine of the Future Life is one which has absorbing interest for large numbers of people. This makes it necessary for the scope and purpose of this study to be clearly stated at the beginning, if only to avoid for the reader the disappointment of discovering that many of his questions are not faced in this book. In particular it is necessary to remember that all philosophical arguments about the reality of the Future Life have been avoided. This is not because all such arguments are valueless, although if pressed I should have to say that in my view the certainty of the Future Life can never be a matter for philosophical demonstration, but must inevitably remain a matter of faith. Equally, attempts to prove a future existence on the basis of psychic phenomena will not, I think, ever be successful. Yet these approaches are not avoided because I have concluded them to be valueless; the reasons for their exclusion are the self-imposed limits of this work. These limits are to inquire what can be discovered from the synoptic gospels about our Lord's attitude on this subject. Without denying the value of other approaches to this subject it must be conceded that the question 'What did Jesus say about the Future Life?' is of the utmost importance to the Christian, and ought to be seriously considered by anyone who is genuinely interested in these matters.

It will be helpful to give here a brief synopsis of the scope and contents of this study. At the beginning I have considered questions which arise when we seek to investigate the words of Jesus. Is the record of these words sufficiently trustworthy to be used as a basis for a detailed consideration of the teaching of our Lord? To answer this question I have briefly stated my views regarding the historicity of the gospels, with special attention to form criticism, typology, and demythologizing. Also in the first chapter I have discussed the relative positions of the individual and the community in our Lord's teaching; a subject which is of special importance because I am trying to answer the question: 'What did Jesus teach about *personal* future life?'

Chapters Two, Three and Four are concerned with the various

uses of the word 'heaven' in the gospels. I have given particular attention to the terms 'Kingdom of heaven' and 'Heavenly Father', for although the New Testament does not use 'heaven' in our modern sense of the abode of the blessed dead, there is considerable value in noticing the 'other-wordly' implications of these terms, which were central in our Lord's teaching.

This is followed in Chapter Five by a study of the fact of death, including our Lord's attitude to the death of others and also his attitude to his own death. In this chapter I have considered the records of the raising of the dead by Jesus, and tried to look at the death of Christ as an indication of the meaning of human death.

Chapter Six is a study of the words used to express the idea of judgement; and also in this chapter I have considered the teaching of the judgement parables. The significant question here is whether the words of judgement and condemnation used by Jesus can be applied to us and to our contemporaries, and to what extent they have a particular reference which forbids a general application.

In Chapter Seven I have discussed what the gospels say about those who do not respond to the offer of the love of God in Christ. This involves a study of the words 'Gehenna', 'Hades', and 'fire'.

The next question to be faced is what is said about the bliss of the saved. In Chapter Eight I have therefore discussed the terms 'Kingdom of God', 'Eternal Life', and 'Blessed'. The first of these expressions is considered in two senses; as that which can be entered, and that which can be received as a gift. Although the term 'Eternal Life' is more fully expounded in the Fourth gospel, we find it in the synoptic gospels, and I have attempted to state what meaning is given to this phrase in the earliest Christian tradition.

The detailed study of the book concludes in Chapter Nine with an exposition of two specially significant passages; namely, the Sadducees' question, and the so called parable of the rich man and Lazarus.

In the concluding chapter I have ventured to sum up my conclusions, and then to suggest answers to the three questions which I judge to be uppermost in the minds of most people as they ponder this subject. These questions are:

(1) Is there a future life?
(2) How is it obtained?
(3) What is it like?

I have thus endeavoured to relate this study to the needs and questions of ordinary men. Of necessity there is much detailed discussion, which I hope will encourage my readers to examine carefully the scriptural evidence I have considered. My hope is that in this way the living truth of the gospel will present itself to those who read. If some find thereby that their way is made a little plainer, and their hope quickened, I shall be well rewarded. I can only say that in the course of these studies I have sometimes felt the division between earth and heaven to be very thin, and the Christian hope in life everlasting has been quickened in my heart. I pray that God will use this study in the same way for those who read, as He has done for him who writes.

The invitation of the Fernley Hartley Trustees to deliver this lecture has provided me with a welcome opportunity and encouragement to pursue these studies, and I thank the Trustees for the honour involved in their generous invitation.

The task of writing this book has been made immeasurably lighter and more pleasant because I have had the generous help and encouragement of my friends. In particular, I have to thank the Principal of this College, the Rev. C. Leslie Mitton, B.A., M.Th., Ph.D., who has read nearly all the work in typescript, and out of his wide knowledge of New Testament study has made many valuable suggestions. The Rev. A. Raymond George, M.A., B.D., has also read the book in typescript, and has helped me in many ways, especially with regard to ensuring a clearer expression of my meaning. At an early stage I had the advantage of an illuminating conversation with the Rev. C. Kingsley Barrett, M.A., D.D. It is perhaps unnecessary to say that none of these scholars can be held responsible for the imperfections which remain; but apart from their kindly and expert help the imperfections would have been far more numerous.

I am indebted to the Rev. Brian E. Beck, M.A., for assistance in making the indices and in reading the proofs, and for the help he has given me in many different ways. I have been very fortunate in the timely help offered to me by Mr Gerald Botteley, who has provided me with the services of a typist, and thus saved me many hours of labour. To him, and to Mrs Mary Perks, who has undertaken the large amount of typing involved, I am very grateful.

But my chief and last word of thanks must be to my wife and son, for it is their encouragement, patience, and love which have made possible the writing of this book.

WILLIAM STRAWSON

HANDSWORTH COLLEGE
*Ascensiontide 1959*

# CHAPTER ONE

# INTRODUCTION

THE aim of this study is to seek an answer to the question 'What did Jesus say about personal future life?' This apparently simple question involves certain assumptions which are seriously challenged by some of the leading tendencies of contemporary New Testament study. This makes it necessary at the outset to state the point of view implied in the attempt to answer this question.

The challenges raised by some present-day tendencies in New Testament study can be expressed in the form of three questions, to which we must essay an answer—

(i) Can we know with certainty what Jesus said on any subject? The answer to this involves the matter of *historicity* in the gospels.

(ii) Are not the terms used in connexion with future life inextricably bound up with a pre-Copernican cosmology which is no longer acceptable? This involves the issue of *mythology*.

(iii) Is not the idea of *personal* future life a false abstraction and perversion of the teaching of the gospels? This raises the question of *the place of the individual and the community* in the teaching of Jesus.

In stating my own views on these issues, it should be emphasized that I am not attempting anything in the nature of a full exposition or critique of the theories involved. My purpose is simply to state the grounds on which I hold this investigation to be legitimate. It is outside the scope of this study to engage in a full appraisal of criticism, of demythologizing and of the place of the individual in the teaching of Jesus. All that can be attempted is a statement of conclusions which seem to be acceptable and which form the basis of this study.

## I. THE QUESTION OF HISTORICITY

The chief challenge to the historical trustworthiness of the synoptic gospels still arises from form criticism. This approach to the gospels emphasizes the several interests and tendencies which were at work in the process by which the gospels came into their present form; and much work has been done on the study of the forms the stories have taken, determined by the various interests of the Church.[1] It is because there is a strong awareness of the life of the early Church in the formation of the gospels, that it has often been supposed that in the gospels, which are admittedly the product of the life of the Church, we have an expression of the mind and interests of the Christian community, read back into the life of Jesus. There is no doubt that this idea of the life of the early Church determining the form of the presentation of the gospel story, has contributed very largely to a feeling of insecurity about the gospel record of the life of Jesus.

It is not necessary to reject all the findings of form criticism in order to see that it is a tool which can easily be over-employed. The strongest single question raised against the wholesale rejection of historicity by some form critics, is an examination of the relation between the thought of the early Church and the emphasis of the gospels. To instance but a few matters which are distinctive of the thought of the early Christian community: there is great emphasis on the Holy Spirit, prophecy, gift of tongues. These distinctive early Church emphases are, however, not at all pronounced in the gospels. In other words, the extreme conclusions of the form-criticism method prove untenable in the light of the known facts of the early Church.[2] The relation between the thought of the first Christians and the records of the life of Jesus is indeed full of interest, and one possibility in this present study is to inquire whether there is discernible a natural development from the basic and germinal concepts of the gospels, to the more fully worked out views of Paul and other early Christian thinkers. But whatever else the relationship may be, it seems no longer possible to hold that the mind of the early Church determined the content as well as the shape of the gospel story. There is without doubt great benefit gained from this study of the influence of the life of the early Church upon the selection and presentation of the records of the life of Jesus; but this method entirely over-reaches itself when it concludes that there is little material of historical trustworthiness in the gospels.

---

[1] See Vincent Taylor, *Formation of the Gospel Tradition*, pp. 22-43.
[2] See B. S. Easton, *The Gospel before the Gospels*, pp. 85ff.

One of the last articles written by T. W. Manson before his recent death is a forceful expression of the view that in spite of form criticism, the historical value of the gospels is to be very highly regarded.[3] The position maintained in this present study cannot be better expressed than by some quotations from this article. Manson points out that after thirty years of form criticism 'it may perhaps be suggested that it has by now done about all that it could do, and more than it ought'.[4] Having recognized the interest of discussion of the units of narrative and teaching, Manson goes on to remind us that while interesting, the discoveries of form criticism are not epoch making, and most of all, they do not invalidate the historical worth of the gospel accounts— 'a paragraph of Mark is not a penny the better or the worse as historical evidence for being labelled "apophthegm" or "pronouncement story" or "paradigm".'[5] Form criticism has in fact become involved with criticism of the trustworthiness of the Marcan outline, and with the question of *Sitz im Leben*: that is, the setting of the gospel narratives in the life of the Church. In both these enterprises Manson believes that a wrong emphasis is very easily expressed. The Marcan outline is to be regarded as basically trustworthy, and the question of the 'setting in life' should be applied to the life of Jesus rather than to that of the primitive Church. Two quotations will be sufficient to indicate Manson's view on these subjects. 'I am increasingly convinced that the Marcan story presents in the main an orderly and logical development; and that this development or framework has as good a title to be considered reliable historical material as any particular anecdote incorporated in it.'[6] 'There is a good deal to be said for treating the gospels as historical documents concerning Jesus of Nazareth rather than as psychological case-material concerning the early Christians.'[7]

Lest these conclusions should give rise to a premature expression of triumph from those who have always said gospel criticism could never come to any good, it is necessary to add that Manson urges that because the gospels have a right to be treated as historical

[3] 'The Life of Jesus: Some tendencies in present-day research', in *The Background of the New Testament and its Eschatology* (1956), pp. 211-21.
[4] Ibid. p. 212. [5] Ibid.
[6] Ibid. p. 213. Vincent Taylor reaches substantially the same conclusion about K. L. Schmidt's alleged shattering of the Marcan outline. VTM, p. 148. (For abbreviations used in footnotes, see Bibliography, pp. 237-9.)
[7] Manson, 'The Life of Jesus', op. cit. p. 215.

documents, this does not mean the abandonment of procedures of historical investigation. 'All this means that we are driven back to the business of treating the gospels (a footnote says 'All four of them') as wholes and in detail—as historical documents, using all the resources of exact scholarship and strict historical method for the task.'[8] Thus we are not committed to avoiding critical questions of authenticity, but we are committed to the basic assumption that in the gospels we have a substantially trustworthy account of what Jesus said and did. This is the position from which this study is undertaken.

Another method of interpreting the New Testament which often appears to raise doubts about historicity is *typology*. Austin Farrer, a leading exponent of this method, has warned us against speaking of 'the typological hypothesis',[9] but we can, nevertheless, characterize this sort of interpretation in general terms. Typology is the method of interpretation which sees resemblances between people and events in the New Testament, and people and events in the Old Testament. It is a method which is used in the New Testament itself,[10] and our Lord's use of the title of Son of Man may well be explained in this way.[11] As Professor Lampe points out,[12] this kind of interpretation was universally employed until the critical study of the Bible rendered it untenable, and in recent years it has gained great importance, especially through such writers as Austin Farrer and L. S. Thornton.[13]

The particular point at issue here is the relation between this kind of interpretation and the question of the historical reliability of the gospels. If we must assume that in records of particular events in the life of Jesus, the authors of the gospels are concerned to demonstrate how Jesus fulfils the type prefigured in the Old Testament, it is not difficult to see how historicity can be pushed into the background. Indeed, Lampe, who is by no means an extreme exponent of typology, can write: 'We learn that they [the compilers and authors of the gospels] felt free to modify the details of *the narrative tradition* in order to bring out the meaning it

[8] 'The Life of Jesus', pp. 219-20.
[9] *E.T.*, LXVII. 228.
[10] An example often given is the interpretation in Hebrews 7 of the priesthood of Christ in terms of Melchizedek.
[11] G. W. H. Lampe, *Essays on Typology*, p. 25. 'Christ must surely have believed himself to be the fulfilment of God's dealings with his ancient people.'
[12] Ibid. pp. 9-14.
[13] See especially their chapters in *Apostolic Ministry* (ed. Kirk).

possessed for them when it was expressed in imagery derived from Old Testament history.'[14] It is no doubt true that some extreme typologists are more interested in the question 'What prefigurement, type and antitype are involved in this incident?' than 'Did these events really take place as they are reported?' Yet it is not properly part of the typological method to minimize the historical element. As Lampe shows, it is its historical foundation which distinguishes typology from allegory, and must also determine the legitimate use of typological interpretation.[15] This insistence that typology must not be assumed to question historicity is also seen in the words of Professor Daube. In connexion with the rabbinic interpretation of an incident in Samuel's life which possibly prefigures the activity of Jesus in the temple, Daube writes: 'We are not concerned with the historicity of the incident reported by Luke. All that is here suggested is that the Jewish model, if it existed in his time, may have contributed to his selection of this scene, and to his manner of depicting it.'[16] It appears necessary to maintain this emphasis upon the historical element if typology is to be kept from those excesses of imagination to which it is especially prone. In this connexion note should be taken of the warning expressed by J. G. Davies: 'It must be frankly acknowledged that only those passages may be deemed relevant [to the Old Testament prefigurement of the Ascension] where the literal and historical sense, as far as it can be discovered, corresponds with and is not contradictory of the typological.'[17]

Opinions will continue to differ about the value of this method of interpretation, and it is often pertinent to ask what insight is gained after the elaborate typology has been worked out. Perhaps the best approach is one of caution, using only those parallels and prefigurements which naturally arise out of the New Testament account.

With this caution must go also a continual watchfulness lest by implication if not by definite statement, the enthusiasm for typology warps our historical judgement, or makes us try to assume that the historical question is really not very important.

---

[14] *Essays on Typology*, p. 19. (Italics mine.)

[15] Ibid. pp. 31, 35ff.

[16] *The New Testament and Rabbinic Judaism*, p. 14. Note that the rabbinic prefigurements suggested by Daube are much more questionable than those drawn from the Old Testament.

[17] *He Ascended into Heaven*, pp. 15-16.

This sense of actual history can, indeed, be a help to typology, especially if there is recognition of what Lampe calls 'the recurring rhythm of the divine activity'.[18] For if it is recognized that the divine activity follows a pattern which has been partially revealed in previous events, we may well find value in the typological interpretation. But the essential basis of this assumption is that real events must be involved; not only expressions of opinion or recognition of recurring expectations, but the very events in history in which God has not only repeated his activity, but in a true sense, completed it. This is the kind of basis which must be assured if typology is to serve a useful purpose in gospel interpretation: 'Typology must rest upon authentic history, interpreted in accordance with the biblical view of the divine economy and with due regard for the literal sense of scripture and the findings of critical scholarship.'[19]

## II. THE QUESTION OF MYTHOLOGY

To many people the statement that something is 'a myth' is exactly equivalent to saying it did not happen, and any supposed record must be 'untrue'. This of course is not the proper meaning of myth, which is well defined by Julius Schniewind as 'the presentation of unobservable realities in terms of observable phenomena'.[20] This approach to the New Testament is specially significant for our study. In the first place, the attempt to 'demythologize' the New Testament must have an effect on any study of the gospels. Secondly, Rudolf Bultmann, the chief exponent of the need for demythologizing, begins his discussion of the subject by referring to the terms used in our present study. 'The cosmology of the New Testament is essentially mythical in character. The world is viewed as a three-storeyed structure, with earth in the centre, the heaven above, and the underworld beneath.'[21] That is, Bultmann regards some of the terms descriptive of the future life, as the first on the list for the process of demythologizing.

The effect of this upon our study can best be seen if we inquire more fully into what this process of demythologizing involves. There is no doubt that this movement has the very praiseworthy

---

[18] *Essays on Typology*, p. 29.      [19] Ibid. p. 38.
[20] *Kerygma and Myth*, ed. H. W. Bartsch (E.T., R. H. Fuller), p. 48.      [21] Ibid. p. 1.

motive of attempting to make the gospels intelligible to modern scientific man. In this, as Schniewind points out in his reply to Bultmann,[22] demythologizing is attempting the very same task which faces every preacher. This task is the necessity of presenting the eternal truth of the gospel in contemporary, understandable terms. The real difficulty about demythologizing is that it seems to be so thorough in its discarding of first-century thought forms, that little of the gospel is left. It is true that Bultmann vigorously denies that demythologizing removes the kerygma along with the myth. And there is truth in the assertion that unlike nineteenth-century liberalism, Bultmann is not trying to uncover a timeless truth which exists apart from historical manifestations. The chief difference is that Bultmann insists on the truth of the saving event of Christ.[23] Yet when this idea of a saving event is discussed, we find Bultmann saying that the human life of Jesus is 'a unique combination of history and myth'. The relation between history and myth is explained by reference to the Cross and the Resurrection. These are regarded as part of the same event; the Cross is 'a permanent historical fact originating in the past historical event which is the crucifixion of Jesus'.[24] The Resurrection is not an event of past history; it is the mythological expression of the victory of Christ over death. By this process Bultmann is seen to demythologize the gospel so thoroughly that there seems little content to the saving event which he so much emphasizes. Barth's criticism appears amply justified when he says that according to Bultmann 'the real Easter event is not something which happened to Jesus but something which happened to the faith of the disciples'.[25]

The value of this brief exposition of Bultmann's views of the event of Jesus Christ is in the insight it gives into the validity of the process of demythologizing. While many would agree with his intentions, few scholars support Bultmann's extreme conclusions. This is all the more so because this process is closely tied to existentialist philosophy, which clearly determines the interpretation of salvation as 'a change of consciousness'. Bultmann is plainly open to the criticism that he rejects the philosophy and thought form of the first century only to replace it with one expression of twentieth-century thought. His attempts to show

---

[22] Ibid. p. 45.   [23] Ibid. p. 34.   [24] Ibid. p. 37.
[25] I. Henderson, *Myth in the New Testament*, p. 41.

that the New Testament and the existentialist philosopher are saying the same thing are not very convincing, and it is possibly true that terms like 'authentic existence' so dearly loved by existentialists, need as much demythologizing as any ideas and expressions in the New Testament.

Nevertheless, it must be acknowledged that this approach reminds us of some of the serious problems to be faced in our study. It is beyond question that the modern view of cosmology has made completely irrelevant, as a cosmology, the conception of a three-decker universe which is assumed throughout the Bible. This means that if there is to be any significance for post-Copernican man in the teaching of Jesus about the future life, that teaching must be carefully separated from the pre-Copernican cosmology in terms of which it is presented in the gospels.

The only way in which this admittedly difficult operation can be carried out is by firstly trying to understand what the terms employed in the New Testament meant to those by whom and for whom they were used. The problem is not to be solved by disregarding or despising what is said in the gospels about heaven and hell. Rather we must seek to clarify the meaning these terms held for Jesus and his contemporaries, and then apply that meaning to our own circumstances, using our own terminology.

In this process of interpretation we may well discover that mythical expressions cannot ever be completely dispensed with. One interesting fact in this connexion is that although every reasonable person knows that 'heaven' is not a place up in the sky, it is extraordinarily difficult to speak of the future life without employing words of exaltation and ascent. This reminds us that it is vain to hope entirely to rid our thinking of the mythological. Modern man, scientific or not, has his myths just as much as first-century man. These are undoubtedly different myths and, as always, hardly recognized as such. We shall be able to present to our generation the truth seen in the fully historical event of Jesus Christ only as we try to appreciate the form in which it was first presented. It is a conviction underlying this study that when full account is taken of the mythological form of the teaching of Jesus, there is abundant material of permanent truth to present to our own generation.

### III. THE QUESTION OF THE INDIVIDUAL
### IN THE TEACHING OF JESUS

If we are to justify the personal approach to the teaching of Jesus about the future life, it must be by showing that his teaching as a whole is directed to the individual. In this connexion it is important to recognize that we are not called upon to assert that our Lord directed his teaching *exclusively* to individuals. Indeed if this were the necessary implication of asserting the place of the individual in the teaching of Jesus, the whole project would have to be dropped. In fact, the words of our Lord are addressed both to individuals and to groups. From different points of view it is necessary to stress both aspects.

On the one hand, against the prevalent notion of individuality, it is necessary to emphasize that there are strong community aspects in our Lord's words and works. The background of this is found in the Old Testament, in which there is a strong sense of community life and responsibility. This background is brought to the forefront in the gospels. When Jesus was baptized by John the Baptist, he was taking part in an activity which was directly related to a community. Through the waters of baptism John was gathering together the nucleus of the New Israel,[26] and our Lord's acceptance of baptism indicates his agreement with this activity. The first activity of Jesus when he began his ministry in Galilee was the calling together of those who were to be his disciples (Mk 1[16-18]). Throughout his public ministry these men, with others who were added to their number, were with Jesus, and an increasing part of his work was directed to their instruction and training.[27] Dr Flew has demonstrated that behind our Lord's activity connected with the disciples was the conception of the formation of the New Israel, a community which being saved, is also commissioned to save.[28] Indeed, if the thesis is correct that Jesus intended to gather together a community of which he is the head, which is the true beginning of the Church, there can be no doubt that our Lord had more than single individuals in mind when he preached the gospel of the Kingdom of God. It is

[26] Cf. C. K. Barrett, *The Holy Spirit and the Gospel Tradition*, p. 32.

[27] R. Newton Flew, *Jesus and His Church*, p. 52: '[Jesus had gathered a circle of disciples about himself] . . . with a deliberateness and sense of purpose which have left an ineffaceable impression on all the various strata of the Synoptic tradition.'

[28] Ibid. p. 54.

undoubtedly true that the clearer conception of the place of the Church in the saving activity of God, which is one noticeable emphasis of contemporary theology, has directed our attention to the community aspect of our Lord's mission.

Another outstanding feature of New Testament interpretation which equally emphasizes the community aspect of the work and words of Jesus, is the paramount position accorded to the Kingdom of God. Vincent Taylor has pointed out how few of the actual uses of Kingdom of God in the Synoptics refer directly to a community.[29] This indicates how wrong it is to equate the Kingdom of God with the Church; the Kingdom of God is the 'domain' in which God exercises his dominion; this has become a present fact in the coming of Jesus, in whom the rule of God is now operative, and through whom that kingly rule will eventually be consummated. But while we must avoid *equating* the Kingdom of God with the community of Christ's disciples, there is every reason for asserting a *connexion* between the two concepts. The announcement of the imminence or actual arrival of the rule of God is made to people in the plural, not to individuals (Mk 1$^{15}$). Again, there are sayings in which Jesus appears to speak of the Kingdom of God as a community (Mt 11$^{11}$, Mk 4$^{30-2}$, Mt 25$^{34}$, 26$^{29}$).

Furthermore, in many instances in which Jesus describes the Kingdom of God by parable, he depicts scenes in which numbers of people are quite naturally involved. When we think of such parables as the Drag Net (Mt 13$^{47-8}$), the Wheat and the Tares (Mt 13$^{24-30}$) and the Talents (Mt 25$^{14-30}$), we notice that these stories belong to community life, to the ordinary activities of people living and working together in towns and villages. It seems evident that when Jesus thought of the Kingdom of God he connected it with communities of people, like those in which he and his disciples lived. This fact is equally evident whenever this gospel of the Kingdom of God is preached today, for it is impossible to limit the meaning of it to exclusively individual circumstances. This is the good news of the way in which God has entered human life in Christ, and is at work in him moulding and transforming all human relations, both corporate and individual. As such, the gospel of the Kingdom of God declares the divine activity, which applies to both individuals and to communities.

---

[29] *Jesus and His Sacrifice*, pp. 8-9. Less than one-sixth (9 out of 60) instances of the use of Kingdom of God have a community meaning.

But when full weight is given to the community aspect of our Lord's mission, it is clear that this does not remove all references to individuals. It is interesting to notice that this can be indicated by further reference to some of the incidents which we have cited as examples of the corporate aspects of our Lord's activity. Thus when Jesus was baptized by John, he submitted to this rite as an individual. There was indeed particular significance in *this* baptism as distinct from the others, as the words from heaven indicate; but all baptisms are individual, for every man must repent for himself, and each one severally must pass through the waters of baptism. In accepting John's baptism, however, Jesus was indicating his agreement with this activity whereby individuals who repented became through this rite members of the community which was being made ready for the Lord.

Again, we have noticed that the first act of Jesus was to begin to form the community of disciples which became the Church. But this was effected by our Lord issuing a personal call to each man separately. In this connexion it is very significant that the disciples are named individually (Mk $3^{13-19}$, Mt $10^{2-4}$, Lk $6^{14-16}$). Another illustration of the same process in which there is an individual relationship in a strongly communal setting is in the account of the Last Supper. The emphasis on the preparation of the Passover meal (Mk $14^{12-16}$, Mt $26^{17-19}$, Lk $22^{7-13}$) suggests that this is to be an act of the fellowship which Jesus had created. Not only was the Passover a striking example of community life, but Jesus was deliberately showing that he and his men formed a proper community, not unlike the more usual family group, and should, therefore, eat the Passover meal together. Yet as soon as they are assembled, Jesus begins to speak of his betrayer. 'One of you shall betray me' (Mk $14^{18}$ and par.). This immediately raises in each man's mind the question 'Is it I?' It was truly 'one of the twelve', one who was dipping bread in the same dish as Jesus, one who was there because of his call. The community is made up of those who one by one have responded to the Lord's invitation to 'Follow me' (Mk $1^{17}$, Mt $4^{19}$). It is not only, however, in the act of betrayal that individual responsibility is seen. The act of receiving bread and wine from the hands of Jesus is of necessity an individual act.[30] No one can eat or drink

---

[30] This is so whether the cup and dish used at the Last Supper were 'common' or individual. J. Jeremias, *The Eucharistic Words of Jesus* (pp. 45-6), thinks both cup and dish were 'common' at any ordinary passover meal, as well as at the Last Supper.

B

for another. To this day this aspect of the individual's relationship with Christ is preserved in Holy Communion, when one by one we receive bread and wine as from the hands of the Lord. It is, of course, significant that this is done in fellowship, in the community of believing people. But this community continues to be a true community because its members severally are in a living relationship with Christ the Head.

It is not only in respect of his relationships with the disciples that we see our Lord's personal attitude to people. Many of the miracles show a careful consideration of the individual's needs and problems. We have only to mention Peter's mother-in-law (Mk 1$^{29-31}$), the paralytic brought by his friends (Mk 2$^{1-12}$), the woman with an issue of blood (Mk 5$^{25-34}$); to show how often Jesus is pictured in a close personal relationship with individuals. Other examples, not from works of healing, but from stories of our Lord's gracious dealings with individuals, are the widow's mite (Mk 12$^{41-4}$) and the anointing at Bethany (Mk 14$^{3-8}$). Of particular interest is the story of Zacchaeus (Lk 19$^{1-10}$) for this contains not only an account of Jesus' personal approach to one unlikely man picked out from the crowd, but also refers to that man's relation to the community of God's people. 'Today salvation is come to this house, since he also is a son of Abraham' (Lk 19$^{9}$).

The impression left by these, and many other instances of Jesus' attitude to people, is of one who was intensely interested in people; to whom people such as the rich young ruler (Lk 18$^{18}$ and par.) naturally came with his pressing individual questions. The impression that Jesus was interested in people just as they were, in whatever need they happened to be, is amply supported on almost every page of the gospels.

The question of how this attitude was combined with the strong sense of community which we have already noticed, requires some further discussion. We have commented on instances in which both the corporate and individual aspects are revealed. This indicates that Jesus did not fluctuate between one aspect and the other, but held both personal and corporate conceptions together. The effect that these conceptions had on each other can be considered under two headings, as follows.

*(a) Jesus commonly turned to the individual when speaking to a crowd*

To take one example of this, the Sermon on the Mount is ostensibly addressed to the disciples as a group (Mt 5$^{1-2}$). In agreement with this introduction, many of the following words are addressed to hearers in the plural. But on several occasions the person is suddenly changed to the singular. Examples can be found at Matthew 6$^1$ (plural), 6$^{2a}$ (singular), 6$^{2b}$ (plural), 6$^3$ (singular); the teaching about prayer in Matthew 6$^5$ is addressed in plural terms. Yet the details in Matthew 6$^6$ are in the singular.

Other examples of the same mixing of singular and plural occur in Matthew 12$^{36-7}$, Mark 10$^{15}$, etc. The usual explanations of these changes of number do not seem entirely satisfactory. To argue that these changes of number are due to the ambiguity of the original Aramaic is hardly satisfactory, as it implies a considerable carelessness on the part of those who translated the supposed Aramaic original into Greek. The argument that these changes arise owing to the composite form of the gospel narratives, has more to commend it. Full account must be taken of the possibility that the change in number is due to the putting together of separate pieces of narrative. But this leaves instances of this phenomenon in passages which bear all the marks of being continuous, homogeneous narratives.

It is, therefore, tentatively suggested that underlying these changes from the plural to the singular, is a strong recollection that whenever possible Jesus deliberately turned the conversation to the individual. It is not impossible that Jesus was remembered as one who spoke directly to individuals whenever he could, and that this memory of him has influenced our gospel records. Then we may be able to picture Jesus as one who was continually striving to get near to men as individuals; who made a man feel that even when speaking to the multitude, he was speaking personally to him. Without such a supposition it seems impossible to account for the overwhelming attraction Jesus had for those who felt they not only could but must come to him for help and guidance.

*(b) Jesus sought to place the individual in his proper context in a community*

We turn here to the three stories of lost things in Luke 15. In each story—of the lost sheep, the lost coin, and the lost son—our

Lord is clearly emphasizing the importance to God of the individual. It is the one lost sheep which the shepherd seeks in the wilderness; the one lost coin that causes the housewife to turn the room upside down until she finds it. There is no doubt a different emphasis in the story of the lost son, which should be called the parable of the Elder Son rather than the Prodigal Son. Yet even in this story, there is the idea of one lost person whom the father waits to welcome home.

But beneath the surface, another truth is being expressed. The individual which is sought is part of a whole, which is incomplete without him. The flock is not a complete flock so long as one sheep is lost in the wilderness. The dowry money is incomplete so long as one coin is missing; the home is not fully a home so long as the prodigal stays away.[31] When this thought is applied to our Lord's relations with men and women, it must surely mean that he sought to place the individual in a community, which is his proper sphere. This can be expressed by the assertion that when dealing with the individual, Jesus was always seeking to help him to take his place in the community of God's people. By so doing, the individual becomes personal; he has relationships with other persons through their common relationship with God in Christ. To be a Christian is to move away from the false abstraction which is individuality, into the true life of man, which is personal life in a community. This indeed is what happened to the disciples. They began as a collection of individuals, and the dispute about who is to have the foremost place in the reign of God (Mk 10[35-45] and par.) shows how difficult it was for them to cease to think of their own position and to begin to think as a fellowship. Even on the night on which Jesus was betrayed, Peter tried to dissociate himself from the others, who unlike himself, might well prove unfaithful (Mk 14[29] and par.). Peter had to learn in the bitterness of defeat that he was not better than the rest. They all had to know the desolation of the Crucifixion before they could begin to say '*We* had hoped that he was the one to redeem Israel' (Lk 24[21]). And only after the Resurrection and Ascension could they boldly say: 'This Jesus God raised up, and of that *we* all are witnesses' (Acts 2[32]).

Thus by the redeeming work of Christ the individual is brought out of his individualism, and introduced into a community whose

[31] I owe the germ of this interpretation to Prof. H. G. Wood.

head is Christ, in which he truly becomes a person. The approach of Jesus to people is neither exclusively individual nor only centred on a community, taking no account of individuals. It is personal, being based upon a personal relation to the Lord himself, and at the same time issuing in personal relations with others in the community of Christ's people.

This conclusion amply justifies the claim of this study to ask the question about man's personal future life. It is also a reminder that as with all his other words and works, when Jesus is speaking of the future destiny of the individual, he is also thinking of the place of that individual in the true community of God's people. For in the future life as well as present Christian experience, to be related to Christ is to be joined in fellowship with all God's people.

To conclude this introduction, a word of explanation about the scope of the study is required. I have chosen to limit this investigation of the teaching of Jesus to a study of the synoptic gospels. I have considerable sympathy with the growing opinion among scholars that the Fourth gospel is more historically trustworthy than used to be supposed. Yet it has seemed best to investigate the teaching of Jesus in those gospels which still have the strongest claim to be regarded as authentic historical records. In adopting this course I hope to reveal what can be regarded as the most primitive tradition of the teaching of Jesus on the subject of the future life. Only when this has been done can we say to what extent the later New Testament teaching arises out of and is a legitimate development from the original teaching of Jesus. In the last chapter I have endeavoured to indicate what grounds there are for saying that the later New Testament teaching is a natural development from the teaching of Jesus. There seems to me to be no doubt that the highly developed doctrine of 'eternal life' in the Fourth gospel belongs properly to later New Testament teaching rather than to the primitive tradition of the teaching of Jesus. It is indeed a most wonderful, and as I think, legitimate development. But we shall only confuse the issue if we regard it as other than developed Christian teaching.

CHAPTER TWO

# HEAVEN

HEAVEN is the most common word used in contemporary speech to describe life hereafter; those whom we have lost are said to be 'in heaven'; when we die we hope to 'go to heaven'. The fact that the word is used in a great variety of meanings, both sacred and profane, makes it urgently necessary for us to see what is meant by the term in the gospels. This is all the more so since, as we shall see, some of the most frequent uses of the word in contemporary religious language are not found at all in the gospels.

But there is another, and possibly more fundamental reason for our study of this word. That reason arises out of the phrase which is found only in St Matthew: 'The Kingdom of heaven.' This title seems to be synonymous with 'the Kingdom of God' which occurs very frequently in St Mark and St Luke and is regarded on all sides as expressing one of the most fundamental ideas of the gospels. The reign of God which Jesus announced at the beginning of his ministry (Mk 1$^{15}$) is the key to the basic understanding of our Lord's message and mission. For the particular purpose of this study the importance of the concept Kingdom of God— Kingdom of heaven is obvious. The New Testament throughout assumes that the rule of God in the present and in the future is the context of man's life. That is, in order to live as he ought here and now, a man must recognize and come to terms with the rule of God which has come into operation in the life, ministry, death, and resurrection of Jesus Christ. Because the powers of the new age have now become operative in the present time, a man must decide on his attitude to this great new fact. In this sense the rule of God is regulative of man's present existence. Only in conformity with the purpose and power of God can a man reach true fulfilment, a life lived as God intended it to be lived. So the announcement of the rule of God includes the call to repentance, and many of the parables of the Kingdom emphasize the urgent need for decision to be taken in the face of the present fact of the rule of God. 'The parables use all the resources of dramatic illustration to help men to see that in the events before their eyes—in the miracles of Jesus, his appeal to men and its results, the blessedness that comes to those who follow him, and the hardening of those who reject him; in the tragic conflict of the Cross and the tribulation of the disciples, in the fateful choice before the Jewish people, and the disasters that threaten—God is confronting them in his Kingdom, power and glory. This world has become the scene of a divine drama, in which the eternal issues are laid bare. It is the hour of decision. It is realized eschatology.'[1]

But it is not only in relation to this present life that the rule of God is significant. The future beyond the grave is also necessarily connected with this rule. Jesus not only announced the rule of God as now present, he also spoke of a future rule of God in which the power and majesty of his Father will be fully revealed.[2] This element cannot be removed from the teaching of the gospels except by making their message radically different from what it is. Very much thought has been exercised, and is still being exercised, on the question of the time references in our Lord's view of the future coming of the rule of God. Fortunately, for our particular purpose it is not necessary to attempt to reach a final decision on this matter. It is sufficient for us to notice that if there is to be, sometime in the future, a consummation of the rule of God which is even now operative in the world, then man's individual future life must be considered against this background. Modern popular thought about a future life too easily assumes that it is some different existence for those who have ended their earthly life, which goes on concurrently with the more or less permanent continuation of this present existence for other succeeding generations. But this is very far from being the view which the New Testament teaches. According to that view, not only must individual life on earth inevitably end, but also earthly existence as we know it must one day cease entirely. The problem of the individual's future life is then to be considered against the background of the end of the ages and the inauguration of the new world

---

[1] C. H. Dodd, *Parables of the Kingdom*, pp. 197-8. See also pp. 198-210, in which the practical implications for this life of the coming of the rule of God are admirably set out.

[2] The idea of the future coming of the Kingdom is rare in the teaching of Jesus, but it does appear significantly in Matthew 6[10], par. Luke 11[2]; Mark 9[1]; Luke 22[18] (cf. Mark 14[25]). See the discussion of these, and other possible references, in W. G. Kümmel, *Promise and Fulfilment*, pp. 25ff.

which God has promised. So the question of the meaning of heaven is a much deeper and wider question than it appears at first sight to be. To this question we must now direct our attention.

The word οὐρανός (heaven) and its cognates, οὐρανοί (heavens) and οὐράνιος (heavenly), occur about 150 times in the synoptic gospels. Of these, by far the greater proportion are in Matthew, who uses οὐράνιος 7 times—the word only occurs in two other places in the New Testament (Lk 2¹³, Acts 26¹⁹)—and οὐρανός and οὐρανοί 84 times. Marcan and Lucan instances of οὐρανός and οὐρανοί are 17 and 36 respectively. It is clear from these statistics that 'heaven' is a favourite word with the author of the first gospel, and this fact has led many commentators to regard the word with considerable suspicion, especially as an authentic word on the lips of Jesus. But as we hope to show, this attitude may do less than justice to this word, and wrongly interpret its place in the records of our Lord's sayings.

As with most New Testament words, 'heaven(s)' is found in the Old Testament, and equally, as with many New Testament words, there are discernible likenesses and differences in the use of the word between the Old and New Testaments. The Hebrew term שָׁמַיִם ('shamayim') is used in two main senses. First, to denote *the sky*; what Genesis 1¹⁴, ¹⁵, ¹⁷ describes as the 'firmament of heaven'. This phrase bears witness to the realism (some would say 'childish realism') of the Hebrew idea of the universe. Everything being what it appeared to be, the earth is flat, and above it is a great dome which appears to be solid and therefore is solid, i.e. a firmament. Beneath this dome there is air, and also at different levels there are 'heavenly bodies'—sun, moon and stars, which, because they move are thought to be 'living'.[3] So the sky is where the stars are (Judg 5²⁰), where the birds fly (Gen 1²⁰), which is darkened with clouds (1 Kings 18⁴⁵), cleared by wind (Job 26¹³), from which comes rain and dew (Gen 8², 27²⁸); the heavens are 'high' (Gen 11⁴), they are over all the earth (Gen 6¹⁷), and are made by God (Jer 51¹⁵, Ps 8³); God has not only created the heavens but He can make windows in them through which heavy rain can pour, either to cause a flood (Gen 7¹¹) or possibly to end a drought (2 Kings 7²). Again, God rained down manna

---

[3] C. Ryder Smith, *The Bible Doctrine of the Hereafter*, p. 1, to which I am greatly indebted at this point, gives a clear and vivid account of the Hebrew idea of the universe.

from the skies and gave his people the corn of heaven (Ps 78²³ᶠ).

In the second place, heaven is *the place where God dwells* (1 Kings 8³⁰, etc.), where He sits enthroned (Isa 66¹); from which He hurls down hailstones (Josh 10¹¹) as well as gives manna (see above). From heaven God talks with Israel (Ex 20²²), and looks down upon them to bless them (Deut 26¹⁵). His might is heard as He thunders from heaven against His adversaries (1 Sam 2¹⁰); He bends the heavens to come to the help of the man in distress (Ps 18⁹), and is urged to rend the heavens and come down to help His afflicted people (Isa 64¹). God is called 'the God of heaven' (Ezra 1²), but this is plainly a post-exilic title. In view of later development we note particularly that 'heaven' is not used in the Old Testament as a synonym for God.⁴ As we shall see when we consider the meaning of 'kingdom of heaven', there was in rabbinical literature a very widespread practice of using a periphrasis for the divine name, which was regarded as too sacred to be uttered, and one of the most common of these circumlocutions was to refer to 'heaven' when God was meant. Because of this it is usually supposed that 'kingdom of heaven' is really a secondary form of the original 'kingdom of God', but in our discussion below we shall take particular note of the fact just stated, that 'heaven' is not used in the Old Testament as a divine title.

It will be convenient to discuss the use of the word 'heaven' in the synoptic gospels under several heads, thus indicating the breadth of meanings which this idea embraces.

## I. HEAVEN(S) AS THE SKY, SKIES

One most interesting use of οὐρανός with the meaning of 'sky' is in connexion with the act of prayer. Especially we notice that in the acts of prayer which accompanied the miracle of the loaves (Mk 6⁴¹ and pars.), and the healing of the deaf-mute (Mk 7³⁴) Jesus lifted up his eyes to heaven. In the first instance this action is accompanied by blessing before he broke the loaves; in the second Jesus sighed as he looked up to heaven. In both cases it is probably right to regard these as expressions of our Lord's perfectly natural attitude. When breaking bread he naturally blesses God, remembering He is the giver of all; when faced with

---

⁴ Brown, Driver and Briggs, *Hebrew and English Lexicon of the Old Testament*, pp. 1029-30 for fuller details.

the double affliction of the deaf-mute his human sympathy is expressed in a sigh. This is not to deny that in Mark's account of the feeding of the five thousand there are several terms which belong significantly to the institution of the Eucharist—i.e. 'took bread', 'blessed', 'brake', 'gave'; and Taylor's judgement about the intention of Mark to interpret the miracle as an anticipation of the Eucharist is convincing.[5] This point of view adds significance to the phrase 'lifted up his eyes to heaven'; for this phrase does not occur in any account of the institution of the Eucharist, and its presence here, among these admittedly liturgical expressions, can best be explained as a genuine reminiscence of our Lord's habit in prayer. There is further use of this expression in the parable of the Pharisee and the tax collector (Lk 18[9-14]). 'The tax collector, standing far off, would not even lift up his eyes to heaven.' Easton comments that raising the eyes is a most natural act in prayer,[6] and Plummer adds that this signifies that he would not adopt any confident or familiar attitude toward God.[7] If it were the habit of Jesus to lift up his eyes to heaven in prayer, we can be sure that his confidence was in God, to whom he prayed as to his heavenly Father. The symbolism involved in this characteristic action must not be treated as if it expressed a literal truth. By looking up to the sky as he prayed Jesus was not indicating that he thought God was 'up there'. But his action means that 'the sky' was perhaps never just 'the sky and nothing more', but represented and symbolized something of the love and power of God.

A second use of οὐρανός with the meaning of 'sky' is in the phrase 'the birds of heaven' (Mt 6[26], 8[20], Mk 4[32], Lk 8[5]). While this expression clearly involves the interpretation of 'heaven' as 'sky', there·are accompanying ideas which should be noticed. In the parable of the mustard seed (Mk 4[30-2]), the reference to the birds of heaven which come and lodge in the branches is thought to indicate that Gentile nations will come to shelter under the tree which in its growth represents the kingdom of God.[8] It may not be too fanciful to say that in the gospel tradition οὐρανός is connected with the world-wide mission of the Church, through

---

[5] VTM, p. 324.

[6] *The Gospel according to St Luke*, p. 269.

[7] *ICC, St Luke*, p. 419. Prayer of Manasses (9) refers to the idea of sins preventing a man lifting up his eyes to heaven.

[8] T. W. Manson, *The Teaching of Jesus*, p. 133 note [1].

this expression 'the birds of heaven'. It certainly is not difficult for us to think of the sky as a symbol of the wide embracing love of God.

> *The glorious sky, embracing all,*
> *Is like the Maker's love,*
> *Wherewith, encompassed, great and small,*
> *In peace and order move.*[9]

The other instances of the use of οὐρανός to represent the sky can be mentioned briefly. First, Mark 8[11] tells how the Pharisees came seeking a sign from heaven. This appears to mean that they demanded some visible token of the validity of our Lord's claim, comparable possibly with the promise made by Theudas that he would divide Jordan as a sign.[10] Secondly, the condemnation of Capernaum (Lk 10[15], Mt 11[23]): 'And you Capernaum, will you be exalted to heaven? You shall be brought down to Hades.' McNeile refers to Psalms of Solomon 1[5] and comments: 'Hades expresses the lowest shame, as heaven the highest renown.'[11] This is a somewhat symbolic use of 'heaven' with a certain flavour of moral judgement. Thirdly, Luke 4[25] seems to be simply a straightforward use of the term in reference to the drought which occurred in the days of Elijah, when the heavens were shut up three years and six months (1 Kings 17[1]). Matthew 16[3] is too questionable on textual grounds to be considered here, but the similar logion in Luke 12[56], 'you know how to interpret the appearance of the earth and sky', uses οὐρανός in the sense of 'sky'.

The outcome of this investigation is mainly negative. There are very few instances in which οὐρανός is used simply and only for 'sky'. This contrasts somewhat vividly with Old Testament usage, in which 'heavens' is quite often simply 'the sky' without any other idea attaching to it. Especially we need to notice that in the use of the expression 'lifting up the eyes to heaven' there are overtones of meaning, no doubt influenced by the contemporary use of heaven as a periphrasis for God.

## II. HEAVEN AND EARTH

Closely connected with the use of οὐρανός considered above, is the expression ὁ οὐρανὸς καὶ ἡ γῆ (heaven and earth). This is used to

[9] John Keble (*Methodist Hymn-book*, No. 43).   [10] VTM, p. 362.
[11] *The Gospel according to St Matthew*, p. 161.

express the lordship of God over the whole creation. Matthew 11[25] reads: 'I thank thee, Father, Lord of heaven and earth.' With this should be considered Matthew 5[34]: 'do not swear by heaven for it is the throne of God, or by earth for it is his footstool'. And a saying recorded in Matthew 28[18], if genuine, has tremendous Christological implications—'All authority in heaven and on earth has been given to me'. McNeile observes that this claim to absolute authority is a fulfilment of a phrase in the Lord's Prayer (Mt 6[10]): 'Thy will be done, in earth as it is in heaven.' 'The consummation for which the disciples had been taught to pray was potentially reached by the Resurrection.'[12]

A further expression of this dependence of heaven and earth upon God is the prediction that they will 'pass away' (Mt 5[18], Mk 13[31]; cf. Lk 16[17]). This means that the heavens as well as the earth are the handiwork of God; they are of limited duration and owe their present existence to God alone. While we moderns may justifiably adopt a superior attitude to the simple cosmology of all this, we ought also to recognize the tremendous faith in God which these conceptions imply. The 'world' of the New Testament may have been physically small; nevertheless the God in whom the first Christians believed was regarded as utterly supreme over heaven and earth. If in modern times we sometimes think the universe is too big for God to know it and control it, the answer to our scepticism lies in seeing again the truth enshrined in our Lord's trust in God, the Lord of heaven and earth.

### III.   THE ESCHATOLOGICAL AND APOCALYPTIC USE OF 'HEAVEN'

There are several instances in the gospels in which 'heaven' is used in eschatological and apocalyptic passages.[13] We have to consider not only the meaning of the particular passages, but also what influence, if any, this use of 'heaven' has had upon other uses of the word, especially in connexion with the phrases 'heavenly Father', and 'Kingdom of heaven'.

The Baptism of Jesus is regarded by many scholars as 'an

---

[12] *The Gospel according to St Matthew*, p. 435.

[13] 'Eschatological' means 'concerning the last things' ($\tau\grave{\alpha}$ $\check{\epsilon}\sigma\chi\alpha\tau\alpha$); Apocalyptic is the term applied to Jewish and Christian pseudonymous writings, which purport to give, through visions of a seer, revelations of the hereafter, as applied to the world, to nations, and to individuals. See G. F. Moore, *Judaism*, II.279-86; H. W. Robinson, in Manson's *Companion to the Bible*, pp. 307-8.

eschatological sacrament'.[14] That is, by undergoing baptism, Jesus is signifying that he approves of the community gathered together by John the Baptist on the basis of repentance, and in himself the promised act of God has taken place, the new age has dawned. For our particular purpose one statement calls for consideration. 'He saw the heavens opened' (Mk 1[10]) or, as St Matthew puts it, the 'heavens were opened' (Mt 3[16], cf. Lk 3[21]). 'The rending of the heavens', as Taylor writes, 'is a common feature of apocalyptic thought, the underlying idea being that of a fixed separation of heaven and earth, only to be broken in special circumstances.'[15] Before we look at some of the Jewish apocalyptic references quoted by Taylor, we should note that this idea is also represented in the Old Testament (Isa 64[1]): 'O that thou wouldst rend the heavens and come down, that the mountains might quake at thy presence.' This passage is part of a prayer to God for deliverance, and bears witness to the conviction that God is able to divide the heavens and descend to save His people.

This idea of sovereignty expressed in rending the heavens is obviously close to the idea of creation. It is because God has created the heavens and the earth that He is able to rend them and give His special assistance to His people. The connexion with creation is made in another way in the baptism story, through the symbol of the Dove representing the Spirit which descends upon Jesus as he comes out of the waters of baptism. In rabbinical literature the dove represents the Spirit of God which moved over the watery chaos and brought order to it.[16]

This concept of divine power evidenced in the rending of the heavens is further illustrated from Jewish apocalyptic literature. Perhaps most significant because practically contemporaneous with New Testament writings, is the Apocalypse of Baruch. This writing is described by R. H. Charles as 'almost the last noble utterance of Judaism before it plunged into the dark and oppressive years that followed the destruction of Jerusalem'.[17] *Apoc. Baruch* 22[1] reads: 'And it came to pass after these things that lo! the heavens were opened, and I saw, and power was given to me, and a voice was heard from on high.' This is the way in which God begins to answer the questions Baruch has raised about the emptiness of this present life and the old problem of the prosperity

---

[14] C. K. Barrett, *The Holy Spirit and the Gospel Tradition*, p. 33.    [15] VTM, p. 160.
[16] VTM, p. 161; C. K. Barrett, op. cit. p. 39.    [17] *A. & P.*, II.470.

of the wicked, about which God seems to do nothing at all. We notice that along with the opening of the heavens there goes the word of God; this is, of course, closely paralleled in the account of our Lord's baptism, for he heard a voice from heaven saying: 'Thou art my beloved Son.' In view of this close connexion between the heavens being opened and a voice being heard, it is not surprising that reference is also made to Ezekiel 1[1]: 'As I was among the exiles by the river Chebar, the heavens were opened and I saw visions of God'. Charles indeed regards this passage as the probable source of both the gospel accounts of the opened heavens and heavenly voice at our Lord's baptism, and the above reference in the *Apocalypse of Baruch*.[18] This comment does not imply that there is no historical basis for the account of our Lord's baptism, but that the form in which the account is presented is influenced by these Old Testament and Jewish passages.

If it is correct to see in these passages some apocalyptic emphasis we can readily admit that here the use of this 'heavenly' symbolism emphasizes the sovereign power of God; and more to the point, that this power has become specially operative in the baptism of Jesus. This indeed is something to remember when the excesses of apocalyptic language seem to remove our Lord far from our everyday world. Beneath all this imagery of clouds, of heaven, of trumpets and a descent from heaven, is the basic conviction of the present and future manifestation of the sovereign majesty of God.

To consider this more excessive apocalyptic language we next turn to a part of the gospels which is a great problem, indeed even a stumbling-block to many. The passages referred to are Matthew 24, Mark 13, and Luke 21. These sections of the gospels are often called 'Little Apocalypses' because to some scholars they seem to bear a close resemblance to the Jewish apocalypses. The day is long past when these chapters could be regarded as alien intrusions in the gospels, their ideas discounted, and their presence more or less ignored in the study of the gospel message. Taylor carefully considers the theory that the basis of these chapters is a short apocalyptic document, to which the gospel writers have attached certain disconnected sayings of Jesus, and he concludes that a far more satisfactory theory is that we have several (probably

---

[18] *A. & P.*, II.479. Cf *Test. Levi* 18[6], *Test. Judah* 24[2].

four) groups of sayings which have been brought together in this chapter. Some of these sayings have definite apocalyptic characteristics, others have a more specific reference to the present situation connected with the imminent fate of Jerusalem. If the composite nature of these chapters is recognized, there is good reason for taking them seriously, although not literally. They represent important factors in the teaching of Jesus.[19]

With this background we can turn to these passages in which the term 'heaven' occurs. The relevant texts are Matthew 24[29-31], Mark 13[24-7], Luke 21[25-8]. The main points at issue may be stated as follows:

(i) As part of the signs preceding the coming of the Son of Man, the following phenomena are described. The stars will be falling from heaven (Mk 13[25], Mt 24[29]). The powers in the heavens will be shaken (Mk 13[25], Mt 24[29], Lk 21[26]). The angels will be sent out and the elect will be gathered from the ends of the earth to the ends of heaven (Mk 13[27], Mt 24[31]). The sign of the Son of Man will appear in heaven (Mt 24[30]).

(ii) There are other closely connected statements which, however, do not use the word 'heaven'. These statements are— The sun will be darkened and the moon will not give its light (Mk 13[24], Mt 24[29]). There will be signs in sun and moon and stars, and upon the earth distress of nations, in perplexity at the roaring of the sea and the waves; men fainting with fear and with foreboding of what is coming on the world (Lk 21[25]). Also following the words about 'heaven' we have in Mark 13[26] and Luke 21[27]: 'Then they will see the Son of Man coming in clouds with great power and glory.'

These sayings, thus grouped together, may well leave us wondering if they could possibly have been spoken by the same person whose other words we find so relevant to our own situation. Our chief purpose in considering them now is to discover what meaning is given to the idea of heaven in the gospels. This purpose means that many of the most trying questions are not our immediate concern. We shall do well to heed the wise words of Professor C. H. Dodd, expressed in broadcast talks given in 1950. This passage, he writes 'is addressed to the imagination, and read with imagination it gives a key to what the coming of Christ meant to the first Christians. It was the final disclosure of the

[19] VTM, pp. 498ff, 636-44.

power and righteousness of God, and the end of history as we know it.'[20]   According to Taylor the section of this composite passage which we are considering may be in substance a genuine prophecy of Jesus,[21] but the apocalyptic imagery probably connects it with 'that glittering apocalyptic robe with which primitive Christianity clothed Him'.[22]

In order to understand the significance of these celestial signs we need to consider some Old Testament passages. For instance Isaiah 13[9-10] refers to the Day of the Lord which cometh, cruel, with wrath and fierce anger, to make the earth a desolation and to destroy its sinners from it. 'For the stars of the heavens and their constellations will not give their light; the sun will be dark at its rising, and the moon will not shed its light.' It is important to notice that all this happens on the day of the Lord— it is not a prediction of what we should call a national catastrophe, but is envisaged in the proper sense of the words as 'an act of God'. In other words, this kind of language is saying in forcible and picturesque terms, that the future lies in the hand of God and that in His activity the heavens as well as the earth, with the people on it, are subject absolutely to the power of God, the Lord of heaven and earth.

In the case of the descriptions in these apocalyptic passages in the gospels, it is likely that the original writer, and the early Christians, thought that real phenomena were being described and foretold. The powers of heaven were regarded as either heavenly bodies or elemental spirits thought to rule over the stars.[23] The early Christians who read this and other passages would take them to mean that the whole universe known to them was under the power of God and was to be violently changed at the coming of the Son of Man in glory. Again we find that by means of the expressions connected with heaven, an emphasis is being placed on the majesty and sovereign power of God. Added to this is the equally tremendous conviction that it is in the coming of Jesus of Nazareth, the Son of Man, that these powers of God will be revealed. It is the Son of Man, who is to 'come' on the clouds of heaven; it is not a general or vague catastrophe which is expected, but the full manifestation of the power and rule of God.

Also we must recognize that what is to be is determined by

---

[20] C. H. Dodd, *The Coming of Christ*, p. 4.
[21] VTM, p. 642.    [22] Ibid. p. 644.    [23] Ibid. p. 518.

what has already taken place. It is Jesus, whom the disciples knew, who is to return with the majesty and power of God. Even if we have to recognize that some apocalyptic notions have become attached to the figure of Jesus, we also must admit that this connexion was not incongruous to the early Church. They did not find any difficulty in thinking of him as one to whom apocalyptic ideas could be attached. Two conclusions follow from this.

First we have to admit that the gospels give evidence which is difficult to discount completely, that Jesus himself used, and encouraged others to use, apocalyptic ideas about his person. This is not to claim that his own teaching was exclusively apocalyptic, but that there are inseparable elements of apocalypse embedded in it. Secondly, the connexion between Jesus and apocalyptic thought is not to be regarded as quite impossible to reasonable people today. If apocalyptic thought is not entirely incongruous with the person and message of Jesus, it cannot be regarded as mere nonsense, nor can it be considered entirely irrelevant or meaningless. This should remind us that apocalyptic language is symbolic. The greatest difficulty Western thought faces here is due to our apparently incurable literalism. We will persist in taking language only at its face value. But we shall never appreciate the meaning of apocalyptic language unless we recognize its symbolic structure. This means that when we try to understand what is meant by such phrases as 'the heavens were opened' or 'the sun and moon and stars cease to shine' we must look beneath the symbol to the idea being expressed. As we have shown, in this case, the idea is that of absolute divine powers exercised over the whole of the universe. The significance of this conviction is not in any way lessened by the recognition that those who expressed it in picturesque language had a very limited view of the universe. It is certain that if their view of the universe had been like ours, they would still have asserted the same conviction of the lordship of God over it.

A further passage to be considered is the account of our Lord's reply to the Chief Priest's question, 'Are you the Christ, the Son of the Blessed?'—'I am, and you will see the Son of Man sitting at the right hand of Power and coming with the clouds of heaven' (Mk 14[62], Mt 26[64]; cf. Lk 22[69]). Luke adds the significant 'from now on', which seems to emphasize the sense of urgency and climax

c

which surrounds the whole passage. Commentators point out that the words of Jesus seem to be a combination of Daniel 7¹³: 'I saw in the night visions, and behold, with the clouds of heaven there came one like a son of man and he came to the Ancient of Days and was presented before him', and Psalm 110¹: 'The Lord says to my lord: sit at my right hand till I make your enemies your footstool.'

Taylor regards this saying as probably based on a genuine saying of Jesus, and rejects the view that the omission by Luke of reference to clouds of heaven makes the saying questionable. He points out that the saying does not necessarily involve the idea of a visible descent of the Son of Man, because the passage in Daniel does not refer at all to a descent, but to coming to the Ancient of Days. The meaning, therefore, is, 'the glorious destiny which belongs to the Messiah, described in different ways by the Psalmist and the prophet, will be seen to be his. The emphasis lies on enthronement, and on enthronement as a symbol of triumph.'[24]

This interpretation is supported by a statement of Rabbi Joshua ben Levi who in the first half of the third century A.D. harmonized Zechariah 9⁹, 'Behold thy King cometh unto thee . . . lowly and riding upon an ass', with Daniel 7¹³ in the following way: 'If they (Israel) are worthy, with the clouds of heaven; if they are not worthy, lowly and riding upon an ass.'[25] According to this view, coming on the clouds of heaven is a triumphal way of coming, dependent indeed on the active response of Israel. In this latter regard, Jesus may be claiming that coming in triumph will not depend upon the right response of all Israel.

On the other hand, if there is a community sense involved in the title 'Son of Man', it may be that Jesus is inferring that the community of disciples will give the worthy response which will ensure that he comes in majesty to be enthroned. In that case we must regard this word of Jesus as full of amazing courage and of faith in God. Here he stood, condemned by the leaders of his people, about to die as a blasphemer. He had spent most of the time in his public ministry training and enlightening his small band of disciples. Now they had all forsaken him; he stood alone. Yet in this desperate situation he dared to believe that his own life would be vindicated in his coming triumph as glorified Son of

[24] VTM, p. 569.    [25] G. F. Moore, *Judaism*, II.334-5.

Man. And not only in the distant future, but now, from the present onwards, this triumph was to begin. This seems reminiscent of the view of the Fourth gospel, that the death of Jesus was indeed his enthronement. Being lifted up on the Cross he was also lifted up in glory. But we probably have to say that for the synoptic gospels this enthronement, while beginning with the Crucifixion, is really manifest in the Resurrection and Ascension. In any case we notice that when the full symbolism of the language is appreciated, 'coming on the clouds of heaven' is not an outmoded expression entirely dependent on a discredited cosmology, but the assertion of the triumph and attending glory of the enthronement of the Son of man.

Other passages with an apocalyptic flavour can be briefly considered. Luke 9$^{54}$—concerning the refusal of the Samaritans to receive Jesus and his disciples as they went on their way to Jerusalem—James and John said: 'Lord, do you want us to bid fire come down from heaven and consume them?' We must remember that the story of the Transfiguration, which includes the appearing of Elijah, has just been recorded by St Luke (9$^{28-36}$). It seems likely, therefore, that the story of Elijah, and his contest by fire with the Baal priests (1 Kings 18$^{38}$) should be considered here. No doubt the Transfiguration caused the disciples to think seriously in terms of apocalyptic appearances, and in such an atmosphere it would not be surprising if they thought they could deal with this indifference as Elijah had dealt with his opponents. If this were so, the rebuke of Jesus shows that the power attendant upon himself as Son of Man is not to be used in a way which contradicts the very purpose of his coming, which was to seek and save the lost (Lk 19$^{10}$, etc.). This must surely provide a lesson for us. We are not to be so immersed in the coming glory of Christ that we neglect the ordinary plain duties of responding to the gospel here and now. The glory of Christ is reached through the suffering of the Cross, not through any short-cut way of calling down fire from heaven. Indeed, we may profitably notice that Jesus, who was so vividly aware of the heavenly powers, was also very careful how they were to be used. This has great significance for us as we consider the practical implications of believing in supernatural powers and our future destiny. It is quite out of harmony with the central truth of the gospel to use our belief in a future life as an escape from the stark realities of the present, or as

a threat through which we hope to drive people into acceptance
of the saving love of God in Christ.

Luke 10[17] records the joy of the seventy disciples when they
returned from their mission, with our Lord's words in verse 18:
'I saw Satan fall like lightning from heaven.' Here we can take
'heaven' as the sphere in which spirits dwell, and in which according to some Jewish writings, Satan was supreme. The *Martyrdom
of Isaiah*, which probably belongs to the first century A.D.,
describes how 'Manasseh forsook the service of the God of his
father and he served Satan and his angels and his powers' (2[2]).
Again in the same work: 'When Isaiah saw the lawlessness which
was being perpetuated in Jerusalem, and the worship of Satan and
his wantonness, he withdrew from Jerusalem and settled in
Bethlehem of Judaea' (2[7]). If this can be taken as typical of
contemporary ideas of Satan, the passage from Luke which is
under consideration suggests that Jesus saw in the victory over
the demons ($\delta\alpha\iota\mu\acute{o}\nu\iota\alpha$) the beginning of the end of the kingdom of
Satan. The powers of Satan are being defeated by those who go
out and heal in the name of Jesus. There are some who find it
difficult to accept the view that Jesus believed in Satan; they
would explain such a word as this as arising from the popular
notions of the first Christians. But it is far more realistic and
significant to see that Jesus did believe in the existence of a supernatural power of evil. The name given to this power is not important; what matters is our Lord's conviction that in himself,
and significantly, in his disciples, the powers of evil were beginning to be defeated. We do less than justice to this exultation of
Jesus if we only think of it in crudely materialistic terms.

The use of 'lightning' in this connexion, especially connected
with the coming of the Son of Man, is also found in Luke 17[24] and
Matthew 24[27]: 'For as the lightning flashes and lights up the sky
from one side to the other ($\acute{\epsilon}\kappa$ $\tau\hat{\eta}s$ $\acute{v}\pi\grave{o}$ $\tau\grave{o}\nu$ $o\grave{v}\rho\alpha\nu\grave{o}\nu$ $\epsilon\grave{\iota}s$ $\tau\grave{\eta}\nu$
$\acute{v}\pi$' $o\grave{v}\rho\alpha\nu\grave{o}\nu$) so will the Son of Man be in his day.' Easton thinks
that this expression illustrates the vivid clarity of the coming of the
Son of Man rather than its suddenness;[26] and in view of the two
illustrations of Noah going into the Ark (Luke 17[26]) and Lot
escaping from Sodom (Luke 17[28]), we may add that the careless
indifference of people is suddenly faced with a catastrophe which
divides one from another. Thus although this is a Son of Man

[26] *The Gospel according to St Luke*, p. 263

passage, it is best to regard the references to heaven as being merely illustrative, and not as eschatological in any developed sense.

We have now surveyed all the instances of the use of 'heaven' in the synoptic gospels which have an eschatological or apocalyptic significance. Our conclusions must be that while the form of expression is necessarily influenced by the current view of cosmology, as well as those of contemporary apocalyptic, beneath these somewhat crude expressions about heaven we see the steady assertion of the power and ruling authority of God, specially manifest in Jesus. The question remains whether every other use of 'heaven' in the gospels must have an eschatological or apocalyptic interpretation. Does the apocalyptic flavour of 'heaven' appear in the phrases 'heavenly Father' and 'Kingdom of heaven'? We cannot answer that question until we have considered more carefully the use of these terms, but we can say at this stage that there is not necessarily such a colouring. Indeed, as we consider the various uses of 'heaven' we seem to discover that with such a wide variety of senses, the word cannot be said always to mean the same thing. This was a term used for several quite distinct meanings. Each meaning must be discovered on the basis of the actual usage, and it is probably misleading to try to find one conception which is common to every occurrence of the word.

## IV.  'IN HEAVEN'—'WITH GOD'

The next group of sayings to be considered are those in which the expressions 'by heaven', 'in heaven', 'from heaven' are used. In all these cases we notice the influence of the Jewish practice of not using the divine name, but substituting for it a variety of circumlocutions, of which 'heaven' was one of the most frequent. Thus swearing 'by heaven' (Mt 5³⁴, 23²²) means swearing by God, and Jesus makes it quite clear that the oath is to be regarded as binding even if no divine name is used. On this basis, Jesus recommends that no oath be taken; but 'against the form of expression as such Jesus urges no objection'.[27]

Again there is the phrase 'treasure in heaven' (Mt 6²⁰, Lk 12³³, Mt 19²¹, Mk 10²¹, Lk 18²²; cf. Mt 5¹²). This means treasure with God. Dalman asserts that 'any mystical pre-existence of

[27] Dalman, *Words*, p. 206.

reward or treasure is in no way contemplated'.[28] The first example comes from Q (Lk 12[33], Mt 6[20]). In the Lucan narrative there is an interesting comparable saying in 12[13-21]. The saying which follows the story of the rich fool is: 'So is he who lays up treasure for himself and is not rich toward God.' This is exactly what is meant also in 12[33]: 'A treasure in the heavens that does not fail, where no thief approaches and no moth destroys.' The second example occurs in all three synoptic gospels (Mt 19[21], Mk 10[21], Lk 18[22]). The occasion is the question of the rich man who inquires the way to eternal life, and is told by Jesus that he lacks one thing, 'Sell all that you have and distribute to the poor and you will have treasure in heaven; and come, follow me'. One of the first facts to note is that here we have an example of Mark using 'heaven' as in effect a synonym for God. This is significant because 'heaven' is so often either an exclusively Matthean word or else is shared only by Luke. The comments which have been made about the other passage in which 'treasure in heaven' is used, equally apply here. The plain meaning is that the rich man, if he sold all his property and gave away the money to the poor, would find true riches with God, and would be able to follow Christ with an undivided heart.

Mark also records, together with the other synoptics, another occasion on which Jesus used 'heaven' as a synonym for God. This is the question Jesus put to the High Priests and the Scribes and the elders when they challenged him to state his authority, apparently having in mind his action in cleansing the temple: 'Was the baptism of John from heaven or from man?' (Mt 21[25], Mk 11[30], Lk 20[4]). Our Lord's questioners show by the consultation together which preceded their answer that they understood 'from heaven' to mean 'from God'. 'If we say "from heaven"; he will say "Why then did you not believe him?".' That is, to admit his heavenly origin is to place oneself under an obligation to obey his words. On the other hand, to say John was from men would appear to deny his prophetic office, which was accepted by all the people. We should notice that 'from heaven' does not mean 'of divine nature'—this was not claimed for John the Baptist. But it was claimed that he came from God or, as this passage puts it, from heaven. Again we notice that Mark uses the phrase ἐξ οὐρανοῦ. Together with his earlier use of the phrase

[28] Dalman, *Words*, p. 206.

this constitutes weighty evidence that Jesus himself probably used 'from heaven' in this sense.

Both instances (Mk 10[21], 11[30]) occur in passages which seem to have all the marks of authentic history, i.e. Mark 10[17-31] contains several indications of being a first-hand narrative—the rich man met him 'in the way'; he 'ran to him and fell on his knee before him'. He addressed Jesus as 'good teacher', calling forth the disclaimer from Jesus, which Matthew's account avoids by changing our Lord's reply to: 'Why do you ask me about the good?' Then Mark alone records that when Jesus looked on the man he loved him. All these seem authentic touches to a lively and utterly reliable story. Regarding the second story, it is, as Taylor says, 'excessive scientific caution' to ask whether Mark 11[28-30] is an historical account or a formation of the community.[29] While the biographical details are not very clear in the story, the circumstances of a clash between the leaders of the Jews and Jesus are entirely understandable, and the reply of Jesus is clearly preserved as the very core of the story; indeed it is the main reason for the story being in the gospel. We have then good grounds for saying that Jesus used 'from heaven' and 'in heaven' with the meaning of 'from God' and 'with God'.

The other passages in Matthew in which 'in heaven' is used require a somewhat fuller treatment. Matthew 16[19] reads: 'I will give you the keys of the kingdom of heaven; and whatever you bind on earth shall be bound in heaven; and whatever you loose on earth shall be loosed in heaven.' This is a specific promise to Peter, and seems to be repeated and applied to the Church in Matthew 18[18]. As the same form of words is used we can safely confine our consideration of the term 'in heaven' to the promise to Peter. There is no necessary contradiction between the two sayings and there is no reason to doubt that the promise was made to both Peter and to the community of disciples.[30] Flew points out that 'heaven' in this saying does not mean the same as 'kingdom of heaven'. 'It [i.e. 'heaven'] is the dwelling-place of God, and so in Matthew, is often used for God himself, in his transcendence.'[31] That this use of 'in heaven' does mean 'before God' is perhaps supported by the rabbinical notion that God and the angels form a heavenly court of justice which ratifies the decisions

---

[29] VTM, p. 469.    [30] R. Newton Flew, *Jesus and His Church*, p. 135.
[31] Ibid. p. 134.

of the Sanhedrin.[32] This likeness cannot be pressed too far, but it may be allowed that on the basis of his faith in Christ as the Son of God, Peter is given the assurance that now that he understands the secret of the kingdom of heaven, he and those who share with him this knowledge of faith, can expect that God will support and ratify their decisions. This is not because some special authority has been granted to Peter which no one else can share, but because Peter has entered into that living relationship of faith in Christ which enables him to judge and decide according to the eternal will of God revealed in Christ. This assurance still stands for the Christian man as well as for the Christian community. Those who have faith in Christ have an understanding and recognition of the will of God. This is not given automatically, nor through any one particular means. But a Christian, when he acts according to his faith in Christ, acts according to the eternal will of God, for this has been made known in Christ. Then the decisions and apprehensions of truth of a Christian man will be ratified and supported by God himself. This can only mean that the heavenly powers are available to support and confirm those decisions and judgements which are taken according to the will of God, as it is revealed in Christ. This does not mean that Christian men and Christian communities are infallible, but that when mistaken decisions and judgements are made, they are precisely not in accord with the mind of Christ. Such decisions will not be ratified and supported by the powers of heaven. But in fact the power of heaven will be known in the awareness of the error. Without making this a claim to any sort of infallibility, we can recognize the great strength and assurance which arises from this conception. It can be put in a form which is recognized as true by all who seriously believe in Christ and walk in the Christian way—namely: 'If a person or people sincerely act according to the will of God, such action will indeed be confirmed, verified and supported by the powers of heaven—indeed by God himself.'

The phrase 'in heaven' is also used in two instances by Luke. We may first consider Luke 10[20]. 'Nevertheless, do not rejoice in this, that the spirits are subject unto you; but rejoice that your names are written in heaven.'

In their return from the mission through the places Jesus himself was about to enter (Lk 10[1]), the seventy report to the Lord

---

[32] Dalman, *Words*, p. 213.

the great success which has attended their work. 'Lord, even the demons are subject to us in your name' (10[17]). Yet they are told that even this triumph is not to be their greatest source of rejoicing, but rather that their names are written 'in heaven'. This is the only reference in the gospels to an idea which was well known in Jewish thought, and became significantly stressed for Christians in the Book of Revelation. The idea is that there is a register of all those who will be saved, what Manson aptly terms 'the burgess roll of the Kingdom'.[33] There is, after all, nothing surprising in the fact that membership in the Kingdom should be somehow recorded. That the idea is an early one is shown by the reference to it in the prayer of Moses (Ex 32[32]). The inevitable complication of the idea in the course of history is seen in the way in which various books are mentioned, and the details contained therein are regarded as secret (see Dan 12[1]). Eventually four such books are described—the first containing the list of the saved, the second a list of the deeds of each man, the third the destiny of each man, and the last the divine plan for all nations and especially for Israel.[34] The rabbis developed the details further, and described how on each New Year's Day, three lists of men were written—those who were righteous, those who were sinners, and those who were not clearly in either category. These last were given ten days in which to repent and then gain inclusion in the list of the righteous, or to be numbered among the condemned. Thus it came about that the ten days between New Year and the Day of Atonement are used by pious Jews as days of repentance, expressed in fasting.[35] In view of these interesting developments, which can, of course, also be illustrated in part from the Book of Revelation (3[5], 13[8], 17[8], 20[12-15]), we may note the simplicity and directness of our Lord's reference to this matter. The point is undoubtedly that the disciples are to rejoice most of all in their salvation. If we recognize the natural and figurative language employed we shall not find difficulty in appreciating the meaning of our Lord's words that the names of the disciples were written in heaven.

There is another reference which ought to be noticed, in view of the fact that these seventy were not only followers, but emissaries

33 *The Sayings of Jesus*, p. 258.
34 Ibid. p. 259; Dalman, *Words*, p. 209.
35 Moore, *Judaism*, II.62-3.

of Jesus. In Ezekiel 13⁹ is a statement that the Jewish prophets who follow their own spirit have seen nothing, and thus have misled God's people. They 'shall not be in the council of my people nor be enrolled in the register of the house of Israel'. In contrast to this, the seventy disciples who have obeyed the instructions given them when they were sent out, will have their names written in heaven. So we can conclude that the phrase 'written in heaven' means counted among those who are saved, with possibly a hint of the place given to faithful servants in contrast to the exclusion of unfaithful prophets. If we are inclined to dismiss this phraseology as too dependent on an outmoded view of a localized heaven, we should notice that other ways of referring to the same idea, such as 'counted among the saved' which we have just used, are equally figurative. Indeed, when describing supramundane realities we are bound to use mundane language, for we have no other, and therefore we must use it in a figurative sense, as our Lord does on this occasion.

Another instance in which the phrase 'in heaven' appears in the exclusively Lucan material is Luke 15⁷: 'Even so, I tell you there will be more joy in heaven over one sinner who repents than over ninety-nine righteous persons who need no repentance.' In the following story of the lost coin, which is a close parallel to the story of the lost sheep, a different phrase is used, apparently to express the same idea. Luke 15¹⁰: 'Even so, I tell you, there is joy before the angels of God over one sinner who repents.' Putting these two similar expressions together, we seem to gain a sense of community involved in the idea of 'in heaven'. The two stories do, in fact, make the point that when the lost sheep is recovered, and the lost coin is discovered, the shepherd and the housewife both call together their friends and neighbours—their rejoicing is on the basis of 'together'. It is surely not pressing the analogy too far to suppose that 'joy in heaven' means not only 'with God' but also in the company of those who are thought of with God. If this is allowed we then find a new insight into the meaning of 'in heaven'. Again, we have in the gospels a simple form of an idea which became very detailed and complicated— for instance the ideas connected with the hierarchy of angels, each with their special responsibility. The difference between the gospels, with their almost stark simplicity, and Jewish (and some Christian) writings, is very remarkable. The gospels always seem to hesitate to fill in the details. Yet the simple truth can be very impressive, as it is in this case. 'In heaven' is 'with God', and because it is 'with Him' it is 'with angels and archangels and all the company of heaven'.[36]

The remaining instance of Luke's use of 'heaven' as an apparent periphrasis for God is in the story of the lost son (15[11-32]). In his carefully rehearsed speech the prodigal says to his father: 'Father, I have sinned against heaven and before you' (15[18, 21]). Dalman admits that this is possibly the only exception to the rule that Luke does not consciously use 'heaven' meaning 'God'.[37] The phrase 'against heaven' could mean 'up to heaven' but as Easton remarks, this is too laboured,[38] and with Dalman we must accept it to mean against God, in spite of the difficulty of style which is involved. Dalman appears to think that the phrase might also mean 'even unto heaven' which implies that the fault of the prodigal was so great that it reached up to heaven. It is possible that Charles Wesley had this interpretation in mind in his lines:

> *My trespass was grown up to heaven;*
> *But far above the skies,*
> *In Christ abundantly forgiven,*
> *I see Thy mercies rise.*[39]

The conjunction of 'against heaven' and 'before you', i.e. before his father, needs also to be noted. The meaning of the story is so clearly based on the fact that the father represents the attitude of God, that we can easily forget that in essence this is a human situation which wonderfully exemplifies the love of God. Sin against God is at the same time offence against another person. Equally, the offence is not limited to the disregard of his father's care and love, but also, inevitably, involves sin against God. This conjunction of 'earth' and 'heaven' becomes important when we consider later the relationship between duties on earth and rewards in heaven. For the present we may usefully note that man and God are intimately bound together in this offence, which being against man is inevitably and equally against God.

Apart from the terms 'Father in heaven' and 'the Kingdom of

---

[36] Dalman, on the contrary, interprets 'joy in the presence of the angels of God' as joy in the presence of God, or strictly, God will rejoice. *Words*, p. 209.
[37] Ibid. pp. 217-18.
[38] *The Gospel according to St Luke*, p. 237.
[39] *Methodist Hymn-book*, No. 77[4].

heaven', which are treated in the next chapters, we have now reviewed all the occurrences of the word 'heaven' in the synoptic gospels. Our review produces some interesting conclusions, which may now be briefly indicated.

(1) The word 'heaven' is used in a variety of ways, all, no doubt, connected with the idea that the skies are especially the abode of spiritual beings, and God is naturally, perhaps inevitably, regarded as 'in heaven'. But the variety of meanings can only be interpreted with due regard for each separate instance. In particular, there seems no reason to think that every instance of the word has an eschatological flavour, although this aspect is dominant in some instances.

(2) While St Matthew is particularly fond of using the term, it does in fact occur, in its varied meanings, in all three synoptic gospels. This leads to the supposition that while Matthew may frequently use the term when another term appeared in his sources, he cannot be accused of complete invention. We can only suppose, in view of its appearance in all our sources, that the use of the word goes back to Jesus. This will inevitably affect the way we approach the phrases 'heavenly father' and 'Kingdom of heaven', for we cannot dismiss the 'heavenly' factor as purely a Matthean invention made for the purpose of dressing up the gospel in Jewish garments so that Jews would more readily understand and accept it.

(3) In few, if any, instances of the use of the word 'heaven' in the synoptic gospels is there any parallel with modern usage. The gospel records of our Lord's life and teaching do not speak of 'going to heaven', as a modern believer so naturally does. Rather is the emphasis on that which is 'heavenly' coming down to man, when any movement is thought of. Again, our modern way of speaking of life with God as being life 'in heaven' is not the way the gospels speak of the matter. Especially is there no suggestion that Jesus is offering to his disciples the certainty of 'heaven' after this life. This is not to say that there is no such assurance in the teaching of Jesus. Whether this is so or not we must further inquire. But certainly the term 'heaven' is not used of that assurance.

(4) The extent to which the phraseology of the gospels is affected by pre-Copernican views of the universe can easily be overstated. If we recognize the limitations of the ideas of the

universe held by the contemporaries of Jesus, we need not think
that these limitations make their ideas valueless to us. They spoke
in a figurative way of God coming down from heaven. We know
what they meant but we must not assume that thereby we know
all that they believed about God in His world. It is very difficult
to think that the first Christians thought God was 'up in the sky'
and nowhere else. We still have to use figurative and symbolic
language to express our views on these matters. We may think of
the universe in a different and undeniably more satisfactory
way than did the first Christians. But still, when we speak of
God and the future life, we must employ figurative language,
based upon the current and contemporary meaning. So we would
maintain that the inadequate cosmology of the gospels does not
invalidate their teaching about the future life.

# CHAPTER THREE

# HEAVENLY FATHER

IF it is true to say that the most usual name for God on the lips of Christians is 'Father',[1] it is also noteworthy that very frequently the adjective 'heavenly' and some personal pronoun (my—our—your) are added in Christian speech. The obvious reason for this terminology which we too easily take for granted, is that Jesus spoke thus of God, and especially in the prayer which he taught to his disciples he used the title 'Our Father who art in heaven' (Mt 6[9]). In view of the universal acceptance of this title it seems almost an impertinence to draw attention to the facts concerning the occurrences of this phrase in the gospels. But it is vital that we should have the facts before us, because only so are we likely to arrive at a just interpretation of them.

The first and most striking thing we notice is that the title 'Father in heaven' or 'heavenly Father' is almost exclusively a Matthean title. In fact the first gospel uses it 20 times, St Mark only once, and St Luke not at all, although he uses a phrase which is almost the exact equivalent of Matthew's phrase and is indeed translated 'heavenly Father' in the Revised Standard Version. The occurrences can be classified by means of the personal pronoun used—as follows:

(a)   *My Father in heaven*—ὁ πατήρ μου ὁ ἐν τοῖς οὐρανοῖς
            (Mt. 7[21], 10[32, 33], 12[50], 16[17], 18[10], 18[19]).
      *My heavenly Father*—ὁ πατήρ μου ὁ οὐράνιος
            (Mt 15[13], 18[35]).

(b)   *Your Father in heaven*—ὁ πατὴρ ὑμῶν ὁ ἐν τοῖς οὐρανοῖς
            (Mt 5[16], 5[45], 6[1], 7[11], 18[14], Mk 11[25]; cf. Lk 11[13]).
      *Your heavenly Father*—ὁ πατὴρ ὑμῶν ὁ οὐράνιος
            (Mt 5[48], 6[14], 6[26], 6[32], 23[9]).

The two instances outside St Matthew are clearly of special significance.

---

[1] J. Moffatt, *Theology of the Gospels*, p. 99: 'For Christianity the supreme title is that of "Father".'

(1) Mark 11²⁵: 'And whenever you stand praying, forgive, if you have anything against anyone, that your Father also who is in heaven may forgive you your trespasses.' This is part of the discourse reported by Mark which follows the disciples noticing that the fig tree which had been cursed had withered away. Jesus tells his men to have faith in God, and whatever they ask, even an apparent impossibility, such as the removing of a mountain, will be possible. The need for faith in asking is further stressed in verse 24. Then follows what seems to be another and possibly separate saying, referring to the need for forgiveness in those who ask for forgiveness for themselves. This seems to have been a genuine word of Jesus, which is also recorded by St Matthew (6¹⁴) immediately after the account of the Lord's Prayer. So Taylor writes: 'The sayings themselves are genuine utterances of Jesus, but the manner in which they are introduced is artificial.'² This remark applies with particular force to the verse we are considering, as it is difficult to see any reasonable connexion between the cursing of the fig tree and the demand for an attitude of forgiveness in those who seek forgiveness from God. The connexion with the Lord's Prayer, through the parallel in Matthew 6¹⁴, is taken by Taylor to indicate that this prayer was known in Rome before A.D. 60.³ We can also, from the evidence, draw the conclusion that Mark knew of this title which Jesus used for God—'your Father in heaven'.

(2) The reference in St Luke is also significant. 'If you then who are evil, know how to give good gifts to your children, how much more will the heavenly Father give the Holy Spirit to those who ask him?' (11¹³). This is also part of a discourse on prayer. In this passage from Q (cf. Mt 7⁷⁻¹¹), our Lord teaches the necessity of asking, seeking and knocking, and points to the certainty of being answered on the basis of the father-child relationship which men know to be operative in their own lives. If they, as fathers, do not give useless or dangerous things to their children, will not their heavenly Father more certainly give the Holy Spirit to them that ask him? There is a significant difference between Matthew and Luke at this point; Matthew says God will give good things, not the Holy Spirit, to them that ask him. The general opinion of interpreters is that Matthew's account is to be preferred here, and Luke has changed the general 'good things'

into the supremely good thing, namely the Holy Spirit, in accordance with his special interest in this direction.[4] If this is accepted, it seems to add more significance to the name given to God; we can say that having altered part of the statement in accordance with his special purposes and interests, it would have been easy for Luke to have changed the divine title as well. The fact that he has not done so suggests that he also, like Mark, knew the tradition that Jesus spoke of God as heavenly Father. Thus, although the great weight of evidence rests on Matthew, there is good reason for accepting the view that Jesus did speak of God in this way.

When the Jewish practice contemporary with Jesus is considered, there is strong reason for saying that he would be likely to use this name for God. Among the Jews it was a title very widely used. Although the term 'heavenly Father' does not occur in the Old Testament, there is a strong tradition bearing witness to the fatherhood of God. In Jewish writings approximately contemporary with the New Testament there are many instances of 'heavenly Father' being used. One significant sense is brought out by Simeon ben Yokhai (c. A.D. 130) who says that a wise man makes glad not only his earthly father, but also his heavenly Father. This expresses something of the warmth and intimacy involved in this name: it can be compared with the relation existing between a child and his earthly father, or, in another sense, the implication is that we need a heavenly Father just as much as, indeed more than, an earthly father. This likeness to an earthly father-child relationship is not allowed to be merely sentimental; the relationship involves rebuke and punishment, as Gamaliel II (c. A.D. 100) indicated in his statement that since the beloved children (i.e. Israel) provoked their heavenly Father to anger, he set over them an impious king. Again, the living reality of the relationship is well illustrated by the words of Nathan (c. A.D. 160) regarding the persecution of the Jews under Hadrian. 'Why art thou scourged?—Because I have done the will of my heavenly Father.' To modern ears the remark of Simeon ben Eleazar (c. A.D. 200) is not so significant, but perhaps tells us a good deal about the attitude of the Jews to requirements of the law. Concerning the mixture of materials in cloth he said: 'Whoever wears this is perverted and alienates himself from his heavenly Father.'[5]

---

[4] C. K. Barrett, *The Holy Spirit and the Gospel Tradition*, p. 127.
[5] See Dalman, *Words*, pp. 186ff.

On the basis of these typical examples it is reasonable to assert that 'Father in heaven' was a popular substitute for the divine name, which in the form of the tetragrammaton[6] had become obsolete. The implication of the title may well have been the simple belief that God did dwell in heaven.[7] Yet there still remains the doubt whether this title is secondary in Matthew, being introduced into his sources because of the author's fondness for the title, and especially for the word 'heaven'.[8]

T. W. Manson has discussed very fully and persuasively the subject of the use of 'Father' in the gospels in his *Teaching of Jesus*, Chapter 4. He carefully considers all the uses of 'Father' in the synoptic gospels and concludes that Mark and Luke are right in reporting that Jesus did not use the title 'Father' for 'God' in any indiscriminate way. Manson maintains, in fact, that our Lord only spoke of God in this way in prayer to God, or to his disciples and close acquaintances, and even to them, only after the confession of Simon Peter at Caesarea Philippi. This reticence in the use of the name 'Father' for 'God', Manson explains as due to the deep significance that the conception had for Jesus. As we have seen, it was nothing new in the thought of Israel to look upon God as Father. What was new was the reality of the experience of Fatherhood known to Jesus, and as with all men, he found it very difficult to speak openly to the crowds of that which was very deep in his heart. This reticence, although somewhat parallel to the secret of his Messiahship, arises from a different cause. It is not so much that the term 'Father' would be misunderstood, as was true of 'Messiah', but that Jesus could only speak of the relationship it implies in the intimacy of the small circle of disciples and even then, only after they had learned enough of his nature to begin to appreciate his meaning.

There are really two main parts to Manson's theory. These are:

(1) That Jesus only spoke about the Fatherhood of God among his disciples or in prayer to God.

[6] The consonants of the divine name were pronounced Adhonai (Lord), when the sacred name itself was thought to be too holy to be expressed. This practice led, in the sixteenth century, to the supposition that the divine name JHVH should be pronounced with the vowels of Adhonai—i.e. 'Jehovah'. But this popular name for God is almost certainly wrong. Yahweh is probably nearer the original form. Cf. O. S. Rankin in Richardson's *Theological Word Book*, p. 96.
[7] C. G. Montefiore, *A Rabbinic Anthology*, p. 23.
[8] T. W. Manson, *Teaching of Jesus*, p. 96.

D

(2) That Jesus did not use this title openly until after Caesarea Philippi.

Now it is true that these two main assertions are joined together very closely in Manson's discussion, but it could be argued that one may be true without the other. Especially the view about the time when Jesus began to speak about God as Father does not seem to be quite so firmly based as that which asserts that this title was not used to the crowds, but only in the prayers of Jesus or among his disciples. This point is particularly relevant for our present purpose in view of the effect it has upon our understanding of the term 'heavenly Father' or 'Father in heaven'. In discussing the question of the timing of the declaration of Fatherhood, Manson considers first the Marcan occurrences and shows that all instances of the name 'Father' for God fall after Peter's confession.[9] Next the witness of Q is considered, and it is suggested that only those sayings should be considered in which both Luke and Matthew use the title 'Father'. This means that in no case does the term 'heavenly Father' or 'Father in heaven' come under consideration in relation to Q's use of 'Father'. How this affects Manson's theory of the timing of our Lord's use of this title does not immediately concern us, but we must notice that by taking only Luke's version of the Q material, the title 'heavenly Father' is placed in a very secondary position. So Manson writes: 'It is evident that "Father", "heavenly Father" and especially "Father in heaven" are favourite words with the First Evangelist and that he was apt to insert them in his text even when some other expression was used in his sources.'[10]

Further, when the distinctive Matthean material is considered, Manson points out that nearly half the occurrences of 'Father' in this source are in the Sermon on the Mount. This being generally recognized as a composite collection, the matter of timing of each saying can only be left in a very undecided state. However, Manson shows that as far as the audience for these sayings is concerned, the few available comparisons with Mark show that the hearers were disciples. Then some of the sayings in Matthew are discounted on the basis of the view that Matthew 26[29] compared with Mark 14[25] shows that Matthew uses 'Kingdom of my Father' as an editorial modification of Mark's 'Kingdom of God'.[11] This means that Matthew 13[43] is regarded as another

[9] *Teaching of Jesus*, p. 95.       [10] Ibid. p. 96.       [11] Ibid. p. 97.

instance of this editorial modification, and the original was 'Kingdom of God'. Thus, apart from three cases dealt with below, all the instances of the use of 'Father' in Matthew are either discounted or else shown to conform to the pattern which applies to Mark and Q; namely, addressed to disciples, or used in prayer, and occurring after Caesarea Philippi. The three remaining passages dealt with rather summarily by Manson are Matthew 12⁵⁰, 20²³, 26²⁹. It will be helpful to look at these passages in some detail.

(a) Matthew 12⁵⁰: *'Whoever does the will of my Father in heaven, is my brother, and sister, and mother.'*
The parallel verse in Mark 3³⁵ reads: 'Whoever does the will of God, is my brother, and sister, and mother.'

The context of this saying is the occasion when our Lord's mother and brothers tried to get into touch with him and were not able to do so because of the crowd which surrounded him. When Jesus was told that they sought him, he replied by looking around at those who were with him and speaking the words we are now discussing. Now Matthew's use of 'the will of my Father in heaven' may indeed be an editorial modification of Mark's 'the will of God'. But we are bound to notice that it fits in very well with the circumstances and gives added point to our Lord's assertion of a new family relationship based on the community which does the will of his Father. The contrast between his earthly family and his responsibility to his heavenly Father is pointed all the more clearly by this title. Of course it can be argued that this very suitability makes it more likely that Matthew made the change for that reason. But it is at least arguable that Jesus himself could see, as clearly as any Evangelist, the apposite nature of his reference to his Father in heaven. It therefore seems that simply on the evidence of this passage, we can discount Matthew's report only if we have already decided that where 'heavenly Father' is used in parallel with 'God' the latter must be the original. Yet this is not immediately obvious, as we shall see below in considering the significance of 'Kingdom of heaven'. At any rate, we would claim that we ought not to dismiss from our consideration of the significance of 'heavenly Father' this passage from Matthew, in spite of Manson's rejection of it.

(*b*) Matthew 20²³: '*He said to them, "You will drink my cup, but to sit at my right hand and at my left is not mine to grant, but it is for those for whom it has been prepared by my Father".*'

The parallel passage is Mark 10³⁹⁻⁴⁰. 'And Jesus said to them, "The cup that I drink you will drink; and with the baptism with which I am baptized, you will be baptized; but to sit at my right hand or at my left is not mine to grant, but it is for those for whom it has been prepared".'

This is our Lord's answer to the request of the sons of Zebedee that they should sit on his right and left hand in his glory. Matthew's account varies from Mark in three particulars, apart from the question of the inclusion of 'Father'. Firstly, Matthew says the request was made by the mother of these two men, a difference which is usually explained by the view that Matthew thus softens the possible criticism which could be levelled against James and John, although this is somewhat weakened by the fact that Matthew as well as Mark reports the reaction of indignation by the other disciples. It might, on the other hand, be argued that Matthew's account is more detailed and realistic, and that Mark omits the reference to the mother of the disciples as an irrelevant detail. One is inclined to think that if the accounts had been reversed, the references to the mother of the sons of Zebedee 'worshipping him' would have been hailed as evidence of Marcan realism and clarity of detail! However, our study so far hardly supports the view that without question Matthew must be regarded as secondary in every detail of this story.

The second difference is that Matthew reports the request as applying to the 'Kingdom' of the Lord (20²¹) while Mark says that the request was for positions in 'your glory' (Mk 10³⁷). In view of the fact that 'in your glory' is an unexpected and unusual phrase in this gospel, and also reflects interest in the parousia, which is a fundamental concept in the teaching of Jesus, it is possible that Mark's account is nearer the original than Matthew's on this point. Nevertheless, it should be noted that some commentators think Matthew gives the original phrase.¹²

The third difference is that Mark includes a reference to baptism which is omitted by Matthew. This is regarded by Taylor as probably an original and creative utterance which

¹² VTM, p. 440.

refers to the coming trouble and suffering which the disciples would indeed share with their Master.[13]

In the variation with which we are particularly concerned, the use of 'by my Father' in Matthew but not in Mark, we notice that some texts of Mark (list in Taylor's Commentary, p. 441) include the phrase from Matthew, or something very much like it. This, of course, does not prove that these words ought to be in Mark, but it does suggest that they have been regarded as entirely suitable. This no doubt is partly due to the abruptness of the ending of the saying in Mark. 'Those for whom it has been prepared' also seems to be unduly impersonal; and one wonders if such an impersonal way of speaking of God is really typical of the sayings of Jesus. If then we feel bound to question Manson's rejection of this saying in its Matthean form, we notice that this does not in any way weaken the theory that Jesus spoke of the Fatherhood of God only to disciples or in prayer, for this is in any case a narrative very intimately connected with the small circle of closest disciples.

(c)  Matthew 26[29]: '*I shall not drink again of this fruit of the vine until that day when I drink it new with you in my Father's Kingdom.*' The parallel in Mark 14[25] reads: 'Truly I say to you, I shall not drink again of the fruit of the vine until that day when I drink it new in the Kingdom of God.'

It would be foolhardy to claim that Matthew is more original here, although in this verse the First Evangelist does give a fuller account, including the words 'with you' which may indicate a separate and reliable source. And again, we notice that in the circumstances of the Last Supper, in close intimacy with the disciples, Jesus might very well have spoken in the direct and personal way which the phrase 'in the Kingdom of my Father' implies. Still, we cannot press the superiority of Matthew here, and we may accept Manson's judgement regarding this instance,[14] but without implying that therefore 'Kingdom of God' is always to be preferred to 'Kingdom of heaven' or 'Kingdom of my Father'.

Manson goes on in a very interesting study to suggest that

[13] Ibid. p. 441.
[14] It is an editorial modification of what is given in Mark. *The Teaching of Jesus,* p. 98.

while Mark and Q are historically correct in indicating the reticence of Jesus in speaking of God as 'Father', Matthew and John are also right in emphasizing the idea of Fatherhood as one of the keys to the understanding of the gospels.[15] In this emphasis, the First and Fourth Evangelists were not inventing something which was not present in the early traditions, but were drawing out the deeper significance of that which was present but not emphasized, either by Jesus or by the earliest sources of the gospels. We have tried to show that this view, especially in regard to the people to whom Jesus spoke about God as Father, does not necessitate regarding Matthew's emphasis on God as Father in heaven as under suspicion of being secondary.

The question of the authenticity of the title 'heavenly Father' on the lips of Jesus can also be approached by a consideration of Matthew's actual usage. He does not invariably use this name, even when God is called Father. The facts may be set out as follows: The first gospel uses 'heavenly Father' 19 times; 'Father' 25 times; 'heavenly Father' never occurs without a personal pronoun; the instances being in detail 'your heavenly Father' 8 times; 'our heavenly Father' once (the Lord's Prayer); 'my heavenly Father' 10 times. Significantly, there are no instances of 'your' (singular) heavenly Father, nor of 'their' or 'his' heavenly Father. The title 'Father' has 'your' (plural) prefixed in 5 cases, 'my' in 7 cases, 'thy' in 5 cases, 'their' and 'his' once each. 'Our' does not occur with 'Father' and there are 6 cases in which the word is used without a personal pronoun. The distribution of the personal pronoun is interesting. 'Your' (plural) occurs 10 times in the Sermon on the Mount, twice in Chapter 10, verses 20, 29, and once in Chapter 23, verse 9. 'My', used by Jesus to describe his heavenly Father, occurs once only in the Sermon on the Mount ($7^{21}$); twice in Chapter 10, verses 32, 33; then at $12^{50}$, $15^{13}$, $16^{17}$, $18^{10, 14, 19, 35}$. When used with 'Father' simply, 'my' occurs once in Chapter 11, verse 27, and all the other instances are connected with the journey to Jerusalem and the account of the last days in Jerusalem. Four instances are in Chapter 26, in connexion with the Last Supper ($26^{29}$), the Agony in the Garden ($26^{39, 42}$), and the arrest of Jesus ($26^{53}$). These last instances seem to suggest that in the hour of his greatest conflict Jesus instinctively turned to his Father, using that most direct

[15] *The Teaching of Jesus*, p. 100.

mode of address 'my Father'. It is no indication that 'heavenly'
was not really part of our Lord's usual name for God, that he did
not use the word in these dreadful hours, because he never uses
'heavenly Father' when addressing his Father in prayer.

It would be extremely difficult to find any simple key to the
puzzle presented by these facts. Indeed, it would probably be
very misleading to try to say in detail on what principles Jesus
sometimes spoke of 'Father' sometimes of 'heavenly Father'. But
unless we are to discount entirely the witness of the First Evangelist, we seem bound to conclude that Jesus did sometimes speak of
God as 'Father', sometimes as 'heavenly Father'. It may very
well be that Jesus used both titles, and we need search no farther
for a pattern of usage than that suggested by a very natural practice of sometimes using the one, sometimes the other.

But if Jesus spoke of God as Father and heavenly Father, why
is there so little indication of this in Mark and Luke? The usual
explanation, as we have seen, is to say Matthew was particularly
fond of this title. This view implies, if it does not openly assert,
that the title is not really authentic. But there is another view,
suggested by Dalman, which merits consideration. This is that
Matthew does in fact faithfully record the practice of Jesus in
speaking of God as Father and heavenly Father. But these titles
could be very misleading to non-Jews, who would naturally interpret
them in terms of pagan notions, which might lead to many wrong
and unworthy views of God. So in presenting the gospels to the
non-Jewish world, Mark and Luke employed the term 'God'
where Matthew reports 'Father' or 'heavenly Father'. This would
be especially true of the latter phrase because, as we have seen,
this is not an Old Testament title for God. Its usage in Jewish
literature outside the Old Testament would not necessarily be any
commendation of it to Gentile Christians. 'A mode of speech
distinctively Jewish and not at the same time biblical had to be
avoided. The Jewish carefulness to make it clear through the
addition of 'in heaven' that 'Father' referred to God, might seem
superfluous to the Hellenist'.[16]

We must note carefully what this view implies. It is not
another attempt to claim that Matthew is the earliest gospel, but
an assertion that in the pre-written stage of Mark and Luke,
there arose this modification of rendering our Lord's 'Father' and

[16] Dalman, *Words*, p. 189.

'heavenly Father' as 'God'. That Jesus sometimes spoke of 'God' is also witnessed by St Matthew. $\Theta\epsilon\delta s$ (God) is used more than 30 times to report the words of Jesus, including five quotations from the Old Testament. These instances occur throughout St Matthew's gospel and present a difficulty to any theory which tries to systematize the divine title used by Jesus. On the basis of the theory we are suggesting we should have to say that not all the occurrences of 'God' as a name for the divine Person in Mark and Luke need be regarded as a change from 'Father' or 'heavenly Father'. Probably we have to admit that the likeliest possibility is that Jesus himself used different words to suit different occasions, and the three gospels taken together faithfully record the fact. But there seems little reason for discounting the title 'heavenly Father' on account of its appearances almost exclusively in one gospel.

Even if we did accept the view that the change is from 'God' to 'Father' rather than the reverse, we still have to account for the change. Supposing Matthew was specially fond of the titles 'Father' and 'heavenly Father' we still may inquire the reason for this fondness. While it is true that 'heavenly Father' was a very popular Jewish title for God in the first Christian century, and this no doubt would commend it to Jewish Christians, it was not the only circumlocution in use at the time. God was also referred to in this roundabout fashion as 'The Highest' (Lk 6[35]), 'The Blessed One' (Mk 14[61]), 'The Power' (Mt 26[64] and parallels), 'The Holy One' (not used in the gospels as a divine title, but see 1 Pet 1[15]); 'The Merciful One' (see Rom 9[16]).[17] It is noticeable how rarely these terms occur in the synoptic gospels, and consequently how little they have been used in Christian language compared with the term 'Father'. Why did Matthew choose this particular Jewish way of speaking of God, instead of one of the others if he is held to have 'translated' 'God' from the language of Mark and Luke into a term acceptable by the Jewish world? In view of the undoubted use of 'Father' by Jesus, to which all the gospels bear witness, surely the best answer to our question is that Matthew reports Jesus using the term 'heavenly Father' because he knew from tradition that Jesus in fact spoke of God in this way. This seems, at any rate, a far more satisfactory view than that which merely says Matthew uses 'heavenly Father' for 'God'

[17] Dalman, *Words*, pp. 198-204.

because he was 'fond of it'. Indeed, this explanation goes perilously near asserting that Matthew was fond of it, as we know from his frequent use of it; and his frequent use is due to his fondness!

If then, we can assert that there is good reason to think that Jesus did sometimes speak of God as 'heavenly Father' we must inquire what content of meaning our Lord put into this phrase. This is important not only for our understanding of Jesus' view of God, but also for appreciation of what is meant by 'heaven' or 'heavenly'.

The passages in which Jesus is reported as speaking of God as 'heavenly Father' are not easy to classify and we may be mistaken if we try to impose too rigid a scheme upon them. The general impression, however, is quite clear, for in this title Jesus brings together two necessary and sometimes apparently irreconcilable concepts of the divine nature. These are the transcendence or 'otherness' of God on the one hand, and His intimacy and nearness on the other hand. While we gratefully recognize the contribution of Jewish thought in making 'heavenly Father' a well-known name for God, we also see that Jesus filled this name with a wonderful new content, which arose out of his own experience. In his conception of God, transcendence and nearness are uniquely combined. This combination comes about through our Lord emphasizing the family relationship between God and man, against the background of the concept of the heavenly divine Being. On the other hand, the heavenly aspect, as in Jewish thought, is made a safeguard against the wrong sort of familiarity. In Jewish parlance it is unusual to refer to God in common discourse as Father, without adding the epithet 'heavenly'.[18] On the other hand, in the language of Jesus, 'the usage of family life is transferred to God; it is the language of the child to its father'.[19] With this general observation we can look more closely at the instances in which 'heavenly Father' is used. The following summary makes no claim to be exhaustive; nor are we asserting that the undermentioned views of God are not found elsewhere in the teaching of Jesus. But with these admitted limitations, we may say that the occurrences of this phrase give something of the following impression of God.

(1) When a man thinks of God, who is in heaven, he should raise his thoughts and expectations above their normal level. So

[18] Ibid. p. 190.     [19] Ibid. p. 192.

the disciples are to let their light shine before men that they may
see your good works and give glory to your Father who is in
heaven (Mt 5¹⁶), or, in the Lord's Prayer (Mt 6⁹), men are to say:
'Our Father who art in heaven, hallowed be Thy name.' The
same idea of the exalted nature of God, and the need for man to
lift up his eyes, is seen in a passage in Luke (6³⁵) in which an
alternative for heaven is used. 'But love your enemies and do
good, and lend, expecting nothing in return, and your reward will
be great and you will be sons of the Most High.' The near-
parallel in Matthew 5⁴⁵ is 'that you may be sons of your Father
who is in heaven'. Those who are sons of the Most High have set
before them the highest aims and ideals of human living. When
Jesus spoke to his disciples of their heavenly Father, he was directing their attention away from their own weakness, to the mighty
power and glory of God.

(2) The heavenly Father is like an earthly father, who in the
eyes of his child is the source of all good gifts. God the heavenly
Father is the Giver of all good things—men can and must believe
this, says Jesus, because they know how to give good gifts to their
children (Mt 7¹¹): 'If you then, who are evil, know how to give
good gifts to your children, how much more will your Father who
is in heaven give good things to those who ask him.' Luke makes
the Holy Spirit the promised gift here (Lk 11¹³) but the principle
remains the same whichever gift is thought of. This assurance of
the care of God, as the care of the heavenly Father, is emphasized
in Matthew 6²⁶, ³²: 'Look at the birds of the air, they neither sow
nor reap, nor gather into barns, and your heavenly Father feeds
them. Are you not of more value than they? ... For the Gentiles
seek all these things; and your heavenly Father knows that you
need them all.' If we compare here Luke 12²⁴, ³⁰, we find 'God'
used for 'heavenly Father' in the first part and 'Father' simply in
the second part. For most people Matthew's way of putting the
matter is much more convincing and reassuring. God our
heavenly Father is able to look after us because his power is
heavenly; it is not confined to this world. But also he is willing,
indeed anxious, to care for us, for he is our Father and we are his
children.

(3) Next we notice that the phrase 'the will of your heavenly
Father' occurs in several places in the sayings we are considering.
Matthew 7²¹: 'Not everyone who says to me, Lord, Lord, shall

enter into the Kingdom of heaven; but he who does the will of my Father who is in heaven.' Again, Matthew 12[50]: 'For whoever does the will of my Father in heaven, is my brother, and sister, and mother.' Mark 3[35]: 'Whoever does the will of God', etc., and Luke 8[21]: 'My mother and my brothers are those who hear the word of God and do it', do not seem to have quite the same force as Matthew's 'heavenly Father'. A saying which is only recorded by Matthew (18[14]) makes the same point of emphasizing the will of the heavenly Father—'so it is not the will of my Father which is in heaven, that one of these little ones should perish'.

These sayings bear witness to a further aspect of the heavenly Fatherhood of God, as it is known by Jesus and transmitted to his disciples. The heavenly Father has a 'will'. This will has to be done by those who seek to enter His heavenly realm; it is the conformity to this will which is the *sine qua non* of entry into the new community of the family of God. And this will is the active concern of the Father in heaven which continually seeks to preserve his little ones from perishing. This is another example of the remarkable duality and balance of this title. God is to be regarded as Father; yet not as Someone who merely tries to satisfy the wish of every petulant child. One who has a purpose, and who demands that those who recognize His heavenly Fatherhood, shall place themselves under the yoke of obedience to His will.

(4) Lastly, we may notice that there is in the use of this title, both a contrast and a comparison between God and man. First, the contrast is emphasized in the following sayings: 'Beware of practising your piety before men in order to be seen by them; for then you will have no reward from your Father who is in heaven' (Mt 6[1]); 'Flesh and blood has not revealed this to you, but my Father who is in heaven' (Mt 16[17]). Possibly also under this heading should be included Matthew 15[13]: 'Every plant which my heavenly Father has not planted will be rooted up.'[20] This is our Lord's comment on the reaction of the Pharisees to his dictum 'not what goes into the mouth defiles a man but what comes out of the mouth, this defiles a man'. In these sayings Jesus seems to be emphasizing the great gulf which is set between God and man. It is dangerous for them to confuse the praise of men with the approval of God; the truth which had come to

---

[20] Cf. Matthew 23[9]: 'Call no man your father on earth, for you have one Father, who is in heaven.'

Simon Peter at Caesarea Philippi was distinctively from God, not from man. This infers that 'heavenly' has a sense of 'not human'; the approval of God is beyond comparison with the praise of men; God the heavenly Father stands over against man, requiring his obedience and setting before him the only true standard, that of God in heaven.

Secondly, God and man are brought together in comparison, and the connexion between the service of God and our duty to our fellow men is made clear. The most striking illustration of this point is in the only 'Father in heaven' saying which occurs in Mark (11[25]): 'And whenever you stand praying, forgive, if you have anything against anyone; so that your Father also who is in heaven may forgive you your trespasses.' Matthew 6[14] reads: 'For if you forgive men their trespasses, your heavenly Father also will forgive you, but if you do not forgive men their trespasses, neither will your Father forgive your trespasses.' Again, Matthew 10[32]: 'So everyone who acknowledges me before men, I also will acknowledge before my Father who is in heaven' (cf. Lk 12[8]). Also Matthew 18[19]: 'If two of you agree on earth about anything they ask, it will be done for them by my Father in heaven', and Matthew 18[35]: 'So also my heavenly Father will do to every one of you, if you do not forgive your brother from your hearts.' In a variety of ways these sayings all make the point of the relationship between our responsibilities to one another and our standing with our Father in heaven. We shall not be forgiven by our heavenly Father unless we forgive each other. Equally our confession of Christ before men is closely connected with his confession of us before our heavenly Father. The conditions under which the promised blessing of our heavenly Father will be granted, are that we should agree together.

Within this category of these sayings, therefore, we see another of these complementary truths. God is other than man; yet the service of God involves the service of man; to live in fellowship with our heavenly Father it is necessary to live in fellowship with each other.

Therefore we may conclude that the heavenly Father was to Jesus the transcendent One, who is yet near to man; the One who bestows gifts, yet at the same time makes demands that His will be obeyed; the One who is other than man, yet whose service must be worked out among men. 'The words "who is in heaven" have in them no suggestion of the remoteness of God, exalted above the world in His celestial habitation; they remove the ambiguity of the bare "father" by thus distinguishing between God and an earthly father.'[21]

We have noted in the previous chapter that the current use of 'heaven' as a description of the future life is not based upon New Testament usage. As a result of these investigations into the meaning of 'heavenly Father', we can see an indirect connexion between the New Testament view of heaven and the Christian hope for the future. This connexion is made through the consideration of God as heavenly Father, for the Christian hope is centred on fellowship with God. If this is accepted, the quality and character of life hereafter depends on the nature of God. From the words of Jesus we learn that our heavenly Father is exalted, he cares for us as children, he has a will which we must obey, and his service is closely connected with the service of our fellow men. These are principles which apply to this present life. It is the growing conviction forced upon us by this study that the same principles apply to the future life. What we call 'heaven' is truly life with 'our heavenly Father', whose nature and purpose are made known to us in Jesus Christ.

[21] G. F. Moore, *Judaism*, II.205.

# CHAPTER FOUR

# KINGDOM OF HEAVEN AND KINGDOM OF GOD

THE last subject in our consideration of the meaning of 'heaven' in the gospels brings us to the question of the significance of the phrase 'the Kingdom of heaven'. It is a fact which cannot escape the attention of even a passing acquaintance with the gospels, that this term is only used by St Matthew. Apart from the first gospel, the only other occurrence of the phrase is in a doubtful reading of John 3[5]. As if to make up for the absence of the words elsewhere in the New Testament, St Matthew uses them very frequently. There are 31 instances of the use of the phrase in the first gospel; in all except two of these the words are ascribed to Jesus. The two exceptions are 3[2], in which John the Baptist is reported saying: 'Repent, for the Kingdom of heaven is at hand'; and 18[1], in which the disciples come to Jesus saying: 'Who is greatest in the Kingdom of heaven?' In neither of these cases are we very far from the main tradition that Jesus spoke of the Kingdom of heaven, for the reference to John is usually regarded as due to the influence of the teaching of Jesus, and in the other case it is perfectly natural that if Jesus spoke of the Kingdom of heaven, his disciples would also. But did Jesus speak in this way? Therein lies the whole crux of the matter, for there is little use in considering what 'Kingdom of heaven' meant to Jesus if, in fact, he did not use the expression.

The last-named conclusion seems to be almost universally accepted and it is not difficult to see why this is so.

First, it is obvious that the term 'Kingdom of God' is regarded as synonymous with 'Kingdom of heaven'. A few examples will show how the two phrases are used in the same passage by different gospels.

Mark 1[15]: The time is fulfilled, and the Kingdom of God is at hand.

Matt 4[17]: Repent, for the Kingdom of heaven is at hand.

Matt 5[3]:   Blessed are the poor in spirit, for theirs is the Kingdom of heaven.

Luke 6[20]:   Blessed are you poor; for yours is the Kingdom of God.

Matt 11[11]:   Among those born of women there has risen no one greater than John the Baptist; yet he who is least in the Kingdom of heaven is greater than he.

Luke 7[28]:   Among those born of women none is greater than John: yet he who is least in the Kingdom of God is greater than he.

A parallel taken from one of the parables might also be added as an example:

Matt 13[31]:   The Kingdom of heaven is like a grain of mustard seed, which a man took and sowed in his field.

Mark 4[30-1]:   With what can we compare the Kingdom of God? . . . It is like a grain of mustard seed. . . .

The other instances in which Matthew has 'Kingdom of heaven' when either Mark or Luke, or both, have 'Kingdom of God' are Matthew 13[11], parallel Mark 4[11]; Matthew 13[33], par. Luke 13[20]; Matthew 19[14], pars. Mark 10[14], Luke 18[16]; Matthew 19[23], pars. Mark 10[24], Luke 18[24]. It is clear from these cases when they are taken together, that the gospels use 'Kingdom of heaven' and 'Kingdom of God' as complete synonyms.

Secondly, it is generally accepted among students of the gospels that Matthew has used Mark as one of his written sources; in which case when there is a difference between the two, we have to say that Matthew has changed something which he found in Mark; it is very difficult to account for the differences between the gospels on any other basis than the priority of Mark. Also, when Matthew and Luke agree together but not with Mark, it is reasonable to suppose that they depend on each other or on a common source. This latter alternative is very widely held by scholars, who give to this unknown, but very important source, the name of 'Q' (from the German 'Quelle'). And as with Mark, so when Matthew shows general agreement with Luke, but difference over such a phrase as 'Kingdom of heaven', we can suppose that Matthew has changed the terminology. Thus we can suppose that both Mark and Q are prior to Matthew, and they both use 'Kingdom of God' rather than 'Kingdom of heaven'. This seems to make a very weighty case against accepting the phrase 'Kingdom of heaven' as in any way belonging to the earliest tradition of the sayings of Jesus. Further, it is urged that in any case the phrase means precisely the same as 'Kingdom of God' so that there is no point in pursuing the matter any farther.

Yet it ought to be noticed that however attractive this theory may be, it does not explain why Matthew made this change. As we noted when considering the title 'heavenly Father', it is really no explanation to say Matthew did this because he was fond of the word 'heaven'. Why was he fond of it? Is it enough merely to say that the phrase would appeal to Jews, for whom Matthew wrote his gospel? It is asserted that in deference to Jewish wishes and practices Matthew used 'heaven' as a roundabout way of referring to God, and there is no doubt that this practice was very common among the Jews at this period. But if this is Matthew's practice, he is by no means consistent in his application of it. We have already considered the evidence about the use of the divine title by Matthew.[1] And can we accept the view that the First Evangelist was quite ready to use his own words when reporting the words of Jesus? The tendency of modern study of the gospels is against crediting the authors with too great freedom in the use of imagination or interpretation in this task of reporting the deeds and especially the words of Jesus.

The statistics we noted at the beginning of this chapter must, at this point, be amplified and commented upon. There are 31 instances of 'Kingdom of heaven' in Matthew. We have seen that in nine of these there is a parallel in either Mark or Luke which uses 'Kingdom of God'. This leaves twenty-two occurrences of 'Kingdom of heaven' for which there is no parallel in the other gospels. There are three cases among these twenty-two which ought perhaps to be regarded as 'doubtful'. That is, while the parallel is not exact, it appears from the context that the same incident or saying is being referred to.

These cases are Matthew 8[11]: 'Many will come from east and west and sit at table with Abraham and Isaac and Jacob in the Kingdom of heaven.' Compare Luke 13[28]: 'When you see Abraham and Isaac and Jacob and all the prophets in the

1 See above, Chapter 3.

Kingdom of God.' Secondly, Matthew 10[7]: 'Preach as you go, saying, The Kingdom of heaven is at hand.' Compare Luke 9[2]: 'And he sent them out to preach the Kingdom of God.' Thirdly, Matthew 11[12]: 'From the days of John the Baptist until now the Kingdom of heaven has suffered violence, and men of violence take it by force.' Compare Luke 16[16]: 'The law and the prophets were until John: since then the good news of the Kingdom of God is preached, and everyone enters it violently.' In all these cases there is not a close verbal similarity, yet it is not unreasonable to say that in each parallel case the same incident or saying is being referred to. So we may add these three cases to the nine already mentioned and say that out of a total of 31 instances, 12 only have a direct or indirect parallel which uses 'Kingdom of God' when Matthew uses 'Kingdom of heaven'. It is, no doubt, a sound principle of interpretation to assume that an author uses a word or a phrase in the same sense throughout his work, and on this basis 'Kingdom of heaven' is interpreted throughout Matthew as merely the peculiar variant of the original 'Kingdom of God'. It is perhaps worth noting that on this view, the meaning of 'Kingdom of heaven' is interpreted on the basis of considerably less than half its occurrences.

It gives added force to this point to enumerate some of the 'Kingdom of heaven' sayings in Matthew which have no parallel in either Mark or Luke. The list includes some very important sayings and parables of Jesus. Firstly, sayings:

5[10]: Blessed are those who are persecuted for righteousness' sake, for theirs is the Kingdom of heaven.

5[19]: Whoever then relaxes one of the least of these commandments, and teaches men so, shall be called least in the Kingdom of heaven (Cf. Mt 5[20]).

13[52]: Every scribe who has been trained for the Kingdom of heaven, is like a householder who brings out of his treasure what is new and what is old.

16[19]: I will give you the keys of the Kingdom of heaven.

18[3]: Unless you turn and become like children, you will never enter the Kingdom of heaven (Cf. 18[4]).

23[13]: Woe to you, scribes and Pharisees, hypocrites, because you shut the Kingdom of heaven against men, for you neither enter yourselves, nor allow those who would enter to go in.

Secondly, the following parables in Matthew come in this category of passages using 'Kingdom of heaven', which have no parallel in the other gospels: Wheat and Tares (13[24]), Hid Treasure (13[44]), Merchant seeking goodly pearls (13[45]), Drag Net (13[47]), Unforgiving Servant (18[23]), Labourers in Vineyard (20[1]), Ten Virgins (25[1]).

It must be admitted that this is a very considerable amount of material. On the basis of consistency we must suppose that 'Kingdom of heaven' means in these passages what it means in those passages in which it is apparently synonymous with 'Kingdom of God'. But it will be necessary to consider further whether this material outlined above has any distinctive teaching about the nature of the Kingdom of heaven. It seems very cavalier treatment largely to ignore more than half of Matthew's statements about the Kingdom of heaven simply because they are not closely paralleled in either Mark or Luke.

To complete this survey of the use of 'Kingdom of heaven' we have to notice the four instances in which Matthew uses 'Kingdom of God'. These are as follows:

(1) 12[28]: *But if it is by the Spirit of God that I cast out demons then the Kingdom of God has come upon you.*

The parallel in Luke 11[20] is the same except that for 'Spirit' Luke reads 'finger of God'. This is an important saying, ostensibly arising out of the discussion provoked by the objection of the Pharisees, that Jesus was casting out devils by Beelzebub, the Prince of devils. As Kümmel points out[2] this logion must be regarded as a detached saying, in view of the point made by Jesus of comparing his own exorcisms with those of 'the sons of the Pharisees'. If the saying really belonged to this context, it would imply that the exorcisms of other people also indicated the presence of the Kingdom of God. The saying is an important assertion of the present reality of the Kingdom of God. The word ἔφθασεν means 'has arrived'. This is all the more important if we agree with Kümmel[3] that Mark 1[15] does not mean, as asserted by Dodd[4] the 'Kingdom has come'. Dodd indeed agrees with Kümmel's view of this passage under consideration: '(It) expresses in the most vivid and forcible way the fact that the

[2] W. G. Kümmel, *Promise and Fulfilment*, p. 105.
[3] Ibid. p. 107.     [4] *The Parables of the Kingdom*, p. 44.

Kingdom of God has actually arrived.'[5] Kümmel connects this very closely with the exorcisms which Jesus has performed. 'From the deeds which can be perceived (i.e. exorcisms) Jesus deduces the fact not perceptible of itself—"then the Kingdom of God has come upon you".'[6] This interpretation is vital for the view which asserts that the Kingdom of God has in a real sense begun to be operative in the activity of Jesus. The following verses, concerning the spoiling of the house of the strong man being preceded by overcoming him, also point the same truth. Thus we can say that in one of the key sayings about the Kingdom, Matthew uses the phrase found in Mark and 'Q'—'the Kingdom of God'.

McNeile's explanation of the occurrence of 'Kingdom of God' in this passage is 'He [Matthew] must have found it in his source and left it unaltered, perhaps in the present case because it formed a better parallel to "by the spirit of God", and also a sharper contrast with "his Kingdom" [12²⁶], the Divine Personality standing over against the Satanic'.[7] Perhaps this is as near as we can get to any explanation of the use of 'Kingdom of God' here, although it seems worthy of note that this is such a clear statement of the presence of the Kingdom of God. Perhaps we can go a little farther along the line suggested by McNeile and say that when the present aspect of the rule of God, evidenced in the mighty works of Jesus, is under consideration, the most fitting term seems to be 'Kingdom of God'. This is only drawing out the implication of McNeile's supposition and drawing attention to an important issue. Apparently Matthew, on this view, did recognize some difference of emphasis between 'Kingdom of heaven' and 'Kingdom of God'. This must surely be the case if, as McNeile says, 'Kingdom of God' forms 'a better parallel' and 'a sharper contrast'. Perhaps after all, even though the phrases mean substantially the same, there is a difference of emphasis. In that case, Matthew's retention here of 'Kingdom of God' is not accidental and may indeed be connected with the main idea of the passage, namely the present fact of the Kingdom of God.

[5] Ibid. p. 43.    [6] Kümmel, *Promise and Fulfilment*, p. 106.
[7] *The Gospel according to St Matthew*, p. 176.

(2) 19²⁴: *It is easier for a camel to go through the eye of a needle than for a rich man to enter the Kingdom of God.* (Cf. Mk 10²⁵, Lk 18²⁵.)

There is some doubt about the text of Matthew in this verse; several of the cursive manuscripts which often depend on a good earlier text, and some versions reading 'Kingdom of heaven'. But the great ancient MSS have 'the Kingdom of God', which fact is reflected in the most recent critical texts and translations.[8] In view of the fact that the more unusual text is generally regarded as most reliable, we seem forced to consider 'Kingdom of God' as the most probable at this point. McNeile's explanation is somewhat unconvincing. 'Its retention here from St Mark may have been an oversight on Matthew's part, but much more probably a harmonization with Mark which has been rightly corrected in the earliest versions.'[9] In view of the comment we made above concerning the passage in Matthew 12²⁸, the view of Taylor on the parallel Marcan passage is interesting. 'Possibly "Kingdom" is conceived eschatologically, but more probably it is thought of as present.'[10] If this is accepted, we note that in this second passage, Matthew uses 'Kingdom of God' where the emphasis lies on the present reality of the Kingdom. Without making this the basis of any theory about the comparative meaning of the two phrases, we do seem to have here further evidence that Matthew could use 'Kingdom of God' when the circumstances made it specially suitable.

(3) 21³¹: *Truly I say to you, the tax collectors and the harlots go into the Kingdom of God before you.*

There is no parallel to this saying in either Mark or Luke, although there are connexions of thought. For instance, the Lucan story of the Pharisee and tax collector at prayer (18¹⁰⁻¹⁴) seems to teach the same lesson, and although the phrase 'tax collectors and harlots' does not appear (except in this passage) there are, of course, frequent references to the tax collectors, and one other reference to harlots in the gospels (Lk 15³⁰). Jeremias[11] says

---

[8] Nestlé's text (23rd edition, 1957); and *RSV* (1952) have 'Kingdom of God' in the text. Although Huck's *Synopse* (3rd edition, 1906) has 'Kingdom of heaven' in the text and 'Kingdom of God' as a good marginal reading, the 9th revised edition (1935, E.T. 1954) has 'of God' in the text and 'of heaven' in the margin.
[9] *The Gospel according to St Matthew*, p. 280.
[10] VTM, p. 431.
[11] *The Parables of Jesus*, p. 64.

that an allegorical reference to John the Baptist is added (Mt 21[32]) because of the likeness to Luke 7[29], which mentions the publicans as among those who heard and responded to the Baptist's message. As far as the inclusion of 'Kingdom of God' is concerned, McNeile says that the reason for it cannot be determined, but it may have been an oversight or an early slip.[12] We must allow for the possibility of this sort of reason and it would be rash to try to build any theory upon this passage. It is perhaps worthy of note that as in the other cases we have considered, 'Kingdom of God' here appears to refer to a present reality. The tax collectors and harlots are already entering the Kingdom of God, for the present tense is used. That which is being entered must be already present.

(4) 21[43]: *The Kingdom of God will be taken away from you and given to a nation producing the fruits of it.*

This saying is only found in Matthew. It is the application of the story of the Wicked Husbandmen (Mt 21[33-43], Mk 12[1-11], Lk 20[9-18]) which, according to Dodd[13] and Jeremias,[14] depicts a realistic situation which could well arise in the prevalent circumstances of landlords frequently being foreigners. Jeremias points out that a process of allegorization is discernible, beginning indeed in Mark (see verse 5b) and extending in the Matthean and Lucan versions. Thus the saying in question is part of Matthew's added allegorical details, and for this reason can hardly be regarded as an original saying of our Lord. Even so, Matthew's use of it here merits our attention, as revealing something of the Evangelist's understanding of the two terms 'Kingdom of heaven' and 'Kingdom of God'. McNeile regards the use of 'Kingdom of God' here as necessary because something other than 'Kingdom of heaven' is meant. The basis for this is apparently the Old Testament use of the vineyard to represent the people of God (Isa 5[7], etc.); so 'the vineyard' which is the community of Israel, is the 'Kingdom of God'.[15] This identification of the Kingdom of God with the people of Israel is very difficult to support from the other words of Jesus. Certainly this assumption tends directly to a very misleading identification between the Kingdom of God and the

12 *The Gospel according to St Matthew*, p. 306.
13 *The Parables of the Kingdom*, p. 130.
14 *The Parables of Jesus*, pp. 55-6.
15 *The Gospel according to St Matthew*, p. 312.

Church on earth, which as Flew shows,[16] has no foundation in the thought of the first two Christian centuries. It is best, therefore, to conclude that Matthew's allegorizing practice has led him into a statement which is not true to the meaning of the parable; which is, in fact, that the privileges of the people of God are to be taken away from those unworthy of them and given to the poor. As far as our present purpose is concerned, we have to conclude that this occurrence of 'Kingdom of God' does not give us any guidance about any difference to be detected between 'Kingdom of God' and 'Kingdom of heaven'.

The other occurrences also, cannot really support any theory that Matthew understood by 'Kingdom of heaven' something entirely different from 'Kingdom of God'. It is indeed not on this basis that we shall gain most understanding of the term 'Kingdom of heaven', but rather, by recognizing that 'Kingdom of heaven' stands for the same reality as 'Kingdom of God', we shall see that each term may contribute something to our understanding of that reality.

That there is a difference of emphasis in the two terms is suggested by Dalman in his careful study of 'Kingdom of heaven' in the gospels.[17] He shows that 'Kingdom of heaven' is an exact equivalent of the Aramaic phrase '*malkutha dishmaya*'. This in turn originates in the Hebrew '*malkuth shamayim*', and in both cases is a periphrasis for 'Kingdom of God'. But Dalman writes: 'Although *malkutha dishmaya* is thus tantamount to "the sovereignty of God", it does not thence follow that all trace of the thought that in the phrase the dwelling-place of God was being named, must have been obliterated'.[18] Dalman carefully guards against any suggestion that the Kingdom is in some way to be regarded as transcendental, which idea, he says 'can only arise out of unfamiliarity with Jewish phraseology'.[19] Yet while it is not the Kingdom which is being designated as transcendent, the idea of transcendence is not entirely absent, for it is the King who is thus regarded. 'The *basileia ton ouranon* is the sovereignty of the transcendent God.'[20] Thus Dalman argues that there is a distinctive quality about 'Kingdom of heaven' which arises out of the idea that it is the rule of the transcendent God. This, we repeat, is not to imply that Matthew claims to be describing a different

---

[16] *Jesus and His Church*, pp. 125-6.     [17] *Words*, pp. 91-6.
[18] Ibid. p. 92.     [19] Ibid. p. 92.     [20] Ibid. p. 93.

reality from Mark and Luke, but that he is, in fact, giving a different emphasis to the one reality.

The work of Rudolf Otto has added considerably to our thought in this connexion. In his fascinating study entitled *The Kingdom of God and the Son of Man*, Otto uses the two titles 'Kingdom of God' and 'Kingdom of heaven' sometimes interchangeably, but usually with the implication of a difference of emphasis. One of the great advantages of Otto's study is that he appreciates the many-sided character of the rule of God, and in this, recognizes the significance of 'heavenly'. In this connexion he writes: 'The idea that righteousness as a state of sanctification, and that blessedness, are not possible in an earthly form of existence, but only in the wholly other form of existence which God will give; that they are not possible in this world but only in heaven, and in a Kingdom of heaven—this idea is the hidden main-spring in the formation of the eschatological, as distinct from merely Messianic conceptions.'[21] Thus to Otto one essential feature in consistent eschatology is 'the idea of a wondrous new creation, i.e. the Kingdom of heaven as a new and different sphere and form for the sanctified, and, therefore, necessarily, no longer earthly existence'.[22] Otto links this closely with the idea which he has developed in *The Idea of the Holy*, that the holy is the wholly other, and expresses his view very forcefully as 'one can only be holy in heaven'.[23]

The value of Otto's thought here is very great, in so far as he has shown that a comprehensive view of the reign of God must take into account the aspect of 'other-worldly'. This indeed is the emphasis which surely belongs to the phrase 'Kingdom of heaven'. It is, of course, the reign of God; the Divine sovereignty is an aspect of the teaching of Jesus which has been properly and impressively stressed in the current emphasis on the Kingdom of God, and if we follow the view of Otto and Dodd, we recognize that part of the message of the Kingdom of God is that in the life and ministry of Jesus, the rule of God has become operative on earth. Here and now, in this present life, among the earthly duties and needs of men, God has begun to reign in Jesus Christ. Because of this fact the message of the Kingdom is an offer of grace. Those who respond to the rule of God in Christ by becoming

---

[21] R. Otto, *The Kingdom of God and the Son of Man*, p. 49.
[22] Ibid. p. 53.     [23] Ibid. p. 50.

obedient to him, here and now, become sons of the Kingdom. It is because of the present fact of the rule of God that the gospel presents men with a decision: indeed with a critical choice. God in His sovereign power has begun in Christ the final process for which all creation has been made. It is not necessary to make this the only message of the Kingdom to see the tremendous 'here and now' significance of 'realized eschatology'.

Yet it becomes increasingly clear that the idea of realized eschatology is not adequate to explain all the aspects of the teaching of the gospels. There is the future aspect, which cannot be ignored if we are to take seriously the gospel accounts of the teaching of Jesus. This future aspect of the rule of God does, of course, raise the very complicated problem of 'When?' And especially the problem of how to interpret those sayings of Jesus in which he seems very clearly to have expected a consummation in his own lifetime.

The alternatives seem to be limited to two—either Jesus was mistaken or else he was misunderstood. Neither conclusion is easy to draw, and the discussion still goes on, with perhaps an increasing tendency to take more seriously the future aspect of the message of the Kingdom. With due deference to the many great scholars who have wrestled with this aspect of the Kingdom of God, one cannot help wondering if the emphasis has not become rather narrow and unbalanced. The future aspect of the rule of God not only involves the question of 'time': it also involves the question of 'sphere' and 'quality'. That is, the aspect of our Lord's teaching which is emphasized in the phrase 'the Kingdom of heaven'. The rule of God cannot be consummated on this earth. If we say then 'in heaven' in our modern sense of the phrase, we must recognize that this is not the sense implied in the gospels. Not 'in' anywhere, but the other world coming down to meet this world, is the sense emphasized by 'Kingdom of heaven'. Otto writes, with complete justification, as I think: 'When it is said that the Kingdom comes, the idea is always present to some extent that it comes down from above. It would perhaps be going too far if one were to say frankly "a new world, which descends from above", but undoubtedly, the idea lies along this line.'[24]

Our conclusion is that 'Kingdom of heaven' and 'Kingdom of God' are intended as synonyms. Yet as with most, if not all,

[24] *The Kingdom of God and the Son of Man*, p. 54.

synonyms, there is a different emphasis attached to each. They
do not in any way contradict each other, but rather, present
complementary truths which combine to reveal something of the
full meaning of this tremendous concept of our Lord. 'Kingdom
of heaven' emphasizes the other-worldly, supernatural, extra-
mundane quality of the reign of God. 'Kingdom of God' emphasizes the truth that it is the reign of God himself which is now
operative and will be consummated in the future.

It is perhaps unnecessary to try to answer the question 'Which
title did Jesus use?' for it is apparent that he filled this idea with
such a richness of thought that more than one phrase would be
needed to convey his meaning. In so far as any judgement on the
matter is possible, it would appear to the present writer highly
probable that Jesus would use the popular expression of his own
day—which was 'Kingdom of heaven'. 'Jesus will have preferred
the popular expression because he also readily abstained from the
use of the divine name.'[25] In this case, the answer to the question
'Why did the first evangelist use "Kingdom of heaven" when it
seems clear that his sources had "Kingdom of God"?', is that in
this phrase is a memory of the actual words of the Lord.[26] The
phraseology of Mark and Q can be explained as a necessary interpretation to meet the needs of the Gentile world, who would not
understand the Jewish, non-biblical phrase 'Kingdom of heaven'.[27]
If this is the real course of events we see here another example of
the way the evangelical needs of the early Church have contributed
to a richer understanding of the gospel. It is indeed fortunate
that we have both titles of the reign of God, for together they
show the divine sovereignty and the beyond-the-earth implications of this teaching.

The relation of this conclusion to our study of the life hereafter
is very significant. Not only are we forcibly reminded that the
environment of the future destiny of man is the heavenly reign of
God, but we are also given a valuable clue to the relation between
this life and the life to come. In the teaching of Jesus about the

[25] Dalman, *Words*, p. 94.
[26] McNeile, *The Gospel according to St Matthew* (p. 25), says Streeter thought the
phrase 'Kingdom of heaven' derived from Q. In fact Streeter asserts that the source
of Matthew's account of the preaching of John the Baptist is Q, but he clearly states
that Q used 'Kingdom of God'. 'On purely critical grounds it is probable that our
oldest authority Q represented John as preaching "the Kingdom of God is at hand".'
*JTS*, XIV.551.
[27] Dalman, *Words*, p. 93.

reign of God there are both present and future aspects. The one aspect is essential to the other, in the sense that we can know nothing of the future consummation except through the present fact. Equally, the present fact is incomplete and beyond full understanding without the future aspect. This is equally true of the life hereafter, for the New Testament knows nothing of a future bliss entirely unrelated to the duties and responsibilities of the present. And equally, the present remains woefully incomplete unless it faces the question of what lies beyond itself. These aspects will become more apparent when we consider the teaching of the gospels concerning the way by which we can obtain fullness of life after death.

# CHAPTER FIVE

# DEATH

IN considering the subject of what happens after death, it is impossible to avoid the subject of death itself. No doubt our attitude to death is largely determined by our belief concerning what happens after it. If this is so, a person's attitude to death may be some indication of his belief about what happens afterwards. With this in mind, we shall consider the evidence of the gospels regarding our Lord's attitude to death. This will necessarily involve also a consideration of the general attitude to death which is inferred or implied in the gospels. Our study can be conveniently arranged under the following heads:

(1) The general attitude to death revealed in the gospels.
(2) Jesus' attitude to the death or the imminence of death of others.
(3) Jesus' own death.
(4) Figurative and symbolic interpretations.

### I. THE GENERAL ATTITUDE TO DEATH
### REVEALED IN THE GOSPELS

In introduction, it is well to adjust our minds to the prevalence of death as a common spectacle in the times of Jesus. Not only was life much shorter;[1] the possibility of violent death was ever present, and death was regarded in a much more realistic fashion than it is nowadays. Few children today think of playing funerals. Not only is the subject frowned upon by adults as 'unnatural', but the children who want to play have little idea what to do because such matters are now carefully kept from them. It is no uncommon thing today for a young minister never even to have attended a funeral until he has to conduct one. But in the days of Jesus it was a common sight to see children playing at 'weddings and

---

[1] Professor P. C. Mitchell wrote in the *Encyclopaedia Britannica* (11th edition, 1911): 'With regard to the human race, there seems to be almost no doubt but that the average duration of life has increased with civilization.' (XVI.976).

funerals' (Mt 11¹⁶, Lk 7³²). Jeremias quotes a rabbinical author for further evidence that funerals were often the basis of children's games.[2] This indicates not only the frequency and open character of funerals but perhaps more significantly, a very natural and uninhibited view of death, which does not seem to have been limited to children.

In the comparatively short space of our Lord's life and ministry, we find a surprising number of references to death. In the first place, death as a perfectly ordinary, indeed inevitable, fact appears in the pages of the gospels. Herod's death is one of the fixed points upon which the historical framework of the gospel is firmly based; it was a death greatly anticipated and rejoiced over among the Jews, a fact not to be wondered at when it is remembered that Herod had not only committed many crimes against his subjects, but had also murdered his mother, one of his wives and three of his sons. The story of the massacre of the Innocents (Mt 2¹⁶⁻¹⁸) is a gruesome reminder of days in which human life was very cheap, and to the natural hazards of human existence was added the continual danger of becoming a victim of Herod's mad passion for blood. As McNeile remarks: 'The killing of twenty or thirty children—and there would hardly be more in Bethlehem—would be nothing to one who massacred on a large scale.'[3] Such circumstances of human life and death must, inevitably, have affected the attitude of ordinary people, who perhaps could be excused if sometimes they harboured bitter thoughts against their persecutors. This fact of long persecution will have to be considered more fully when we come to the question of retribution and punishment.

In a happier vein we come next to the reference to Simeon in Luke 2²⁵⁻³⁵. Here we have the first account of the effect of Christ upon a man's attitude to death. Simeon, one of the small number who waited patiently for the coming of God's Deliverer, had been supernaturally informed that he would not 'see death' until he had 'seen' the Lord's Christ. The use of 'see' is interesting here, especially as it applies to two 'experiences'—the experience of death and of meeting Christ. In spite of the very widespread idea that Simeon was an old man, an 'aged Saint',[4] there is

---

[2] *The Parables of Jesus*, p. 121. McNeile, *The Gospel according to St Matthew* (p. 157), suggests the game involved rhymes being sung or said in rotation, but Jeremias's explanation seems more in accord with the purpose of the parable.
[3] *The Gospel according to St Matthew*, p. 19.  [4] *Dictionary of Christ and the Gospels*, II.62 8.

nothing in the account which really says this. The origin of this
idea is probably twofold. On the one hand the opening words of
Simeon's song are often wrongly interpreted as a wish, using the
imperative of the verb (i.e. 'May I be allowed to depart in peace').
In fact the Greek is an indicative and means literally: 'Now thou
art releasing thy servant.' This does not necessarily mean that
Simeon is about to die, or praying to die; it does mean that he
is ready to die, having found that for which his whole life was a
search. This need not imply that he was old. On the other hand,
the story of Anna the prophetess immediately follows the story of
Simeon (Lk 2³⁶⁻⁸). It appears to be the intention of the third
gospel to indicate that Simeon and Anna received knowledge of
the identity of the Christ at the same time (Lk 2³⁸). So Anna and
Simeon are closely linked and it may be that Simeon is thought to
be old because we are told explicitly, if not too clearly, that Anna
was aged (Lk 2³⁶).

The main interest for our particular study lies in the opening
words of the *Nunc Dimittis*. As already pointed out, the verb is in
the indicative and seems to describe the action God is now taking.
'Απολύω, the verb used, means to set free or release; as, for
instance, when the woman who was crippled was cured by Jesus,
who said: 'Woman you are freed from your infirmity' (Lk 13¹²).
It is also used of release of a debtor (Mt 18²⁷) and of forgiveness
(Lk 6³⁷). The sense of 'dismiss' is seen in Matthew 15²³, when the
disciples urged Jesus to 'send away' the Canaanite woman; also
in cases of divorce, of a man 'putting away his wife' (Mt 5³¹). In
view of the occurrence in Luke 2²⁹ of δοῦλος (slave) and δεσπότης
(master) we can assume that there is a sense of superiority involved in the action of dismissal. That is, the verse recognizes the
authority of God, who is supreme over life and death. But it is
pressing inferences too far to suggest that life is regarded as a
bondage or burden from which Simeon can now be released.
Such a view is really foreign to the whole sense of the passage.
Simeon represents rather the sense of achievement, of full satisfaction, which seeing the Lord's Christ involves. While there is
nothing said here about what happens after death, we must
assume that Simeon's departure in peace indicates confidence in
God, which is surely not limited to this life. The connexion with
Jesus is, of course, the most significant factor of all; it is in contact
with Jesus that Simeon's life has reached its fulfilment. It is

because he has 'seen' Christ that he is now quite ready to 'see death'. Simeon will always be a shining example of what Christ does for men; like Simeon, the man who has seen the Lord's Christ dies 'in peace'.

Yet we must not forget that Simeon's words did not end with the *Nunc Dimittis*. There are also his words of prophecy, which include a reference to the coming tragedy which will befall Mary. The coming of Christ is an event which will cause the falling and rising again of many in Israel; he will be a sign spoken against, and in connexion with the event which will pierce Mary's heart like a sword, the thoughts of many hearts will be revealed (Lk 2³⁴ᶠ). This obvious reference to the passion and death of Christ is a stern reminder to us that in order that Christian men may depart in peace, it will become necessary for the Son of God to go the way of the Cross in agony and shame. It is not a valid argument against this to say that apparently Simeon could die in peace without Christ dying on the Cross, for this mission of Christ, involving his death, is already present in his life, and already foreseen in part by Simeon.

Mark 9¹, Matthew 16²⁸, Luke 9²⁷, is a famous *crux interpretum* in connexion with the eschatology of the gospels, and is also important for our present purpose. The Marcan version reads 'there are some standing here who will not taste death before they see the Kingdom of God come with power'.

Matthew has 'before they see the Son of Man coming in his Kingdom' for the last phrase. Luke's variant is also to be noted, 'before they see the Kingdom of God'. The main question relative to this text is whether it can be used to illustrate the view that Jesus announced the presence of the Kingdom, or whether it refers to a future coming of the Kingdom. In spite of the very weighty opinion of Dodd, Kümmel seems to have established that this verse refers to the future coming of the Kingdom.⁵ If we accept this, we can consider the implications of the prediction in connexion with the question of death.

To 'taste of death' means to 'experience death' or more directly 'to die'. The other passages in which 'taste death' is used are John 8⁵² and Hebrews 2⁹.⁶ 'To taste' also means to experience, in

---

⁵ *Promise and Fulfilment*, pp. 25-8.

⁶ Plummer, *St Luke (ICC)*, p. 249, says 'taste death' implies the bitterness of death, but there is no evidence for this in the New Testament, apart from Hebrews 2⁹, which gives doubtful support.

connexion with 'the heavenly gift' and 'the word of God', in Hebrews 6⁵. Apart from these metaphorical uses, 'to taste' usually means 'to eat', rather than strictly 'to taste', in the New Testament. The exceptions to this are Matthew 27³⁴: 'They offered him wine to drink mingled with gall; and when he tasted it, he would not drink it'; and possibly Luke 14²⁴: 'None of those men who were invited shall taste my banquet.' In view of the close proximity of the story of the Transfiguration (Mk 9²⁻⁸ and parallels) to the saying we are considering, it is noteworthy that the Jewish Apocalpytic writing 4 Ezra (2 Esdras in Apocrypha) refers to 'the men who have been taken up, who have not tasted death from their birth' (4 Ezra 6²⁶). The two most popular figures who were considered not to have died and who were expected to return with the Messiah were Elijah and Enoch.[7] Elijah, of course, is one of the two figures who appeared with Jesus at the Transfiguration. If then this connexion is pressed there may be some grounds for the view of Kümmel that 'it is declared of definite people that they will not need to die, because the King-dom of God will have come $\dot{\epsilon}\nu$ $\delta\upsilon\nu\acute{a}\mu\epsilon\iota$ whilst they are still alive'.[8] Kümmel further insists that the future sense of this saying involves the meaning that some of those who stand by will not only live until the coming of the Kingdom, but 'they are not to die because the Kingdom of God will previously have been made known to them'.[9]

If this view is accepted, it makes all the more severe the problem of the apparently mistaken view Jesus had of the imminence of the Kingdom; for not only did the Kingdom not come in the way Jesus seemed to expect, but all who were standing there did, in fact, die. Yet it may be questioned whether this is what Jesus meant. According to the grammatical evidence, we must insist on 'until' (RSV, 'before') being given its full meaning here. There are no grounds in grammatical usage for taking the pre-position $\dot{\epsilon}\omega s$ $\ddot{a}\nu$ in any other way.[10] The ordinary sense of 'until' or 'before' they see the Kingdom of God come with power is that *after* this event there is no reason why those referred to should not die. Kümmel, it is true, refutes this on the grounds that the coming of the Kingdom is not to be regarded as an historical

---

[7] *A. & P.*, II.576. Cf. *Strack-Billerbeck*, I.751, for further examples.
[8] *Promise and Fulfilment*, pp. 25-6.
[9] Ibid. p. 26.
[10] J. H. Moulton and W. F. Howard, *A Grammar of New Testament Greek*, II.330.

event.[11] But it is difficult to understand anything of the Kingdom, either as present or future, if it is thus separated absolutely from the events of history. Indeed, the historical realism of this prediction needs to be carefully noted. To say that *some* will not taste of death until the Kingdom of God comes with power, is to infer that *others* will do so. This is probably the significance of the Greek construction which normally in classical Greek means 'certainly will not'.[12] Kümmel is therefore justified in saying that this prophecy indicates some interval before the coming of the Kingdom—not, as Schweitzer argues, that the Kingdom is expected by Jesus before his own death.[13] Some interval must be implied, in which a proportion, possibly the majority of those present, will die; but not so long an interval that all will have died.

On this interpretation, therefore, we are justified in concluding that death is here regarded as a datable event, which Jesus thought some would not experience before the Kingdom of God has come with power. This obviously leaves unanswered the question whether Jesus was wrongly understood or whether he himself was indeed mistaken about the time of the end. Into this very difficult and important question, we cannot here enter. Our special interest being the interpretation of the meaning of death, we can conclude that Jesus was thinking of death as an inevitable event, not far distant, but equally not in the immediate future. It is possible that the particular phrase 'taste of death' owes something to the connexion with Elijah, through 4 Ezra; but this connexion does not require that Jesus was here promising that some of his hearers would never die.

Before we go on to consider the references to violent death we must draw attention to an interesting fact concerning the instances of descriptions of the dead. In almost every case 'the dead' is a plural expression; in fact, the few exceptions are all explicable in terms of their implication being other than actual death. Νεκρός is used in the singular at Mark 9[26], describing the state of the boy from whom the deaf and dumb spirit had been exorcised—'the boy was like a corpse, so that most of them said, "He is dead".' Similarly, the singular occurs in the story of the raising of the son of the widow of Nain (Lk 7[15]): 'The dead man sat up and began to speak.' Clearly here νεκρός means 'he who was dead but is

---

[11] *Promise and Fulfilment*, p. 26, note 23.
[12] VTM, pp. 384-5.        [13] *Promise and Fulfilment*, p. 29.

dead no longer'. The other occurrences of 'the dead' in the singular are in the parable of the Prodigal Son (Lk 15²⁴, ³²)— 'this my son—this your brother was dead'; here clearly the word is used in a metaphorical sense. The conclusion of this investigation is that 'the dead' is normally a plural term. It would be going beyond the evidence to suggest that this implies a 'community of the dead', for all we can say is that the dead are 'lumped together'. Possibly the more justifiable inference would be that the dead are regarded as less than individuals because they have no body, and a man is not a real individual without a body.[14] In this fact of the consistent use of the plural for 'the dead' is perhaps also a reminder that however strongly the individual aspect of this subject is emphasized, this must not obscure the equally important fact that we die together just as much as we live together (cf. Rom 14⁷).

There are many forcible reminders in the gospels that life for many people was very insecure, and violent death was only too common. Herod the Tetrarch figures in the story of the shameful death of John the Baptist. This Herod was the son of the so-called Herod the Great, whose own death has already been noted. If the story of the execution of the Baptist (Mk 6¹⁴⁻²⁹ and parallels) serves no other purpose, it certainly provides a forcible reminder of the all too prevalent fact of violent death which must be remembered in considering death in the gospels. Other reminders of the prevalence of violent death are found in the teaching of Jesus; both in parables and in more direct words. Thus the parables of the marriage of the king's son tells how those invited to the wedding showed their contempt of their king by even killing some of his messengers (Mt 22⁶). The same point is made in the parable of the wicked husbandmen (Mt 21³⁹).[15] In both parables a good deal of the point is lost if the situation described is wholly unreal; and it is indeed symptomatic of the time that Jesus could naturally refer to such brutal and unprovoked attacks. Again, in his stern words to the scribes and Pharisees, Jesus makes it clear that violence and murder are in fact only too likely (Mt 23³⁴); he laments over Jerusalem 'killing the prophets and stoning those who are sent to you' (Mt 23³⁷). His disciples are warned of the coming tribulation and persecution in which some of them will be killed (Mt 24⁹, Lk 21¹⁶).

[14] C. Ryder Smith, *The Bible Doctrine of the Hereafter*, p. 94.     [15] See below, p. 115.

F

In the discussion which arose because of the massacre by Pilate of some inhabitants of Galilee, Jesus raised the important question of the relation between these violent deaths and the character of the victims (Lk 13$^{1-5}$). Neither these Galileans, nor those in Siloam who were killed by the fall of a tower, are to be regarded as the most wicked of their contemporaries. The main point of these two stories and of the parable of the unfruitful fig tree, which follows them (Lk 13$^{6-9}$), is the urgent necessity of repentance, but Jesus does make it clear that violent death does not indicate special wickedness in the victim. Some commentators think that the whole basis of these two stories is fictional, there being no other certain mention of either of these two tragedies. But neither is inherently unlikely, as Josephus records equally brutal massacres by Pilate, and the incident of a tower falling upon some workmen would not necessarily be significant enough to be recorded by any historian. The motive of those who reported the massacre of the Galileans may also be interpreted in different ways. Some think it was merely out of interest that this tragedy was reported to Jesus; others suppose that the questioners were ardent nationalists who were trying to trap Jesus into a violent condemnation of Pilate, or show up his refusal to identify himself with their aspirations. Again, it may be argued that the report implied a question similar to those problems raised in the Book of Job. If this is so, it is noticeable that like the Book of Job, Jesus does not attempt to expound in detail a philosophy of disaster. All he positively says is that the popular notion which related such tragedies to the special wickedness of the victims, is wrong. Instead of giving an explanation Jesus takes the opportunity of declaring the necessity of repentance; otherwise all will perish, as the Galileans and those eighteen killed at Siloam have done.

The other question relevant to our study is what is meant by 'perish' in this context? Does it mean simply 'die' as could be supposed on the basis of the comparisons with the victims of these tragedies? But in that case, it seems difficult to understand what repentance has to do with this. Certainly repentance does not make anyone immortal! Possibly the reference is to the coming destruction of Jerusalem, but in that case it is by no means clear of what those who heard were required to repent. But, on the other hand, can we suppose that the meaning is 'perish everlastingly'? If so, this would obviously add a very important factor in our understanding of Jesus' view of death.

The verb used to indicate 'perish' in the English version is ἀπόλλυμι. This verb has a variety of meanings in the synoptic gospels, which can be outlined and illustrated as follows:

(1) *To destroy, annihilate completely.* This meaning is often found when the object of the verb is some inanimate or non-personal thing—e.g. Matthew 5²⁹: 'It is better for you that you lose one of your members.' Mark 1²⁴: 'The unclean spirit said to Jesus, "Have you come to destroy us?"'; cf. Taylor (*Mark*, p. 174)— 'The destruction of evil powers in the Messianic age was widely expected.' Luke 5³⁷: '(The wine) will be spilled and the skins will be destroyed.'

(2) *To kill.* Matthew 2¹³: 'For Herod is about to search for the child, to destroy him.' Matthew 12¹⁴: 'The Pharisees took council against him how to destroy him.' Matthew 21⁴¹: 'He will put those wretches to a miserable death.' Mark 9²²: 'And has often cast him into the fire and into the water to destroy him'—here again 'destroy' seems clearly to mean 'kill'. Cf. Mark 12⁹ for the same meaning. Luke 17²⁷: 'The flood came and destroyed (i.e. killed) them all.' Cf. Luke 17²⁹, 19⁴⁷, 20¹⁶. Along with this meaning we can take the middle and passive forms which mean to die—e.g. Matthew 8²⁵, Mark 4³⁸, Luke 8²⁴. In all the accounts of the storm on the lake the disciples use the expression ἀπολλύμεθα, we are perishing, that is—about to die. Matthew 26⁵²: 'All who take the sword will perish by the sword.' Luke 13³³: 'It cannot be that a prophet should perish away from Jerusalem'—again the meaning is 'die', whether violence is implied or not.

(3) The word often means '*to lose*', as for instance the eight occurrences of it in Luke 15. The phrase 'the lost sheep of the house of Israel' (Mt 10⁶, 15²⁴) also uses the participle of this verb. The same meaning is found in the difficult sayings about losing one's 'life' or 'soul'—(Mt 10³⁹, 16²⁵, Mk 8³⁵, Lk 9²⁴), in the logion describing the mission of the Son of Man to save the lost (Lk 19¹⁰), and in the word about not losing their reward (Mt 10⁴², Mk 9⁴¹).

The only instances in which ἀπόλλυμι is applied to men with the possible meaning of destroy completely are Matthew 18¹⁴; Luke 13³, ⁵. In the passage from Matthew, Jesus is discussing offences against little children, emphasizing that God's care over one child is like a shepherd's care over one lost sheep. The saying quoted can hardly mean 'perish' completely', i.e. be annihilated, in view of the earlier references to their angels in heaven. (Mt 18[10]). Therefore we seem left with these two occurrences in Luke 13 as the only places in which 'to perish' could conceivably mean to perish 'everlastingly'. This must clearly dispose us toward the view that the meaning in these verses is agreeable with the other passages considered, although it must be allowed that another meaning is not impossible. But in view of the almost complete unanimity of meaning in all three gospels, we seem bound to conclude that here also 'to perish' when referring to a man, means simply 'to die'. There is in fact no basis in this passage for the view that Jesus taught that the end of an unrepentant man was complete annihilation. We must conclude that in this passage is some definite contemporary reference which it is now impossible to specify; probably Jesus was, in the manner of the prophets, warning his hearers that national disaster could only be averted by national repentance. It may well be that he did not actively engage in the politics of his day because he realized that the political solution was false; the people could not be saved by different political schemes worked out by their leaders, but only by true repentance before God and obedience to the one whom God had sent. As the succeeding parable shows, there comes a time when unfruitfulness cannot any longer be tolerated; when the fruitless tree must be cut down and burned. Likewise, this people, so long unfruitful, must inevitably fall under the condemnation of God. Perhaps the greatest emphasis then rests on the idea of the nation rather than of individuals perishing.

Another reference to death which may be termed 'incidental' is in one of the seven woes pronounced against the Pharisees by Jesus. This is recorded in Matthew 23[27]: 'You are like whitewashed tombs which outwardly appear beautiful but within they are full of dead men's bones and all uncleanness.' Luke 11[44] has a somewhat different version of this saying: 'You are like graves which are not seen, and men walk over them without knowing it.' These two versions of the same saying are clearly connected with Numbers 19[11-22], which gives elaborate directions about the ceremonial purification necessary after contact with a dead body or with a grave. Because of this regulation, which forbade any person so defiled from entering the temple after walking over a grave, it was the custom to mark the graves plainly with white

chalk.[16] 'Whitewashed tombs', however, as McNeile points out,
can hardly refer here to this custom, for the whole point of the
reference is that the Pharisees were not what they appeared to be:
they were not plainly marked so that men could avoid them.
On the contrary, outwardly they appeared pure, but inwardly
they were 'graves'—full of the bones of dead men and of all uncleanness. The reference in other words, seems to be rather to the
contrast between the outward appearance of the tombs, which
might sometimes appear very bright in the sun, and their gruesome interior.

Does this reference imply that Jesus accepted the contemporary
view that death caused ceremonial uncleanness, and that dead
men's bones are necessarily connected with that uncleanness?
We should not hesitate to admit that in many things Jesus did
hold the views of his contemporaries and this may well be one such
case. But the particular use of this illustration does not imply this.
The point of the illustration would be well understood by our
Lord's hearers. At this point he was not teaching anything about
the proper attitude to the dead, but illustrating his condemnation
of the Pharisees. It is not necessary for the effectiveness of the
illustration that it should accurately express our Lord's view on the
question of the uncleanness of dead bodies. This question was discussed by the rabbis, who expressed their view regarding it in
terms of divine sovereignty. So Johanan ben Zakkai said:
'Death does not make unclean, nor the water make clean. It is
the decree of the Sovereign King of Kings.'[17] We may well
suppose that if he had been pressed on this mattter, Jesus would
have expressed at least as thoughtful a view as that of Rabbi
Johanan. All we can fairly assert on the basis of this saying is that
Jesus used accepted contemporary ideas in order to illustrate his
view of an entirely different matter, namely the contrast between
the appearance and true nature of the Pharisees.

To sum up these general references to death we can note the
straightforward realism of the attitude revealed. Death is a fact to be
faced without too much special concern; it is important, but there
is no need to be continually thinking about it. Especially important
is the fact that death is not 'spiritualized': there is no implication
in the term except plain, inevitable physical death. Jesus apparently did not encourage too much thought about it, nor seek

[16] McNeile, *The Gospel according to St Matthew*, p. 337.    [17] Moore, *Judaism*, II.7.

himself to explain it. Here is a salutary reminder of the healthy realism of the Christian view, for in the end we must all face death. Even a successful attempt to explain it will not alter that fact.

## II. JESUS IN THE PRESENCE OF DEATH

(a) *The Raising of Jairus' daughter* (Mt $9^{18-19, 23-6}$, Mk $5^{21-4, 35-43}$, Lk $8^{40-2, 49-56}$).

This story, which is closely linked with the account of the healing of the woman with the issue of blood, is one of the most moving accounts of a miracle performed by Jesus. While we shall take note of the accounts of Matthew and Luke, we shall base our observations mainly on Mark, because this is not only the fullest account, but bears many signs of being the more original narrative. It will be well also to remind ourselves of the purpose in hand. This is to consider our Lord's attitude to death; while his action in raising the daughter of Jairus is, of course, of the utmost importance, especially when we are thinking of the healing work of Jesus, this is not our first interest here. We are firstly concerned with the question 'What was Jesus' attitude to death?'—we shall do well to keep this special interest very clearly in mind.

This approach affects very considerably, although it does not entirely dispose of, the first question to be raised. That is 'was the girl really dead; is this then one of the very few accounts, or possibly the only certain account, of Jesus raising the dead?' In seeking to answer this question we must record our great indebtedness to Taylor's careful and finely balanced discussion in his Commentary on St Mark.[18] In view of the extreme importance of this miracle story, it is necessary to consider very carefully the evidence about the girl's assumed death. If we take all three gospels together, we are left in no doubt that this is an account of the raising of the dead. But if we consider Mark alone, the evidence is not so clear. In the first place, the ruler of the synagogue, in his first approach to Jesus, says that his daughter is 'at the point of death' (*RSV*). It is to be noted, therefore, that at this stage Mark does not regard the girl as dead. This is further strengthened and verified by the request of the ruler that Jesus should come and lay his hands on her 'that she may be made whole and live'. There has been some discussion among scholars

[18] VTM, pp. 285-8; 293-8.

regarding the last two verbs 'be made whole' ($\sigma\omega\theta\hat{\eta}$) and 'live' ($\zeta\acute{\eta}\sigma\eta$); the conclusion of a rather technical matter concerned with the possible Aramaic originals is difficult to dogmatize about, but it seems fairly certain that 'live' does not imply that the child is dead. Yet it ought to be noticed that in the other instances in which Mark uses $\zeta\acute{\alpha}\omega$ there is a direct contrast with death (cf. Mk 12²⁷—'He is not God of the dead, but of the living'; and Mk 16¹¹, 'when they heard that he was alive'—i.e. after the resurrection). In Matthew and Luke the word is generally used in contrast with death; the exceptions, in addition to the parallel accounts of this incident, being Matthew 4⁴, Luke 2³⁶, 10²⁸, 15¹³, where the implication is ordinary existence, and Matthew 26⁶³, in which the term 'living' is applied to God. Thus on the basis of synoptic usage, there is perhaps some basis for wondering if 'live' here has an implication of contrast with death. Yet even if this is not allowed, we should notice that death, especially in such tragic circumstances, does cast its sombre shadow before it, and even if the child were not yet dead, it might still be apposite for her father to request that she might 'live'.¹⁹

Passing on farther, in Mark's account we notice that Jesus accepted the urgency of the father's plea, at least to the extent of accompanying him to the house where the child was. While this act cannot of necessity imply that Jesus accepted the view that the child was 'at death's door', it does show that Jesus recognized the seriousness of the matter. This was not one of those cases where Jesus would effect a cure from a distance, as he did in the case of the daughter of the Syro-Phoenician woman (Mk 7²⁴⁻³⁰; cf. Mt 15²²⁻⁸), and the story of the Centurion's servant (Lk 7²⁻¹⁰, Mt 8⁵⁻¹³). If Jesus did in fact regard this as a real meeting with death, his going to the child is a telling illustration of his determination to meet the enemy and to conquer it. In passing we should notice that the account of the healing of the woman with an issue of blood adds veracity to the whole story, for there is no attempt to fit these stories together by any literary artifice, and by far the most acceptable explanation is that the events took place as they are reported. We can then possibly see a greater significance in our Lord's words to the distracted father, when messengers tell him that his daughter is dead (Mk 5³⁵). It is a

¹⁹ M. Black inclines to the view that 'be made whole' and 'live' are 'translation-variants' of one Aramaic word, although allowing the possibility that they might have different shades of meaning (VTM, p. 288, note).

common experience that a delay such as was caused by the interruption by the woman will add very considerably to the distress and anxiety of the sort of situation the father now faced. In this event, we can sense the understanding involved in the words of Jesus: 'Do not go on fearing; only continue to believe' (Mk 5[36]). We shall have to consider these words more fully in our attempt to interpret our Lord's attitude in the face of death.

But the messengers who came to the synagogue ruler brought the news that his daughter was dead. We notice that Mark carefully avoids saying that Jesus accepted this as true. Mark uses a difficult expression: ὁ δὲ Ἰησοῦς παρακούσας τὸν λόγον λαλούμενον. Παρακούσας can mean either 'overhearing' or 'not heeding'. Taylor prefers the latter meaning; Jesus did not heed what was said by the messengers, which can mean either he did not believe that the child was dead, in spite of what they said, or else, although he accepted it as true, he was not deterred by it. But it is clear that this part of the story *could* be interpreted to mean that Jesus did not think the child was dead; this, of course, involves the assumption of supernatural knowledge by Jesus, but this, after all, is not unknown in the gospels (cf. Mt 9[4], Lk 9[47]).

The next point to consider in regard to the question whether the girl was really dead is the comment by Jesus on entering the house and seeing a tumult and many weeping and wailing greatly (Mk 5[38]). Jesus said to them: 'Why do you make a tumult and weep? The child is not dead, but sleeping.' It is scarcely adequate to regard this without further question as a plain indication that Jesus did not think the girl was dead.[20] While this conclusion is certainly not impossible, there are others which merit consideration.

Death was often referred to as a sleep. The various connexions between sleep and death in ancient Hebrew thought are described by C. Ryder Smith in *The Bible Doctrine of the Hereafter*, pp. 42-5. The origin of the description of death as 'a sleep' most probably can be traced to the similarity between a sleeping man and a dead man; both are still, and in early historical Old Testament literature, the assumption is that to be dead is to lie down in peace; this view in its early stages concentrates on 'the good side' of death and is an optimistic account.[21] Thus in the historical

---

[20] Leslie D. Weatherhead, *Psychology, Religion and Healing*, p. 74.
[21] *The Bible Doctrine of the Hereafter*, p. 43.

books the phrase 'slept with his fathers and was buried' indicates
natural death, without any implication of what happens after
death. But in the later books, especially the Psalms, there is a
different emphasis; 'to sleep' indicates the violent death of sinners,
and sometimes also it means premature death. This is part of the
growing feeling that in the complete equality and implied inactivity of Sheol there is injustice; it is not fitting that the good
man should merely sleep alongside the bad man. This develops
into a desire that the saints should be delivered from the sleep of
Sheol. On the question of the place of sleep, whether the grave or
Sheol, there seems to have been some vagueness, and it is, as
Ryder Smith says, a question to which even today, if we describe
death as sleep, it would be hard to find a consistent and clear
answer. Ryder Smith sums up the matter thus: 'Under the word
"sleep" the Hebrews united two beliefs, that a dead man was at
rest, body and *nephesh*; and that it was the LORD's will that he
should never do anything more. He had passed out of history.'[22]

It should be noted from this summary that in describing death
as 'a sleep' there is originally no idea that one day the dead will
wake. Indeed, the only possible connexion here is with the work
of the necromancer, who was supposed to be able to waken the
dead. But necromancy was forbidden in Israel, at least from the
days of Saul (1 Sam 28[3]) and it was regarded as entirely repre-
hensible to try to waken the dead, who were to be left to sleep.

The connexion of thought between sleep and death seems to be
more developed in the later literature of Judaism, and in view of
the fact that much of this literature is roughly contemporaneous
with the New Testament, this is important for our consideration
of this saying of Jesus. Thus the idea of the righteous not remaining asleep for ever is expressed in the *Book of Enoch*, and this is
linked with the view that the righteous are guarded in their sleep.
'And over all the righteous and holy He will appoint guardians
from among the holy angels to guard them as the apple of an
eye, until he makes an end of all wickedness and all sin, and
though the righteous sleep a long sleep, they have nought to
fear.'[23]

This idea of awaking from sleep is applied by 4 Ezra (2 Esdras)
to both 'the Age' and the righteous dead—'And it shall be after
seven days that the Age which is not yet awake shall be roused,

[22] Ibid. p. 45.     [23] *Enoch*, 100[5].

and that which is corruptible shall perish. And the earth shall restore those that sleep in her, and the dust those that are at rest therein'.[24]

It is noticeable too, that Sirach indicates that 'to sleep' had become in some sense equivalent to 'to die'—'And Solomon slept in Jerusalem, and left after him one that was overbearing'.[25] As Charles points out,[26] this marks a considerable development from the Old Testament, where 'sleep' never means 'die' when it stands alone; it is always followed by some words which explain it as referring to death.

To return to the saying of Jesus, we can say that while there is clearly some connexion between sleep and death in the thought of the time, the form of this saying makes a complete identification of 'sleep' and 'death' impossible. Otherwise the saying could only mean 'she is not dead but she is asleep' (i.e. dead). But even so, it is not entirely easy to take sleep in a natural sense. For Jesus had not yet seen the girl, and it was not his practice to engage in anything comparable to medical diagnosis.[27] The reaction of the mourners (Mk 5[40]) who 'laughed him to scorn' seems to emphasize this point, for, after all, they were in a position to know. Possibly some of them at least were close friends and neighbours, and could very well have been present when the girl died.

Another possibility to be considered is that Jesus was in fact expressing a different view of death; namely that from God's point of view it is a sleep from which God will awaken the dead in His own time. This, after all, is the natural development of the later Jewish ideas we have noted. Man calls it death—but from the divine point of view it is a sleep—not the sleep of eternal inactivity, as when the idea of death as a sleep was first advanced, but a temporary state, by implication peaceful; from which there will be an awakening to a full existence with God. If this view goes a little beyond the evidence of the saying we are considering, it must be admitted that it accords more fully with all the facts. For whatever critical opinion may declare about the reality of the girl's death, there is no doubt that the gospel records intend to say that she was really dead and that this was a case of restoring the dead to life again. If this implication is not as clear in Mark as in Matthew and Luke, nevertheless it can be argued that this is

[24] 4 Ezra (2 Esdras), 7[31-2].   [25] *Sirach* 47[23].   [26] *A. & P.*, I.499.   [27] VTM, p. 295.

what Mark means to convey. The fact that it is possible to interpret Mark as not strictly meaning the child was dead, is very strong evidence of the evangelist's care in presenting his material accurately. So if we cannot say without any doubt that the child was really dead, we may conclude that the evidence points very strongly in that direction.

And further, without avoiding the difficult issue we have been considering, we can note that from the point of view of our special interest, it is sufficient to be able to say that most, if not all, the people involved thought the child was dead. To the readers of the gospel the inevitable implication would be that the child was dead. Therefore this story can be taken as an illustration of the attitude of Jesus to apparent death, even if a doubt remains whether it was 'real' death.

The main emphasis of the story lies on the response Jesus made to the urgent plea of the child's father. Indeed, the chief concern of our Lord seems to have been for the parents in their loss. There is no suggestion that the child, if dead, was in any desperate or tragic state. We are in fact told nothing about what death means to the girl; only what her death means to her parents. Yet Jesus does not ignore the seriousness of the situation, nor give any impression that death is to be lightly regarded. Instead he responds quickly to the father's request; yet in no sense did he show panic. The incident with the woman on the way powerfully illustrates this. Although Jesus was in a hurry, he was not in too much of a hurry to be able to pause and hold this conversation with her. The disciples might think his attitude unreasonable, but he had time to stay, even in the face of death. Again, Jesus' words of encouragement to the ruler of the Synagogue can be thought to serve a double purpose. Although nothing is said about the need for faith at the time of the miracle, we can well believe that the faith of the father, joined with the confident trust of his three closest disciples, would be a great assistance to our Lord when he raised up the child. But he spoke these words to Jairus also to help him; to encourage and strengthen him in this distressing experience. Throughout the whole incident we seem to detect an air of quiet confidence and understanding sympathy emanating from Jesus. From this we can conclude that in the very presence of death, Jesus still acted with that supreme confidence which can only indicate real mastery. Here indeed is the

Lord of life and death, showing forth his unmistakable power over man's last enemy.

The next words spoken by Jesus are addressed to those who were making a tumult, and weeping and wailing greatly. 'Why do you make a tumult and weep?' (Mk 5³⁹).

We must conclude that the attitude of Jesus implies disapproval. Those involved were either professional mourners,[28] as Matthew 9²³ states (αὐλητής is a flute player, and implies that those present were the mourners who commonly attended such an occasion), or else close relatives and neighbours, who may be meant, in view of the difficulty of assembling professionals at such short notice. In either case we can assume some element of artificiality in these noisy proceedings. It is interesting to note that immediately Jesus said 'She is not dead but sleeping', 'they laughed him to scorn'. Κατεγέλων has an implication of jeering or derision,[29] and seems to suggest a too sudden change of tone for the earlier weeping and wailing to be really genuine. The very fact that professional mourners were customary, even if not present on this occasion, suggests an expression of somewhat un-real emotions—the proper thing to do, whether felt or not. We may well believe that in this case, the crowd of mourners would add to, rather than give genuine expression of, the grief of such a man as Jairus. And Jesus definitely opposes this with his usual insistence on that which is genuine.

One of the most interesting features of the whole incident is the way in which Jesus progressively excludes people from the scene. Only Peter, James, and John are permitted to accompany him to the house; then at the house all are excluded except the three disciples and the girl's parents. Whatever significance this has for an interpretation of the method of healing used by our Lord, it also implies that he looked upon death as something to be faced calmly and realistically. It is not to be falsified by artificial emotion, nor should there be any attempt to obscure its reality by noisy demonstrations. It is indeed true to our own circum-stances that however great may be the ceremony of a funeral, however much the stark reality may be obscured by the meeting together of relatives and friends, there comes a time of testing,

[28] According to the rabbis, burial of and mourning for the dead was a good deed which might even in some circumstances be allowed to interrupt study. Montefiore and Loewe, *A Rabbinic Anthology*, pp. 185, 437.

[29] VTM, p. 296.

when all but the closest have gone home and those most affected
are left to face the reality of their loss. In such a situation a
Christian may well realize the presence of his Lord, who faced
death in its true reality, without any false pity or empty
sentimentality. The abiding impression of the gospels is that death
is to be faced as a fact; we are not to run away from it nor try to
persuade ourselves that it doesn't really happen; we are to face it.
Yet this is, of course, only truly possible because death has been
faced and overcome by Jesus.

(b)  *The Raising of the son of the Widow of Nain* (Lk 7[11-17]).

This miracle is only recorded by Luke, and to many commentators this immediately raises doubts about its historicity. Yet it is
surely not seriously maintained that only those incidents recorded
in more than one gospel are to be accepted. The difficulty that
is raised on the basis of the supposition that the other evangelists
would hardly have failed to record so remarkable an event if it
had really happened, perhaps has a little more weight. Yet as
Plummer remarks, to anyone believing in the possibility of
miracles, raising the dead may be no more remarkable than
cleansing a leper.[30] There is some point in the suggestion that this
story owes its present position in Luke to the following account of
the reply to John the Baptist, which includes as signs of the
Messianic activity 'the dead are raised up' (Lk 7[22]); but this does
not of itself invalidate the story as history. It has been suggested
by others that the man was not dead, but in a trance, but this is
very difficult indeed to fit into the stated events; the story makes it
as plain as possible that the man was dead, and only that attitude
which is sceptical about all miracles will find a way round the
plain implication of the account. Easton remarks: 'The miracle,
as a miracle, is neither more nor less difficult than the raising of
Jairus' daughter, and discussions as to the physical condition of
the body, etc., are idle.'[31] Easton also remarks upon the unusu-
ally Hebraistic style, the mention of Nain, otherwise not mentioned in the New Testament, and regards the latter as an indication that some notable miracle of Jesus was probably the cause of
the otherwise unknown name being remembered. As a result of
this brief survey, we seem justified in proceeding to look at this
as another account of our Lord in contact with death.

[30] *ICC, St Luke*, p. 197.     [31] *The Gospel according to St Luke*, p. 99.

We notice that Luke uses ὁ κύριος here for the first time in his gospel; the implication may well be, as in the case of Jairus' daughter, that the Lord of life was here in contact with death, and in that case the title draws attention to his lordship over death. Again, as in the case previously considered, we notice that Jesus' main concern was with the one who is bereaved. The circumstances here were particularly tragic, for the dead man was the only son of his widowed mother. These sad circumstances are underlined by the comment that a considerable crowd of her fellow inhabitants of the town were accompanying her, presumably because they were so sorry for her. We note also that there is here no rebuke by our Lord of those who were expressing their grief. The funeral ceremony is more advanced than when Jesus came into the house of Jairus, and the story gives a remarkably clear picture of the sad procession leaving the town as Jesus and his disciples met them. Again, as in the case of Jairus' daughter, Jesus' first concern is with the bereaved parent, and his word is one of encouragement: 'Do not go on weeping—cease to weep.'[32] But how empty an exhortation unless something is going to happen to change the circumstances which cause the sorrow! There is, therefore, implied in our Lord's greeting a promise to do something. He went forward and touched the bier—possibly to cause the bearers to halt, or perhaps more symbolically, to indicate his claim to that which had been claimed by death.[33] This simple action is immediately followed by the dead man sitting up; there is a noticeable lack of any description of a complicated technique. The words used by Jesus are as few and simple as could be imagined—'Young man, to you I say "Get up!" ' (Lk 7[14]). The action of Jesus in giving back the man to his mother (7[15]) seems further to emphasize the main concern of our Lord with the bereaved widow.

As in the case of Jairus' daughter, the main teaching of this miracle would seem to point to our Lord's recognition of the need of the bereaved, rather than any implication that death itself is evil or to be avoided. Death is conquered for the sake of the sorrow it has caused. But death appears to be a very different

[32] Plummer, *ICC, St Luke*, p. 199.

[33] Ibid. Note the suggestion of A. J. Grieve (Peake's *Commentary*, p. 730), that the form of the story has been influenced by the accounts of raising the dead in 1 Kings 17[17-24] and 2 Kings 4[32-7]. Even if accepted this does not necessarily involve doubt about the historicity of the account in St Luke. Cf. comments on typology in Chapter 1.

matter when Jesus deals with it. He can recall the dead to return
to life, as if, indeed, the fact of death is not so great an obstacle to
God as it inevitably seems to man. Our Lord's action here is
very much like that of arousing someone from sleep, although the
idea of sleep is not mentioned in the passage. It did not, however,
appear so to the bystanders, who understandably were gripped by
fear, and said that God had raised up a great prophet among them,
and that He had visited His people. This reaction is perfectly
natural, and fits very well into what we should expect to be the
reaction of the Jews. It is perhaps worth noting that the natural
tendency of a people with a long tradition of faith in God, is to
think God is the cause of this remarkable event. This cannot be
used as an argument against the story, however, for this is precisely the response we should expect. There is no attempt in the
story to heighten this natural sense of wonder, but an implication
that God is at work through Jesus. Also we must note the extreme
rarity in the gospels of these stories of raising the dead. We may
well suppose this to be due to the infrequency of such an act by
Jesus. It seems best to understand this miracle as our Lord's
response to the tragic plight of the widow, and as an indication
of his mastery over death—a mastery never idly displayed to the
curious, but all the more real by being kept under control.

We may note, in connexion with these two accounts of our
Lord's raising the dead, the possibility that they might cause
bitterness rather than comfort to persons bereaved in equally sad
circumstances. No doubt some people do react in this way to
these miracles. 'Jesus raised from the dead the daughter of Jairus,
and the widow's son, why does he not restore my child, my loved
one?' Yet by far the greater majority of those who read these
accounts from the point of view of their own sorrow, find comfort
rather than bitterness. This must surely be because they dimly
but certainly realize that beyond the circumstances of physical
death, there is a greater power of God at work in Jesus. Jesus
did not come to take away from anyone the inevitable fact of
mortality. He was not concerned to make anyone escape physical
death. There were doubtless many cases of equal sadness with
which our Lord did not deal in this way, although he could have
done so. But he does mediate, through these accounts, his power
to make death an important, yet not a tragic event. Many people
of all sorts have turned from the grave of their loved one without

bitterness because they know that he who could conquer physical death can overcome the sharpness of death and has indeed opened the kingdom of heaven to all believers.

There are two other incidents connected with our Lord's attitude to the apparent death of another, or the threat of it. In the story of the healing of the epileptic lad (Mk 9¹⁴⁻²⁹ and parallels), we are told that at the climax of the miracle the lad fell down like a dead person, so that the majority of those present said 'he is dead' (Mk 9²⁶). This is clearly not a case of raising the dead; only the appearance of death is meant. It seems difficult to compare this and the subsequent action of Jesus with Jairus' daughter,[34] for here there is no suggestion that the boy really was dead; but we have suggested above that a different conclusion is possible in the case of Jairus' daughter.

The other reference to Jesus facing the possible death of another person is in the story of the healing of the nobleman's slave at Capernaum (Lk 7²⁻¹⁰). The condition of the slave is described in Luke 7² as 'sick and at the point of death'. But it is not suggested at all that the slave died before Jesus healed him. This, therefore, cannot be considered as a case of raising the dead.

On the basis of this consideration of the stories of the raising of Jairus' daughter and the widow's son at Nain, we can see the following implications in our Lord's attitude to the death of others.

(1) Death is regarded by Jesus as an important and significant matter; it is not ignored, nor treated lightly.

(2) Jesus is revealed as the master of death. We have suggested reasons for asserting that these accounts of the raising of the dead are historical. In them we see the calm assurance with which Jesus faced death and overcame it.

(3) Our Lord's chief concern seems to have been for those who were bereaved. While we cannot suppose that it was pity alone which prompted his action, we see Jesus filled with concern for the bereaved in their sorrow.

(4) Jesus gives no hint that the persons who had died were in any tragic or unfortunate state. This is all the more remarkable in view of the youth of the girl, and the implied not very great age of the widow's son. Jesus plainly did not regard it as his work to deliver men from physical death. As far as we know those who

[34] VTM, p. 400.

were raised from the dead were still mortal, and in due course
they died like other people.

(5) This last point indicates that the 'life' Jesus came to bring
to men was not deliverance from physical death. The followers
of Christ must not expect to be delivered from mortality, but from
sin. This point is reinforced by the fact of the rarity of these
miracles of raising the dead.

### III.   JESUS' ATTITUDE TO HIS OWN DEATH

There is no more important or fruitful subject in the whole range
of Christian thought than the death of Christ. This phrase is
immediately and necessarily linked with the conception of man's
salvation through Christ's atoning work. Without in any way
suggesting that this is not entirely proper, we may add a further
comment. The tremendous, overwhelming significance of Christ's
death as Saviour very easily overshadows the aspect of his
death as a man. Obviously from the point of view of our present
study, there can be no more important subject than that dealing
with our Lord's attitude to his own death. We have tried to
consider his attitude to the death of others, and this is, indeed, of
great importance. But nothing can be quite so important to our
study as Christ's own view of death, and his dealing with it.
Can we adduce as evidence of the meaning of human death,
Jesus' attitude to his own death? Immediately some will say that
we cannot, precisely because Christ's own death was not an
ordinary death like ours. He did not die, it will be said, just to
show us how to die; we are not asked to face death bravely because Christ did the same, but because he died 'for us', not just
'before us'. Yet it may still be asked whether there is not a significant meaning of the death of Christ on the level of human
death. Certainly we cannot *limit* the significance of Christ's
death to an example of how we are to die. Indeed, it may be
seriously contended that we do not begin to appreciate the saving
work of Christ, which culminates in his death and resurrection,
until we see that it is exactly as something done for us that this
work is effective. But we need not deny any of the truth of the
atoning significance of the death of Christ in saying that also his
death teaches us much about the meaning of our own death.
After all, it is part of the orthodox Christian faith that Christ was
truly a man; therefore his death is human death. It is, we may

G

repeat, infinitely more than an example; but whatever this 'more' involves, it does not in any way lessen the significance of Christ's death as human death. The same point can be made with regard to the frequent assertion that Christ's death was not just physical death—it involved a spiritual 'death' and desolation such as could only be experienced by the Incarnate Son of God. This may be fully granted, but it does not lessen the meaning of Christ's death as human death. Sometimes commentators refer to 'mere physical death' as if it is really a matter of no account at all. This, at any rate, can be refuted from a consideration of the references in the gospels to Christ's death. Whatever deeper significance can rightly be ascribed to that death, it is also to be considered as a significant human death.

In our consideration of Christ's death as human death we shall first briefly consider the references to it in the synoptic records.

(1) His death was prophesied and anticipated by Christ himself. The three prophecies of the Passion (Mk $8^{27-33}$, $9^{30-2}$, $10^{32-4}$) with parallels to each prophecy in the other two gospels, are sometimes thought to be three versions of one statement. There are, however, noticeable and important differences, so that we may well conclude that on three different occasions Jesus spoke in this way to his disciples.[35] The main feature of these sayings can be summarized as follows. The predictions, which only begin after Simon Peter's confession at Caesarea Philippi, show Jesus under a strong sense of compulsion. It is necessary for him to go to Jerusalem. There he will meet the leaders of the Jews, who are to be the cause of his death. The coming death will be preceded by suffering which will be caused by various acts of physical violence; mocking, spitting, scourging being specially mentioned. After the death, there will be a resurrection. All this is a mystery to the disciples, to whom the idea of a suffering Messiah was a complete novelty. This mystification of the disciples is well symbolized by the picture of Jesus leading his men up to Jerusalem, they following him in wonder and fear (Mk $10^{32}$).

Not only in these three announcements of the passion, but in many other sayings, Jesus foretold and anticipated his coming death. When the three disciples came down from the mount of Transfiguration he referred to the Son of Man rising again from the dead (Mk $9^9$). His reply to the request of the sons of Zebedee

[35] VTM, p. 377.

for a premier place in his kingdom, includes reference to the
baptism he is to undergo, which plainly means his coming death
(Mk 10$^{38-9}$). Again, in the same passage, he refers to his coming
death as a ransom given for many (Mk 10$^{45}$). We can at least
say that these references show that Jesus faced the prospect of death
a considerable time before he entered Jerusalem. His death was
neither a sudden surprise nor an accident.

(2) Christ's death was deliberately planned and brought about
by the actions of his enemies, the leaders of the Jews. We must
certainly say more than this whenever we try to answer the
question: 'Why did Christ die?' A full answer to that question
requires references to the will of God and the sin of man. But
again, we insist that this does not invalidate the truth, so clearly
stated in the gospels, that Jesus died at the hands of lawless men.
His death was planned by the Jewish leaders who tried to take
him by subtlety and kill him (Mk 14$^1$); the betrayal by one of the
twelve was an important factor in the events which led to his
arrest (Mk 14$^{44f}$); once he was arrested, the leaders of the Jews
provided false witnesses to condemn him, and in spite of the
judicial decision of Pilate, that Jesus was innocent, he was
delivered up to be crucified. The remarkable fact about the
recording of these events in the gospels is that they are presented
as that which might well have happened to anyone. The gospels
do not present these distasteful facts in order to elicit our pity for
the victim, nor our condemnation of his enemies. The emphasis
is upon the stark facts—facts, we must remember, in their outward
appearance, not uncommon in those times. Indeed, looked at
from the point of view of a Roman these events would probably
be regarded as sordid and boring; the sort of thing that did happen
from time to time in those remote corners of the empire. Again,
we insist that this is certainly not all there is to be considered in
the death of Christ—all subsequent Christian history shows that
to be false—but in its simplest outline here is a man facing death.
Whatever else it is, it is brutal, sordid, painful human death;
not the worst kind of death anyone could face, but bad enough to
be considered one of the most brutal and unjustified, even on the
grounds of common decency and justice.

(3) His death took place outside Jerusalem by crucifixion.
The question here is perhaps the most significant of all we consider in this study. It is, after all, of the greatest value to know

how Jesus himself faced death. This, even more than his teaching, tells us what he thought about death, and how it should be faced. We have already noticed that Jesus did not come unprepared to the point of crucifixion. Nor had he ever taken the road out which was open to him, of turning away from his responsibilities. He had come here, deliberately, acting according to what he knew to be the will of God. This needs to be taken into account in our consideration of his attitude to his own death.

Next, we must consider an extremely important saying which occurs in the story of the Garden of Gethsemane. The words are addressed to Peter, James, and John, whom Jesus had taken with him away from the rest. 'My soul is very sorrowful even to death; remain here and watch' (Mk 14[34]); cf. Matthew 26[38], which adds 'with me' to the Marcan form. The first part of this saying is an echo, rather than a quotation,[36] apparently based on Psalms 42[5] and 43[5]. 'Why are you cast down, O my soul?' These two Psalms both deal with the disquietude, or in modern terminology, 'depression' of a man who normally enjoys fellowship with God. In the first instance the depression is caused by a loss of the sense of God's presence. 'My soul thirsts for God, for the living God.' 'When shall I come and behold the face of God?' (Ps 42[2]). This desolation is increased by the jibes of those who continually say unto him: 'Where is your God?' In the second instance, it is more plainly stated that it is a man's enemies which cause him 'to go mourning'. In both cases the solution to the difficulty is the same. 'Hope in God; for I shall again praise him, my help and my God.' These points are important because it may be assumed that such thoughts would be in our Lord's mind when he used this phrase from the Psalms.

The second part of the saying, 'even unto death', also occurs in the Old Testament and in the Apocrypha. The most instructive Old Testament occurrence is Jonah 4[9]. Jonah, fainting under the scorching heat of the east wind, asked that he might die, and said: 'It is better for me to die than to live.' When God asked Jonah whether he does well to be angry for the gourd that has withered, Jonah replies: 'I do well to be angry, angry enough to die.' In the LXX the last phrase is ἕως θανάτου, as in this saying of Jesus. We should also note its occurrence in *Sirach* 37[2]. 'Is it not a grief to the death (ἕως θανάτου) when a companion and friend turns

[36] VTM, p. 553.

to enmity?' In both these cases the implication is that there is an emotion, whether anger or grief, which is comparable in bitterness with death itself. Thus many commentators, applying this sense to the saying of Jesus, take it to mean 'so that I am almost dying of sorrow'.[37] There is a slight difference between the interpretation which takes the meaning to be a 'sorrow equal with death' and that which implies 'a sorrow which threatens life itself',[38] but the meaning is substantially the same in both cases. The sorrow which Jesus feels, caused, according to many commentators, by the shock of realizing that Messiahship involves suffering, was so great as truly to endanger the life of Jesus at this point. It is agreeable with such an interpretation to add that the mystery of this sorrow is beyond our understanding, but we dimly conceive that it must have been connected with the weight of the world's sin. In other words, Christian thought usually asserts that this deadly grief of the Lord was not caused by fear of death or pain or shame; but by the great burden of human sin which he knew he had to carry. It is usually part of this assertion to deny that Jesus was afraid of death. We may quote a verse from a hymn to illustrate this:

> *The awful sorrow of His face,*
> *The bowing of His frame,*
> *Come not from torture nor disgrace:*
> *He fears not Cross nor shame.*[39]

On the basis of this kind of exegesis, it is generally held that a Christian should have no fear of death, but rather face it with the courage and fortitude shown by Christ. The difficulty which faces many Christians at this point is that, try as they will, they cannot avoid a sense of fear in the face of death. Sometimes this fear is admittedly due to lack of faith, but it has to be admitted that even in many whose faith is very firm, this fear persists, and can, indeed, be the source of much distress, especially when it is assumed that fear of death must imply lack of faith in Christ. These preliminary remarks have seemed necessary in introducing another view of Christ's attitude to death, which will seem strange and even offensive to some. This is the view of Oscar Cullmann,

[37] Grimm-Thayer, *Greek-English Lexicon of the New Testament*, p. 282.
[38] VTM, p. 553.
[39] Thomas Benson Pollock (*Methodist Hymn-book*, No. 175[2]).

in his recent book, *Immortality of the Soul or Resurrection of the Dead?* (English Edn, 1958).

The author of this book remarks in his preface on the open hostility the book has engendered among many people, and this can be well understood if not shared, when we quote some of his words: 'Jesus is afraid, though not as a coward would be of the men who kill him, still less of the pain and grief which precede death. He is afraid in the face of death itself. Death for him is not something divine; it is something dreadful. . . . He is afraid of death.'[40] What makes Cullmann's view even more objectionable to many is his comparison between Socrates and Jesus as they face death. Socrates is calm, composed, talking freely with his disciples about immortality until the moment when the poison finally makes him unable to speak. Jesus on the other hand, is distressed and greatly troubled, in agony of prayer, needing the companionship of his intimate disciples to help him to face this dreadful experience; in the end crying out in agony: 'My God, my God, why hast thou forsaken me?'

While this comparison between the death of Socrates and the death of Jesus raises the level of interest in Cullmann's discussion, it is to be doubted whether it is either justifiable or helpful to the main argument. As far as the justification is concerned, it must be remembered that there are several points at which the parallel between Jesus and Socrates fails. Jesus was in the prime of life; Socrates was an old man; Jesus faced one of the most brutal forms of execution ever devised; Socrates' death by self-administered poison was civilized and gentle in comparison. Jesus faced his death alone, having been forsaken by his followers. All our Lord could hear were the scornful criticisms of the high priests and their friends and the angry cry of the vacillating mob. Socrates was permitted a quiet conversation with his friends, which continued until he gently passed away.

Further, it is doubtful if Cullmann's point really helps his argument, for this can stand without the comparison with Socrates. This argument is that Jesus was afraid of death. This may well be true and needs no bolstering by an unfair comparison.

Cullmann discusses this account of Jesus in Gethsemane and interprets it in terms of our Lord's trembling in the presence of death. The meaning of Jesus' trembling and being distressed is

[40] O. Cullmann, *Immortality of the Soul . . . ?*, pp. 21f.

that 'Jesus is so thoroughly human that he shares the natural fear of death',[41] Cullmann rejects the view that the sorrow of Jesus endangers his life, on the ground that at this time Jesus knew he was going to die. He therefore accepts the interpretation of Johannes Weiss: 'My affliction is so great that I am sinking under the weight of it.'[42] The sense then, seems to be: 'My soul is exceeding sorrowful, in the face of death.' Death is certainly not regarded as a friend in this interpretation, but rather as an enemy. Cullmann further asserts that this interpretation is supported by Mark 15[34], 'My God, my God, why hast thou forsaken me', and Luke 12[50]: 'I have a baptism to be baptized with, and how I am constrained until it is accomplished.' This is taken to refer to our Lord's distress, which will not be ended until death has been experienced.

In seeking to assess this view alongside the more usual interpretation outlined above, we need to take account of more than the strict grammatical usage. There is no doubt that the other uses of ἕως θανάτου do suggest a meaning of 'I am troubled to the point of dying of trouble'; but Cullmann is justified in pointing out that this meaning does not really suit the circumstances, in which Jesus knew he was going to die, and would hardly have been troubled that sorrow might cause his death. Again, we have to notice that in all these references to the death of Jesus, whether it is prophesied, expected or plotted, there is no emphasis on anything but physical death. To the disciples as well as to the Jews, Jesus was going to Jerusalem to die—in an ordinary, if brutal and tragic sense of the word. The implication of the saving significance of his death is a perfectly proper and necessary interpretation; but at the time, it is physical death, plain human death, that our Lord is facing. If this can be accepted, then we have to say that it was human, physical death from which Jesus recoiled in horror. This would also mean that the cry of dereliction, 'My God, why hast thou forsaken me', is the cry of one who faces the death we have to face. He does not so cry out because he is a coward, but because he is a realist. Later Christian thought rightly interpreted this as a sign of his sin-bearing and this is a necessary implication. But in the first place it was death as we have to face it, that caused Jesus such anguish.[43]

[41] Ibid. p. 21.     [42] Ibid.
[43] Daniel-Rops, *Jesus in His Time*, p. 438: 'Jesus died the death that waits for all of us.'

Against this assertion that Jesus was afraid of death may well be quoted the Q passage in Matthew 10²⁸, Luke 12⁴: 'And do not fear those who kill the body but cannot kill the soul; rather fear him who can destroy both body and soul in hell.' Superficially this passage seems to show Jesus exhorting his followers not to be afraid of death, which is strange indeed if he himself feared it when he approached it. But this is not the meaning of these words of exhortation, for in them Jesus is counselling his disciples not to fear *their persecutors and opponents*. This advice to others, Jesus certainly applied in his own life, for he never showed the slightest sign of fear for the Jews and Romans. There is in fact a great difference between being afraid of men and being afraid of death. Jesus in no way conflicted with his own teaching when he passed through anguish and fear as he approached the hour of death.

Does this make Jesus any less a brave man or less worthy of our utmost devotion? Surely not, for the truly brave man is the one who goes on, although he is afraid. Often the absence of fear indicates lack of true sensitiveness; the callous, hard-hearted, unfeeling man may indeed feel less of any emotion, but that makes him neither brave nor exemplary. We must, of course, be careful not to look for an interpretation of this saying which will merely confirm us in our stereotyped views of Jesus; we must try to follow the evidence, whether it confirms our opinion or not. Yet the conclusion of any particular interpretation must somehow accord with the general picture of our Lord. This point of sensitivity and fear may help at this juncture. Was Jesus of such a sensitive character that we can well think of him as being specially aware of the horrors of death? The answer can only be: 'Certainly he was.' We cannot imagine him facing the horror of death without a shudder, if, indeed, death is the ultimate, the last enemy of God. We have then no need to say it was because of the weight of the world's sin that Jesus was so much in agony in Gethsemane. It was because death is a horrible thing when faced realistically. This, in fact, is the witness of many doctors and others who often see men and women die. While after death there often appears to be a great serenity discernible in the features, many good and noble people die in agony and some in terror.

If this is the right interpretation of this saying of Jesus, we must accept it, whatever the consequences for our faith. But fortunately those consequences need not be at all disastrous. It does not take away the ground of Christian hope if we accept that Jesus was afraid of death. Rather it places that hope on a sure and utterly realistic ground. It turns the eyes of a Christian to face this unavoidable fact of death, and his natural fear of it. It does not say: 'You ought not to be afraid, and if you are, you show un-belief.' Instead, it says it is perfectly natural for you to be afraid, for Jesus, the perfect man, was also afraid. But in the hour of death, facing its horror you will know that your Lord knows exactly what this is, and will help you with sympathy. But far more than sympathy, with victory! For the Christian view of death is not complete when we look at Jesus in the Garden of Gethsemane; it must also see Jesus in the Garden of the Empty Tomb; see him as the conqueror of death. His victory is all the more valuable to us because it is a victory over the death we have to face; from which he shrank, as we know we may.[44]

We next consider the account of the death of Jesus which is in Mark 15$^{33-7}$ and Matthew 27$^{45-50}$. We should remember that according to Matthew 27$^{34}$ Jesus had refused the friendly narcotic offered to him on his way to crucifixion. This means that at the last he was fully conscious of death. The gospels do not encourage us to dwell upon the dreadful details of the death of Jesus by crucifixion; indeed, one of the outstanding facts in the gospels at this point is their almost unbelievable restraint. No attempt is made to arouse emotions of pity for Jesus, or anger against the Jews or Romans; the facts are simply, almost baldly stated. The two parts of the narrative of particular interest to us are the Cry of Dereliction (Mk 15$^{34}$, Mt 27$^{46}$), and the statement that Jesus, having cried out with a loud voice, gave up his spirit (Mk 15$^{37}$, Mt 27$^{50}$, Lk 23$^{46}$).

(a) *The Cry of Dereliction* ('My God, my God, why hast thou forsaken me?'—Mk 15$^{34}$, Mt 27$^{46}$).

There seems no reason to doubt that this is a genuine saying of Jesus, and we do well to remember the warning of Taylor here: 'The depths of the saying are too deep to be plumbed.'[45] Obvi-ously the saying has great significance in connexion with the

---

[44] Note Daniel-Rops, ibid. p. 435: 'Death had its way, and in that terrible face-to-face encounter which we must all experience when our time comes, Jesus is seen only as a man broken by suffering.'
[45] VTM, p. 594.

doctrine of the atonement; our more immediate task is to attempt to interpret its relation to the view of death expressed in the gospels. The crucial question is whether this saying can be understood as our Lord's reaction to death alone, or whether we must suppose that it was human death allied with man's sin, which caused the cry. A decision on such a matter must always be tentative and individual. If the point made above is accepted, that Jesus was troubled and afraid of death itself, then it is not impossible to interpret this saying in terms of our Lord's attitude to death, without including the question of sin. It is to be noted that those who do include sin as a relevant factor are not unanimous in their interpretation. Some say that Jesus feels himself forsaken because he is a substitute for sinners, and so is rejected by the Father. This is denied by many modern interpreters on the grounds that it implies a division between the Father and the Son in Atonement, which is not the true Christian interpretation. Others accept the connexion with sin without implying God the Father has rejected the Son, by saying that Jesus felt the horror of sin so deeply, and was so closely allied with sinners, that for a time his sense of fellowship with God was dimmed. It is to be noted that it is not really so far from this view to say, as we have implied, that the horror of death is so great that while it is being experienced the sense of the presence of God is dimmed. Cullmann expresses this very forcibly—'Because it is God's enemy, it separates us from God, who is Life and the Creator of all life. . . . To be in the hands of the great enemy of God means to be forsaken by God. . . . Jesus must suffer this abandonment, this separation from God, the only condition really to be feared.'[46] The only hesitation which may be felt about this is the statement that the Father abandons Jesus in death. This hardly seems a necessary view; if it were really true, there would be no hope for us in death. But we may say that Jesus, as all other men, *felt* himself to be abandoned by the Father. Then to Jesus, death means that sense of desolation, and if Jesus is here meeting death as we have to meet it, we must also be prepared for this sense of desolation. But not, it must be emphasized, the reality of abandonment. To die may mean to feel abandoned by our Father; if we are to have any hope at all, it cannot mean that we are actually abandoned.

[46] *Immortality of the Soul or Resurrection of the Dead?*, pp. 24-5.

*(b)* '*He gave up his spirit*' (Mk 15³⁷, Mt 27⁵⁰, Lk 23⁴⁶).

There are slight, but significant, differences in the three accounts. The stark realism of Mark suggests the most original account: 'And with a loud cry, Jesus expired' (ἐξέπνευσεν). The implication is that death was violent and sudden. This in itself was unusual in the case of crucifixion, and Pilate and the centurion both remarked upon the fact that Jesus was so soon dead (Mk 15³⁹,⁴⁴).⁴⁷ There is nothing in the Marcan account to suggest that the death of Jesus was a voluntary act, as is implied by Matthew's phrase: 'He gave up his spirit.' Luke also seems to indicate the same thought in his report of the last words of Jesus: 'Father, into thy hands I commit my spirit' (23⁴⁶). Thus in comparison with Matthew and Luke, Mark plainly states that this was 'human death' for we do not give up our spirit when we choose; we die at a time when we do not choose, except in the case of suicide. This seems to support the contention made above that Jesus faced and experienced death as any man has to face it. He was not given, or certainly did not use, any supernatural power in order to terminate his life. This seems to suggest that if the Christian follows the example of Christ, he will not wish to decide the point of termination of his life. He will pray for patience to endure until the time which God will choose. Death is one of the things which God has not given us to control—we may not decide when we are to die, for that is something not properly in our power to choose.

This study of our Lord's attitude to his own death suggests the following conclusions about the meaning and significance of death in the gospels.

(1) The death of Jesus is, like other deaths recorded in the gospels, physical death. Nowhere in the accounts of the death of Jesus is it said that he faced 'spiritual' death.

(2) Jesus shrank from contact with physical death, and in the agony of death felt himself abandoned by God. This is explicable without reference to spiritual death, when death is regarded as the enemy of God.

(3) The circumstances and conditions of the death of Jesus on the Cross were much more terrifying and distressing than human death normally is. Yet it is a great help to Christians to know that Jesus has tasted the bitterness of death, and shares our natural

⁴⁷ VTM, p. 601.

fear of death. Even more, a Christian is upheld in the hour of death by the knowledge that our Lord has conquered death, this last enemy of God, and offers a share in his victory to those who believe in him.

### IV.  POSSIBLE FIGURATIVE OR SYMBOLIC USES OF DEATH

Thus far in our study of death in the synoptic gospels we have noticed that the emphasis falls upon the realistic matter-of-fact use of death; the meaning is plain physical death, the end of this present existence. It will be observed that this is an important emphasis, and further, that it is in some ways different from the rest of the New Testament, in which 'death' often has a figurative meaning. So far we have not discovered in these gospels any reference to the relation between sin and death, nor have we found any references in which death seems to mean something in the spiritual realm. But to complete our study, there are a few passages in which it might well be thought there is a spiritual meaning of death, and the physical aspect appears to be secondary. These occurrences must now be briefly considered.

(a) Matthew 4$^{16}$: '*The people which sat in darkness saw a great light. And to them that sat in the region and shadow of death, to them did light spring up.*' (*R.V.*)

There is a similar reference, in a different setting, in the song of Zacharias (Lk 1$^{79}$). The Matthean use of this quotation from Isaiah 9$^{1-2}$ is part of an editorial explanation of how Jesus fulfilled a prophecy by leaving Nazareth and going to live in Capernaum. This is a very apposite use of the prophecy, for it originally referred to the coming of a great light to a land which was in continual darkness owing to the oppression of Assyria. The continual threat of death at the hands of the invader is well expressed as 'living in the land of the shadow of death'. This is, as we have said, a very fitting application of the prophecy, because the gospels tell how the Saviour has come to dispel the darkness of the times. In this sense, death is used in a somewhat figurative way, although we must remember that in the prophetic utterance it was real, physical death which was meant. And the 'spiritual' sense of death is not expounded by Matthew who, as we shall see below, recorded words of Jesus about death which must be taken realistically, even though it would seem to be easier to interpret them spiritually. In view of this lack of any development of a spiritual interpretation of death, we must conclude that although there is an undoubted element of such an idea in this passage, it is not influential in the gospels.

(*b*)  Matthew 8²² (cf. Lk 9⁶⁰): '*Follow me, and leave the dead to bury their own dead.*'

This is one of the replies Jesus gave to those who wished to follow him, but had not sufficiently counted the cost of doing so. Tradition based on Clement of Alexandria, says the disciple in question was Philip. Whoever it was, he said: 'Lord, let me first go and bury my father.' The reply of Jesus raises great difficulty as it stands, because it seems impossible to avoid a 'spiritual' sense of 'dead', and then the reply of Jesus seems unnaturally harsh. It will be well for us first to set out the possible interpretations.

(i) 'Leave those who are spiritually dead to bury the dead.' This, as we have noted, seems somehow out of harmony with the usual attitude of Jesus, who was not in the habit of treating anyone in this fashion. And what is also significant for our present purpose, this would be one of the very few occasions on which Jesus used the word 'dead' in a non-physical sense. Manson points out: 'It is not likely that there is a distinction in meaning between the dead who are to bury and those who are to be buried, the former being the spiritually dead, the latter the physically dead.'⁴⁸

(ii) 'Leave the dead to their burier of the dead.'⁴⁹ The basis for this is an interesting conjecture that the original Aramaic had this meaning and was wrongly translated into Greek. This also seems rather a harsh and unkind thing to say, especially as Jewish law laid it down that the son was primarily responsible for his father's burial, and burial of the dead was reckoned a great act of piety. It is interesting that one text quoted to support this assertion, Genesis 50⁵, is a very close parallel to the present passage. On the death of Jacob, Joseph requested Pharaoh: 'Let me go up, I pray thee, and bury my father and I will come again.' It would be surprising if such a close parallel did not occur to the writer of the first gospel; and we may wonder if there is not an implied contrast between the service of Pharaoh and the demands made upon a disciple of Jesus. We can return to this suggestion later.

⁴⁸ *The Sayings of Jesus*, p. 73.
⁴⁹ I. Abrahams, *Studies in Pharisaism and the Gospels* (Second Series), p. 183.

The emendation proposed in this theory is attractive, but it is not usually wise to rely too much upon supposed Aramaic originals, however brilliant the supposition may be.

(iii) 'Let the dead past bury its dead.' This seems too vague and general a statement to be our Lord's personal reply and cannot attract much support.

(iv) 'Let me wait until my father has died' being the request of the disciple, Jesus saw therein a strong tendency to procrastinate, and in reply uttered this sharp reminder of the urgency of the call to discipleship. Even apart from this possible view, that the disciple's father was still living, this may lead us near to the sense of the passage. That is, this call is so compelling and urgent that whatever your responsibility, it has to be set aside for the more important work you have to do. This interpretation really leaves unanswered the question 'Are the dead the spiritually dead?' although it is strongly in favour of a realistic sense. If indeed the disciple was making an excuse for avoiding the immediate claims of Jesus, it may be that he was answered in paradoxical fashion in order to emphasize the urgency of his call, and the cost of his discipleship. This would seem to be the most satisfactory explanation. It does not deal specifically with the literal meaning of the words of Jesus, because they were not meant literally but paradoxically. So Manson writes: 'The utterance is a paradoxical way of saying "That business must look after itself; you have more important work to do".'[50]

We need to note the limitation of this saying; it is a particular word given to an individual in one specific situation. It does not imply that a disciple of Jesus must never carry out this, or any other, pious duty to his parents. Nor does it imply, as some have supposed, that our Lord was critical and impatient of the Jewish burial customs. As the main intention is to awaken the would-be follower to a real sense of the urgency of the call to follow, and the cost of following, the details of the paradoxical expression must not be taken at their face value.

(c)  Matthew 10[8]: '*Heal the sick, raise the dead, cleanse lepers, cast out devils. You received without pay, give without pay.*'

These are words addressed by Jesus to the twelve disciples whom he chose and sent out. A similar expression occurs in Matthew

[50] *The Sayings of Jesus*, p. 73.

11[5], in the answer to the disciples of John the Baptist, who are told to observe the signs of Messianic activity: 'The blind receive their sight and the lame walk, lepers are cleansed and the deaf hear and the dead are raised up' (cf. Lk 7[22]). Does this mean that Jesus commissioned his disciples to raise the dead and pointed to the raising of the dead as a sign of Messianic activity? There is a strong natural tendency to suppose that 'the dead' here means the spiritually dead, who are raised to new life in Christ. This is indeed a perfectly legitimate way of speaking of the effects of Christ's work, not only as he himself did it, but as his disciples still do it. But we have to admit that this is not the sense implied in these statements. There is no more reason for taking 'raise the dead' figuratively than there is 'cleanse the lepers' or 'cast out devils'. As if to emphasize that the raising of the dead did happen, Luke precedes his account of the reply to John the Baptist with the story of the raising of the son of the widow of Nain. However difficult it may be to apply these words, especially as a commission, we are bound to say that when Jesus said 'raise the dead' he meant the physical dead; when he pointed to the fact that the dead are raised up, he meant the physically dead. There is, therefore, no ground in these sayings to modify our conclusion that death in the gospels is predominantly physical, not spiritual.

(d) Luke 15[24, 32]: '*For this my son was dead and is alive again; he was lost and is found.*' Verse 32 is the same, with '*thy brother*' instead of '*my son*'.

Clearly the meaning of 'was dead' here cannot be 'physically dead', for the younger son is throughout the story described as active, whether in going away, wasting his substance, or returning home. In view of this, and of the fact that this Parable of the Elder Son is so wonderful an epitome of the gospel, 'was dead' can very easily be interpreted as dead in trespasses and sin. But it is doubtful whether this is allowable as the true meaning in the parable, however true it may be to the facts of human experience. We are often rightly warned against allegorizing the parables, and making a detailed meaning apply to every separate part. That warning applies here. The plain meaning of these words in the setting of the story is 'my son was as good as dead'— not 'was spiritually dead'. This is the true situation portrayed in the parable. A separation in a far country, with no communication and no prospect of return is, to the father, almost the same as if the boy were dead. The implication may well be that life consists in living relationships; but it cannot be that the father means his son was spiritually dead—he was 'to all intents and purposes as good as dead'.

The conclusion of this discussion is very interesting and important. Death in the gospels is the physical end of life; it is not, as in Paul particularly, also being dead toward God. That is not to say that Paul's emphasis on spiritual death is wrong; it is, perhaps, to say that our modern attempts to minimize the significance of physical death are wrong. The fact is that when man becomes unsure of what happens after death, he tries to persuade himself that death is not really very important and is best ignored. Conversely, if there is a realistic awareness of the fact and importance of death, we may be confident that this indicates a sure belief about what happens after death. In this regard the witness of the synoptic gospels is of the utmost importance. In them we are recalled to an open-eyed facing of the fact of death; not as a friend to be welcomed, but as an enemy to be faced and to be conquered in the power of Christ. The Christian is often accused of being an escapist; if he remains true to the facts of the gospels he will be, of all men, the realist about the inescapable fact of death. And equally he will find fullness of life here and now, for there is no doubt that one condition necessary for a full life is to come to grips with death. This is what we see Jesus doing in the gospels; it is what every Christian also must do.

# CHAPTER SIX

# JUDGEMENT

THE two ways of considering judgement in the synoptic gospels are:

(1) The use of terms which mean judgement or something associated with it.

(2) The parables of judgement which express the idea without necessarily using the word.

## I.   USE OF TERMS

With regard to the terms used, we note that although several words should be considered, the words by themselves do not give an adequate picture of the prevalence of the idea of judgement in the teaching of Jesus. This is one of the cases where we must look beyond the actual terms to the idea, which is expressed in various ways. The verb which is at the root of most of the 'judgement' words is κρίνειν. This means 'to judge', 'to condemn', 'to hand over for judicial punishment'. It is used with God as the subject only in Matthew 7[1, 2], with a parallel in Luke 6[37-8]: 'Judge not, that you be not judged. For with the judgement you pronounce you will be judged, and the measure you give will be the measure you get.' Luke's version is slightly fuller: 'Condemn not, and you will not be condemned; forgive and you will be forgiven; give and it will be given to you; good measure, pressed down, shaken together, running over, will be put into your lap. For the measure you give will be the measure you get back.' It is indeed possible to interpret all this without reference to God as the One who judges, gives, forgives, etc. But this reduces the saying to mere worldly-wise advice, with a view to being treated well by others. Not only does this often not happen, but it is hardly the sort of attitude Jesus commended. On the other hand, it is the limitless forgiveness of God which must impel our forgiveness of others, as it is the unrestricted generosity of God which should determine our attitude to others.

If then, these are references to divine forgiveness and divine generosity, we must assume this is also a reference to divine judgement. It is typical of the general teaching of Jesus that the emphasis lies on the conditions for avoiding the judgement of God rather than on the details of that judgement. As we consider further instances of our Lord's teaching on this subject, we shall find this principle reappearing continually. Jesus refers to the judgement of God as something well known to his hearers, but about which he does not give many details.

Κρίμα is a noun derived from κρίνειν, which means condemnation, that is, an unfavourable judgement.[1] The tendency toward thinking of κρίμα in an unfavourable light can be seen in the papyri: 'From denoting "judgement" "sentence", the word came to denote the "offence" for which one is sentenced, and hence in modern Greek is frequently used as the equivalent of sin.'[2] The word appears to be used of divine condemnation in Mark 12⁴⁰ (parallel Lk 20⁴⁷). The scribes who devour widows' houses and for a pretence make long prayers shall receive 'greater condemnation'. This condemnation is the condemnation of God.[3] Again we notice a clear statement of the ground of the condemnation but absolutely no description of the details of it. The other occurrences of κρίμα refer to human condemnation, Luke 23⁴⁰: the rebuke of the thief to his companion who railed on Jesus; and Luke 24²⁰: the description by the disciples on the way to Emmaus of how the rulers gave condemnation and crucified him.

Κρίσις is also derived from κρίνειν. Sometimes it is used of 'legal proceedings' (Mt 5²¹).[4] The second occurrence of the word in this passage (5²²) means the 'divine judgement'. This latter sense is certainly intended in those passages which have the phrase 'in the day of judgement' (Mt 10¹⁵, 11²²,²⁴, 12³⁶). The 'day of judgement' is a very common phrase in Jewish Apocalyptic writings, in which the emphasis is on the condemnation of sinners. There are at least four meanings applied to the phrase in this literature—(i) The deluge, (ii) final world judgement at the beginning of the Messianic kingdom, (iii) judgement of the sword

---

[1] W. F. Arndt and F. W. Gingrich, *A Greek-English Lexicon of the New Testament*, p. 451.
[2] J. H. Moulton and G. Milligan, *The Vocabulary of the Greek Testament*, p. 360.
[3] VTM, p. 495.
[4] So Wellhausen, quoted by McNeile, *The Gospel according to St Matthew*, p. 61.

executed by the righteous, and (iv) final world judgement at the
close of the Messianic kingdom.[5] In a very interesting passage,
4 Ezra (2 Esdras) $7^{38-44}$, there is a detailed description of the
unusual natural phenomena on the Day of Judgement, and the
statement that 'on that day' it will not be possible for the righteous
to intercede for the wicked. The reason for this is persuasively
argued in terms of our inability to be ill, to eat, sleep, or be healed
for anyone else. So, according to this view, we cannot expect the
righteous to do anything for the wicked on judgement day.[6]
This brief reference to the idea of the day of judgement in Jewish
literature draws attention to the place this notion held in the
thought of our Lord's contemporaries. Again we can say that
Jesus was using a well-known idea, without at all insisting on
every detail as presented in this literature.

In Matthew $12^{18-20}$, is a use of κρίσις in a rather different sense.
The word translates מִשְׁפָּט (mishpat) which normally has a wide
meaning, almost equivalent to 'religion'. This idea is indeed
present in Matthew $23^{23}$ (parallel Lk $11^{42}$): 'The Pharisees
neglect justice and the love of God.' Here the meaning seems to
be 'care that the rights of others are respected'.[7] But in Matthew
$12^{18, 20}$, the intention seems to be 'the fast approaching judgement
day'. Possibly the inference is that mishpat has some influence on
the sense of κρίσις, i.e. the ethical and religious basis of judgement
is being stressed.

In Matthew $12^{36, 41-2}$, there is a reference to the conditions of
attitude to Christ which will operate at the judgement (cf. Mt
$12^{32}$). Idle words, spoken against the Son of man will condemn
this generation in the judgement.

The other words, not cognates of κρίνειν, which should be
considered in this context, are ἐκδικεῖν and ἐκδίκησις. These
occur only in the parable of the Unjust Judge (Lk $18^{1-8}$) and in
Luke $21^{22}$. While the main meaning of this parable is discussed
below, we should note here that the meaning of these words is
closer to 'vindicate', 'vindication', than to 'avenge', 'vengeance'.[8]
The thought of 'avenge' (AV, RV) is not necessarily primary in
Luke $18^{1-8}$, but rather of 'do right to' and so 'protect' the

---

[5] A. & P., II.214.
[6] 4 Ezra (2 Esdras), $7^{102-5}$.
[7] McNeile, The Gospel according to St Matthew, p. 335.
[8] C. Ryder Smith, The Bible Doctrine of the Hereafter, p. 193. Cf. Moulton and Milligan,
The Vocabulary of the Greek Testament, p. 192.

wronged party. In view of this meaning the emphasis of the story tends to be on God's deliverance of the poor and needy, rather than on His 'vengeance' against His enemies. On the other hand Luke 21[22], 'for these are days of vengeance, to fulfil all that is written', does seem to be a reference to the Last Judgement.[9] The context of this saying is the prediction of the destruction of Jerusalem by Roman armies. This destruction was to fulfil the many prophecies against God's wayward people.[10] The only question which arises is the suitability of describing this as the 'last judgement'. It is not the 'last' in the usual sense of the final judgement at the end of the ages, but rather a particular judgement which is to come upon Jerusalem in the immediate future. This being so, these words do not add anything to our picture of the Final Judgement which Christian thought asserts awaits men after death.

The words κατακρίνειν ('condemn'), and κατάκρισις ('condemnation'), do not occur in the gospels with God as subject, so they are not relevant to our present purpose. 'Punishment' (κόλασις) (Mt 25[46]), 'torment' (βάσανος) (Lk 16[23, 28]), and 'tormentors' (βασανισταί) (Mt 18[34]) are treated below, under the consideration of the Great Assize, Dives and Lazarus, and the parable of the Unforgiving Servant, respectively.

## II.   THE PARABLES OF JUDGEMENT

According to Ryder Smith there are at least eighteen parables which express the idea of judgement.[11] It will help toward an appreciation of the importance of these parables in the study of ou Lord's teaching about judgement if firstly we set down some statements in them. In particular we can notice what these stories appear to say about the fate of the wicked.

In the parable of the Wicked Husbandman, the fate of the rebellious tenants is: 'He will come and destroy the tenants and give the vineyard to others' (Mk 12[9]). Matthew's account is more forcible: 'He will put those wretches to a miserable death, and let out the vineyard to other tenants who will give him the fruits in their seasons' (Mt 21[41]; cf. Lk 20[16]). The fate of the Unrighteous Servant is described in Luke 12[46]: 'The master of that servant will

---

[9] Arndt and Gingrich, *A Greek-English Lexicon of the New Testament*, p. 238.
[10] T. W. Manson (*The Sayings of Jesus*, p. 330) cites Hosea 9[7], Jeremiah 5[29], 26[4–6], Daniel 9[26]; cf. Enoch 25[4].
[11] *The Bible Doctrine of the Hereafter*, p. 194.

come on a day when he does not expect him and at an hour he
does not know, and will punish him and put him with the unfaithful.' Matthew's account is again more forcible—one might
even say more bloodthirsty: 'He will cut him to pieces and put
him with the hypocrites; there men will weep and gnash their
teeth' (24⁵¹). The parable of the Unfruitful Fig Tree is usually
taken in a personal sense, so that the words of Luke 13⁷ seem to
describe the fate of the wicked: 'Cut it down; why should it use up
the ground?' In the story of the Great Supper, Matthew records
that as a result of the shameful action of those who were invited
and refused to come to the marriage feast of his son, 'The king
was angry and he sent his troops and destroyed those murderers
and burned their city' (22⁷). Luke's account of what seems to be
the same story is somewhat milder in the condemnation of the
unresponsive guests, and instead goes on immediately to emphasize
the action of the nobleman in calling others to fill the banqueting
hall (14²¹). The twin parables of Wheat and Tares and the
Drag Net seem to describe the fate of the wicked briefly but
succinctly in terms of destruction: 'Gather the weeds first and
bind them in bundles to be burned' (Mt 13³⁰). When the net
was full 'men drew it ashore and sorted the good into vessels,
but threw away the bad' (Mt 13⁴⁸). The Unforgiving Servant
arouses the anger of his master because of his unmerciful attitude
towards his fellow servant, and as a result 'in anger his lord
delivered him to the jailers [the Greek is literally 'tormentors']
till he should pay all his debt' (Mt 18³⁴). The condemnation of
the Labourers in the Vineyard is brief, but extremely biting:
'Take what belongs to you and go' (Mt 20¹⁴). In the two stories
of the Talents and Pounds, which must surely come from the same
original, the servant who had received one talent and had done
nothing with it, is described as 'You wicked and slothful servant'
(Mt 25²⁶; cf. Lk 19²²), and his fate is not only to be deprived of
his one talent (Mt 25²⁸), but to be cast into outer darkness where
men will weep and gnash their teeth (Mt 25³⁰; cf. Lk 19²⁴). The
fate of the five foolish virgins is exclusion from the marriage feast
and more seriously, to be disowned by the bridegroom. 'After-
ward the other maidens came also, saying Lord, Lord, open to us.
But he replied, Truly I say to you, I do not know you' (Mt
25¹¹⁻¹²). Lastly, in the story of the Great Assize, the nations
which had not served the Lord in the service of the poor and needy

are condemned: 'Depart from me, you cursed, into the eternal fire prepared for the devil and his angels' (Mt 25$^{41}$; cf. 25$^{46}$: 'And they will go away into eternal punishment').

When these words of condemnation are thus put together, it is easy to understand the common view that Jesus said some very hard things about the destiny of the wicked, which seem difficult, if not impossible, to reconcile with his declaration of the love and patience and kindness of God. It must be admitted that the words we have quoted raise some of the most difficult questions a Christian exegete has to face. The ways out of the difficulty are various: some dismiss all these statements as 'Jewish', and assert that these dreadful ideas have no place at all in the genuine teaching of Jesus. Others take the opposite extreme and almost seem to enjoy the prospect of the justifiable condemnation of the wicked. Between these two extremes there are a large number of sincere Christians whose attitude is mainly characterized by bewilderment. The most dangerous effect of this bewilderment is that it naturally develops into carelessness and indifference. In the face of these puzzling sayings, which we find hard to link with Jesus of Nazareth, we very easily adopt the attitude that we cannot know anything at all about future judgement, and in any case, it is not at all important.

In the following study of the parables of judgement we must bear in mind that, in some of the parables we consider, there is no positive teaching about judgement applicable to the present day. In other parables we shall find teaching about judgement which applied originally to specific groups of people, but not to everyone. We shall assume that before we can decide the present-day application of any of these parables, we must first determine, as far as possible, to whom the story was first addressed. Only then shall we be able to say what meaning the teaching holds for today. This approach means that at the end of some of our studies of the parables we shall have to admit that no definite teaching about judgement applicable to present-day conditions can be discovered. But each parable must be considered separately, for we cannot determine beforehand which parables contain applicable teaching about general judgement and which do not.

In order to interpret the meaning of the parables in question, it will be convenient to keep in mind the following questions:

(1)  *To whom is the parable addressed?*

We cannot assume without further question that all the parables contain teaching which must apply to everyone, in all circumstances.

(2)  *What is the time referred to in the prediction of judgement and condemnation?*

This question is often very difficult to answer, but we must not assume that all predictions necessarily apply to the Last Judgement at the end of the ages.

(3)  *What is said about the destiny of the good alongside the statements concerning the bad?*

In other words, we must not isolate the teaching about future punishment from that concerning future bliss.  If we do, we shall gain a very unbalanced view of the teaching of Jesus about judgement, for it involves the good as well as the bad.

(4)  *What standards of judging are stated or implied in these parables?*

This question is easily forgotten if we give too much attention to the details of the judgement or condemnation itself.  As already suggested, the emphasis in the teaching of Jesus falls more upon the conditions to be fulfilled in order to avoid condemnation, than upon the description of what the condemnation is to be.

In seeking to apply these questions to the parables of judgement, very considerable help is available from the recent studies of the parables, especially the work of C. H. Dodd,[12] and Joachim Jeremias.[13] The value of these studies is increased by the fact that they are concerned with the widest implications of the parables and not only with the particular question of judgement, with which we are dealing.  By following the argument of these general studies we are saved from that isolation of our subject to which we have already referred.  Dodd has shown that the parable is a story with one specific point to make, and that allegory or an attempt to find meanings for every detail of a parable will only mislead us by obscuring the one main point.  Dodd further insists that the main point emphasized in many parables is that a crisis has arrived, in which men must take appropriate action.  It is indeed

[12] *The Parables of the Kingdom* (1935).          [13] *The Parables of Jesus* (E.T., 1954).

mainly on the basis of his study of the parables that Dodd asserts his belief in realized eschatology. It is also apparent that Jeremias has been very much influenced by the work of Dodd, which he has carried farther by a detailed study of the structure of the parables. As a result of this study, Jeremias has shown how the circumstances of the early Church have influenced the form in which the parables are now presented in the gospels. As we shall see, this study bears very closely on our concern with the teaching of the parables about judgement. It is precisely in such things as the application of the parables, and the introduction to them, which often radically affect their time reference, that Jeremias discovers the influence of the early Church. We can best illustrate these, and other points, by considering in some detail the 'parables of judgement'.

### THE PARABLE OF THE WICKED HUSBANDMEN.

This is the only one under consideration which appears in all three synoptic gospels (Mk 12[1-11], Mt 21[33-43], Lk 20[9-18]). Jeremias argues that while as it now stands 'the whole parable is evidently pure allegory', it is possible to see what was the original, non-allegorical core of the parable. This is to be seen in the simple story of Luke 20[10-12], which tells how on three successive occasions, the owner of the vineyard sent a single servant to collect from the husbandmen his dues.[14] The sending of the son of the owner is not regarded by Jeremias as having any Christological significance in the original story, for our Lord's hearers would not connect 'the son' with any Messianic claim, and further, the story of the son closes with his death, without any reference to resurrection (Luke 20[15] and parallels—'the stone which the builders rejected has become the headstone of the corner'—is clearly a later interpretation, and not part of the original parable). If this story of the threefold sending of a servant, followed by the sending of the son, is the original core of the parable, we can detect the process of allegorizing beginning in Mark, and coming to full flower in Matthew.[15] Thus Mark 12[5] adds 'many others' to the single servant, apparently implying a reference to the prophets who were sent to Israel. In Matthew, the single servant has become plural; the treatment even at this early stage includes some

---

[14] *The Parables of Jesus*, p. 55. The simple story, however, really begins at verse 9.
[15] There is of course much interpretative material in Luke as well; this view does not mean that Luke is prior to Mark.

of them being killed, in some cases by stoning (Mt 21[35]). Jeremias thinks that this, and the later, more numerous mission, refers to the earlier and later prophets, some of whom were indeed killed by stoning. By his reference to the killing of the son, whom the husbandmen seized and cast outside the vineyard and killed, Matthew seems deliberately to be referring to the circumstances of the crucifixion which took place outside the city wall. The more original account in Mark 12[8] merely says that the husbandmen killed the son and then cast his body outside the vineyard, which seems to be an indignity added to the murder, to emphasize the enormity of the offence of the husbandmen.

The conclusion of this very interesting study is that the original parable 'vindicates the offer of the gospel to the poor'.[16] The leaders of the people, who have been entrusted with the care of the vineyard, have proved rebellious and untrustworthy. Therefore God will now give the vineyard to the poor. That the original parable was spoken against the leaders of the people, they themselves recognized, as recorded in Mark 12[12]. Jeremias further suggests that probably the parable was spoken in connexion with the cleansing of the temple, in which case it is particularly directed against the priestly members of the Sanhedrin.[17] We can, then, answer our questions in relation to the original form of this parable as follows:

(1) The parable is addressed to the leaders, not to all the people. The condemnation it contains, which is terrible enough, and must not be minimized—'He will come and destroy those tenants, and give the vineyard to others' (Mk 12[9], Lk 20[16], Mt 21[41])—applies to the leaders, not to the whole people. This implies that the condemnation cannot be applied to the general fate of the wicked.

(2) The time referred to is not the end of the ages, nor the parousia, nor the last judgement, but NOW! Jesus is vindicating his offer of the gospel to the poor, which is *now* being made. It may be that the terrible events of A.D. 70, when Jerusalem was besieged and captured by the Romans were regarded as the fulfilment of this prediction of the kingdom of God being taken from the Jews and given to the Gentiles.[18] One valuable part of

[16] *The Parables of Jesus*, p. 60.
[17] Ibid. p. 124.
[18] C. Ryder Smith, *The Bible Doctrine of the Hereafter*, p. 194: this parable 'primarily refers to the judgement of A.D. 70'.

the interpretation outlined above is that it does not attempt to explain away the words of condemnation, but rather explains the particular application of them to a clearly defined group of people in a definite historical situation.

(3) In regard to our third question, we note that nothing is said about the destiny of the good, unless we include under this head the promise of the kingdom of God being given to others.[19]

(4) In the nature of the case, we can infer from this parable nothing about the conditions of general condemnation. The basis of the condemnation of the Jewish leaders is plain. It is because they have proved unfaithful and rebellious leaders that they are condemned. In different circumstances we can perhaps infer that the same standard of judgement will be applied to people in equal position of leadership and responsibility, but we cannot assert that these conditions and this condemnation apply to all and sundry.

### THE PARABLE OF THE WAITING SERVANTS (Mk 13[33-7]).

This is the only other Marcan passage to be considered here. With it is often linked Luke 12[35-8], for although several details are different, the general situation is the same in each parable; servants are awaiting the return of their lord, and have instructions to be ready to receive him, however late in the night he may return.[20]

There are difficulties inherent in both accounts, revealed in several details. Taking Luke's account first, the statement in 12[37] is to be regarded as an allegorization which breaks the sequence of the story and adds a detail, which although wonderfully true of Jesus, would not be a natural event in the situation depicted in the story. Again, by referring to all the servants, Luke has missed the point which is clear in Mark, that only the doorkeeper was instructed to watch. The other servants were each given their own task. So it is thought that the nucleus of the parable is the story of the doorkeeper, awaiting the return of his master from a wedding. In this case Mark's introduction is misleading, for the description of the master of the house as 'a man

---

[19] See below, pp. 156-77, for a discussion of the kingdom as an expression of the future life.

[20] C. H. Dodd, *The Parables of the Kingdom*, p. 160; Jeremias, *The Parables of Jesus*, p. 43.

going on a journey' conflicts with the idea of the doorkeeper keeping watch all night. It would be extremely improbable for a man to return at night from a long journey, in view of the eastern dislike of night travel.[21] The situation is perfectly natural if, as Luke says, the master of the house had gone to a wedding, not on a long journey. It seems as if the motive in Mark's description of the long journey is to emphasize the delay in the coming of the parousia, which Jeremias believes was a very powerful influence in determining the form of some of the parables.

If the original parable did not contain any reference to a long delay, we can accept the view of Dodd[22] that the story really emphasizes the necessity of watchfulness in view of the critical situation which the coming of Christ has brought about. This story refers to that critical situation in which anything might happen at any time, and requires watchfulness in the face of this fact. But who is being instructed to watch? Dodd suggests either the general public or the disciples may be meant.[23] Jeremias has the very interesting suggestion that the parable originally was addressed to the scribes, who claimed to possess the keys of the kingdom of Heaven.[24] In any case, it seems reasonably clear that this is a 'crisis parable' rather than a 'last judgement' or 'parousia' parable.

For our own special purpose we note that the part of it which could describe future destiny—(Lk 12³⁷) 'Truly I say to you, he will gird himself and have them sit at table, and he will come and serve them'—is in all probability not part of the original story. We conclude that this parable contains no teaching about the destiny of men, good or bad, which has a general application. The emphasis lies on the sort of wide-awakeness which is necessary to a good doorkeeper. But this is to be applied to the present critical situation, caused by the coming of the Son of Man, rather than to future destiny beyond this life.

### THE LUCAN PARABLE OF THE RICH FOOL (Lk 12¹⁶⁻²¹).

This is interesting from our point of view because it contains condemnation of the rich man's self-sufficiency and the demonstration of the emptiness of his way of life. 'Fool! this

---

[21] Jeremias, *The Parables of Jesus*, p. 44.     [22] *The Parables of the Kingdom*, p. 167.
[23] Ibid. pp. 165-6.     [24] *The Parables of Jesus*, pp. 44-5.

night your soul is required of you; and the things you have prepared, whose will they be?' Again, while the story refers to an individual's death, the main import is that all this regard for property, which has caused the dispute on which Jesus refuses to adjudicate (Lk 12¹³⁻¹⁵) is pointless in view of the crisis which has arisen because the kingdom has drawn near.²⁵

This is a crisis story rather than a judgement story, referring to the present situation rather than future destiny, but we can also notice that there is an implication regarding death. Not punishment, but emptiness seems to be the fate of the man who foolishly relies on material things as the basis of his life. Perhaps there is an implication of punishment in the fact that the man who has cared so much for possessions will find it very hard to leave them behind, and even harder to contemplate other people having the use of them. The parable certainly reminds anyone who reads it that if he makes temporal things the basis of his life, he can expect that in the end he will, in fact, be left with nothing at all. All these issues are brought into sharp focus by our Lord's insistence that the times are so critical that care for possessions and the disputes which almost inevitably go with that care, are vain and useless.

### THE PARABLE OF THE SERVANT
### ENTRUSTED WITH AUTHORITY (Lk 12⁴¹⁻⁸, Mt 24⁴⁵⁻⁵¹).

This is presented in a context which interpets it in relation to the coming of the Son of Man (Mt 24⁴⁴, Lk 12⁴⁰), and naturally in this context, ends with a prediction about the fate of the unfaithful disciples at the sudden coming of the Son of Man (Mt 24⁵⁰⁻¹, Lk 12⁴⁶). There are several indications that a process of interpretation has been at work, which radically affects the meaning of the original story. Matthew's version implies that there are two servants (24⁴⁵, ⁴⁸) and concludes with an application which jumps from an earthly setting to a supramundane one, using the terms 'weeping and gnashing of teeth', which can be recognized as a stereotyped expression relating to the eternal punishment (cf. Mt 8¹², 13⁴², ⁵⁰, 22¹³, 25³⁰, Lk 13²⁸).²⁶ The process

---

²⁵ *The Parables of Jesus*, p. 123. 'The possession of property is irrevelant to the life of the Age to come.'

²⁶ This phrase was probably a well-known saying in the time of Jesus, and may have originated in the punishment given to a naughty child, who might be put outside the single lighted room, to work off his childish rage.

of interpretation is seen even more clearly in Luke 12⁴¹, which is an editorial introduction with the effect of interpreting the parable in relation to the special responsibilities of the apostles. This point is further emphasized by Luke 12⁴⁷⁻⁸, which is composed of separate sayings, brought together and added to this parable. We notice also that Luke expands the description of the misdemeanours of the unfaithful servant, who beats the manservants and the maidservants, spending his time eating, drinking, and getting drunk. Jeremias asserts that the context of these stories must be entirely disregarded,[27] and makes out a good case on the basis of the points we have noted, for saying that this parable 'is seen to be one of (Jesus') many stern words of warning to the scribes that the day of reckoning was at hand, when God would reveal whether they had been faithful to the trust committed to them or had abused it'.[28] The basis for asserting that this parable is directed to the scribes is the belief that when the people heard Jesus speaking of a servant entrusted with responsibility, they would naturally think of their own leaders. 'For them the scribes were overseers appointed by God, to whom the keys of the Kingdom of Heaven had been entrusted.'[29] The condemnation of Matthew 24⁵¹ and Luke 12⁴⁶ is, therefore, directed toward the scribes. Even so, it seems unduly severe to speak of the untrustworthy servant (the scribes) being 'cut asunder' (*RV*)—καὶ διχοτομήσει αὐτόν. There is, however, an interesting conjecture that the Aramaic behind this word may mean: 'He will beat him and treat him as a profligate.'[30]

If the above explanation is accepted, we have to say that this parable, in the form in which Jesus spoke it, does not tell us anything about general destiny after death, nor of the judgement which awaits all men. It is another parable of present crisis, and therefore cannot be used as evidence of our Lord's teaching about general judgement.

### THE UNFRUITFUL FIG TREE (Lk 13⁶⁻⁹).

This is another Lucan parable which must be interpreted as a parable of crisis. That this refers to the people of Israel is

---

[27] *The Parables of Jesus*, p. 46.     [28] Ibid. p. 47.     [29] Ibid.

[30] Ibid. p. 46, note 99. N.B. *RSV*—'will punish him, and put him with the hypocrites'. Cf. Arndt and Gingrich, *A Greek-English Lexicon of the New Testament*, p. 199: 'Cut in two, of the dismemberment of condemned persons—in the context of these two passages the meaning "Punish with the utmost severity" is possible, though no exact linguistic parallels for this meaning have been found.'

clear from the frequent identifications between Israel and a fig
tree (Hos 9[10], Mic 7[1], Jer 8[13]). The action of the vinedresser in
pleading for another opportunity for the barren tree to produce
fruit emphasizes the aspect of the patience of God in this time
of crisis. The time is NOW! The condition of continuity is fruit-
fulness, and the penalty of continued barrenness is to be cut down.
Too much must not be read into this concerning the future of the
wicked, for we have to remember that the parable is realistic,
and when it refers to the tree being cut down, it does not necessarily imply the total destruction of sinners. We notice once
again that the emphasis in our Lord's teaching lies on the reason
for people being condemned (unfruitfulness) rather than on the
details of what condemnation involves.

### THE PARABLE OF THE UNJUST STEWARD (Lk 16[1-13]).

This provides a most interesting study of the way in which
careful thought about a parable can help to disentangle the
nucleus from the later additions, and reveal the teaching of Jesus
in a clearer light. As with the other examples already considered,
we can start with the difficulties. The story begins with an
account of what may well have been an actual incident known to
Jesus. The unjust steward, faced with the prospect of dismissal
on account of his irregularities coming to light, takes swift action
to meet the crisis. He offers a substantial discount to his em-
ployer's debtors, either in order to regain the favour of his master
by showing how he could collect debts; or possibly in order to
gain friends who might help him when he was dismissed. The
story in fact does not say why the steward took this action, nor
what he gained from taking it; it simply records his swift action in
the face of a critical situation.

Jeremias insists that Luke 16[8] refers to Jesus, not to the rich
man of the parable, who would hardly be expected to approve the
action of his unscrupulous servant. It is pointed out that ὁ κύριος
used absolutely always means either God or Jesus in Luke.[31]
In other words, this is the comment of Jesus on the story, with his
application that his hearers ought to take a lesson from the steward
and act wisely in view of the situation caused by his presence
among them.

[31] *The Parables of Jesus*, p. 33.

This interpretation does mean that the story of the unjust steward seems strangely incomplete. We are left completely in the dark about the motive and effect of the steward's action, and this is very difficult to understand unless, as we have said, this is our Lord's re-telling of an incident about which he has heard, and which may have caused a good deal of amazement among those who heard it. But with this hesitation, there is, nevertheless, good reason for accepting the view of Jeremias that this is another parable of crisis. It is a summons to those who hesitate, to decide on a fresh start, in view of the threatened crisis.[32]

We have to notice that two different and additional interpretations have been annexed to the story. Firstly there is the interpretation in Luke 16[9], 'make friends for yourselves by means of unrighteous mammon, so that when it fails they may receive you unto the eternal habitations', which may have been addressed originally to tax farmers or others thought to be dishonest persons.[33] Secondly, there is the interpretation which makes the steward a warning against dealing unfaithfully in worldly things, which indicates how unworthy one is to be given charge of heavenly things (Lk 16[10, 11]). This, too, is a parable of crisis; it urges upon men the need for wise action in face of the eschatological crisis which now confronts them. It does not say anything about eternal destiny.

### THE PARABLE OF THE TALENTS, OR THE POUNDS (Mt 25[14-30], Lk 19[11-27]).

We can readily enunciate the question which must be faced in this parable. In the condemnation of the servant who kept his master's money safe, but did not make any effort to increase it, to whom is Jesus referring? It is interesting to notice that modern study of this parable places the centre of interest in the servant who received one talent, as, for a different reason, a moralizing interpretation stresses that those who receive small endowments should nevertheless make the best use of them. This latter interpretation is surely far from the original meaning of the parable, however true and practical a point it may be. On

---

[32] Ibid. p. 87.

[33] Ibid. p. 34. There is an inferior reading which has the plural ἐκλίπητε ('when you fail'). But in any case this does not affect the sense. Cf. J. M. Creed, *The Gospel according to St Luke*, p. 205.

the basis of the tradition that it was the scribes' chief duty to 'fence the law'—i.e. to keep it safe from wrong interpretation— it is suggested by Jeremias that the one-talent servant is the scribe.[34] This parable then is regarded as addressed to the scribes. It is a warning to them that if they prove unproductive they will be condemned like the unproductive servant. The fate of such a person is stated by Luke to be deprivation of the little he has (Lk 19[24]: 'Take the pound from him and give it to him who has the ten pounds'). Matthew adds what we can only regard as a typical condemnation: 'Cast the worthless servant into the outer darkness; there men will weep and gnash their teeth' (Mt 25[30]). As this condemnation is not found in Luke we must assume that it is added to the original story by the First Evangelist, who as we have seen is rather fond of this phraseology.

The hesitation which may be felt about accepting this interpretation of Jeremias is due to the fact that by concentrating on the single-talent servant no account is taken of the blessing promised to those who had made good use of their opportunities, and received the commendation of their lord. Are we to ignore completely the well-known and much-loved words of Matthew 25[21, 23]: 'His master said to him, "Well done, good and faithful servant; you have been faithful over little, I will set you over much; enter into the joy of your master" '? Hard as it may seem, we are forced by notice of Luke's parallel verse to question whether these words were really part of the original parable. Luke records the commendation of the profitable servants in much more realistic terms: 'Well done, good servant! because you have been faithful in very little, you shall have authority over ten cities' (Lk 19[17], cf. 19[19]). It is clear that this is much more likely to have been what the original story said, for it keeps the reward linked with worldly realities. The Matthean version is, on the other hand, strongly Christological, a fact which is partly obscured by the *RSV* translation of τοῦ κυρίου σου as 'your master'. It is rather to be taken in the sense of 'the Lord', and thus a reference to the coming bliss of the Messianic kingdom. This is further emphasized if, with Dalman, we translate χαρά as 'banquet' rather than 'joy'.[35] We have, therefore, to conclude that the account of the activity of the productive servants is not really the point emphasized in this parable, and we cannot build

[34] *Th Parables of Jesus*, p. 50.        [35] *Words*, p. 118.

a theory of the rewards of heaven upon this picture of faithfulness rewarded with greater responsibility.

## THE PARABLE OF THE TEN VIRGINS (Mt 25$^{1-13}$).

This passage is an interesting example of the way in which the presentation of a parable may considerably affect its meaning. The context of this story in Matthew is made up of sayings about the parousia (Ch. 24) and the parables of the Talents and the Sheep and Goats, both being connected with the coming of the Son of Man. In the same way this parable teaches that although the bridegroom is delayed (Mt 25$^5$) the virgins must be ready and watching, for they do not know the day or the hour (Mt 25$^{13}$). The clear intention is to interpret the story in allegorical fashion, with Christ as the bridegroom and the Church as the attendant of the bride. It does, in fact, argue strongly for the genuine nature of the parable as the teaching of Jesus, that the bride is not mentioned. The idea of the Church as the bride is a common-place in the thought of the early Church (2 Cor 11$^2$, Eph 5$^{31-2}$), and we could well have expected a reference to the Church under the allegory of the bride in this story. It is consistent with the teaching of Jesus that the disciples are thought of as the attendants but not as the bride.[36] Jeremias further shows that the representation of the Messiah as the bridegroom is 'completely foreign to the whole of the Old Testament and to the literature of late Judaism'.[37] On this ground he asserts that in the original parable the bridegroom was not an allegorical representation of Christ. The story is, in fact, not an allegory at all, but a parable describing an actual situation preparatory to the wedding feast.

In this case the meaning of the parable must be found in the situation described. This meaning is that there comes upon the waiting bridal attendants a sudden call to action: 'Behold the bridegroom! Come out to meet him!' The lesson is 'the crisis is also upon you'. Matthew 25$^{13}$ cannot be the original lesson, for as Jeremias points out, all the virgins slept; the application that men must 'watch' does not really arise out of the story. But the lesson that all must be ready for this crisis is clear from the parable. The preparation is the attitude of repentance and readiness

---

[36] *The Parables of Jesus*, p. 42, note 83.
[37] Ibid. p. 41. Reference is made to the evidence presented in *TWNT*, I.1094-5.

to receive the offer of God's invitation as it is being presented in Christ. The parable is addressed to all who hear, but it is not a parable of the last judgement. Therefore the words in $25^{10-11}$ cannot be used to describe the destiny of good or bad. However attractive and suitable it may be to describe the joys of heaven as a marriage feast, this interpretation cannot be based on Matthew $25^{10}$, which is simply a natural part of the realistic story Jesus told to make the point of the imminence of the eschatological crisis, and the necessity of preparing to meet it. Equally, the description of the attitude of the bridegroom to the five virgins who were shut out is not to be taken as indicative of what it means to be excluded from heaven. The bridegroom would have nothing to do with the foolish virgins because in the story they failed in their responsibility. This means, indeed, that this time of crisis is a time of decision and separation. But it cannot be made the basis of a description of the fate awaiting the wicked as 'being shut out from the presence of Christ', however right it may be on other grounds to describe the destiny of the wicked in these terms.

There are three other parables which, according to Jeremias, are intended to be a vindication of the offer of the gospel to the poor—the Great Supper (Mt $22^{1-14}$, Lk $14^{16-24}$), the Labourers in the Vineyard (Mt $20^{1-16}$), and the Importunate Widow (Lk $18^{1-8}$). In each of these stories are words which can readily be taken to indicate some aspect of future destiny, so we must briefly consider each in turn.

### THE PARABLE OF THE GREAT SUPPER (Mt $22^{1-14}$, Lk $14^{16-24}$).

In this story a comparison between the two synoptic accounts shows clearly that a process of allegorization has taken place. Matthew especially reveals this in his reference to the king, whom Luke calls merely 'a certain man'; the feast is the wedding of the king's son, instead of, as in Luke 'a great supper'. Matthew makes much more of the number of servants sent out by the king, and the treatment of them by the invited guests, which included killing some. By these extra details Matthew seems clearly to be referring to the coming of the prophets and the treatment they received. Luke's account does not show such clear traces of allegorical interpretation, but there is probably the underlying notion that the feast is the feast of salvation. The matter which Matthew includes which has no parallel in Luke is the description of the punitive action taken by the king, in which the unresponsive guests were killed; this must be regarded as an embellishment of the story, if for no other reason because it is inconceivable that all this could go on while the wedding waited to be supplied with guests. It hardly needs to be added that the conclusion of Matthew's account, the story of the Guest without a wedding garment (22[11-14]), is an entirely separate story, whose introduction may well have become detached, and is now found in Matthew 22[1-2]. This second story of a marriage can be disregarded in our attempt to interpret the first story.

This first story, especially as presented by Luke, is an account of the measures taken to fill the dinner party with guests when those who had been invited would not come. It was an understandable and wise thing to do, even if somewhat unusual. In the circumstances of our Lord's telling of this story there can be little doubt that it makes the point that the Jews having refused the invitation by their rejection of him, the Gentiles are being invited to share the blessings of salvation. God is doing what is after all perfectly natural, if in some ways surprising. This is, in other words, a vindication of the offer of the gospel to the poor and needy.[38] The parable must be regarded as addressed to the critics of Jesus, who murmured because he associated with publicans and sinners (Mt 9[11], 11[19], 21[31]). The implied time reference is NOW!—for at this very time Jesus was in fact offering the good news of God to these outcasts of men.

If we accept the fact that some allegorical interpretation is inevitable, and Jesus expected it, then we can say that this parable describes the joys of heaven in terms of a banquet. This involves gladness and fellowship. The conception of a Messianic banquet was prevalent in the Jewish expectations of the future, and had a large number of ideas connected with it.[39] This means that our Lord's hearers would easily connect what he said with the idea of future destiny, and would note that it involved the amazing notion that the poor, needy and outcasts were to be included in this banquet; which is different from the narrow and exclusive conceptions of contemporary Jewish ideas. Indeed, if

[38] Jeremias, *Parables of Jesus*, pp. 102-3.
[39] See index, *A. & P.*, II.859, under 'Messianic Banquet'.

we are looking for a new contribution made by Jesus to the idea of the future blessedness of the righteous, we shall find him to be more concerned with the issue of who will receive the blessing than with the details of what the blessing of future bliss is to be. This parable shows our Lord concerned with the way in which God is bringing in the outcasts to fill the places which the invited guests were not prepared to occupy.

### THE PARABLE OF THE LABOURERS IN THE VINEYARD (Mt 20$^{1-16}$).

It is easy to see how this parable should come to be regarded as expressing a lesson about judgement and the future. Not only is it presented as an extended comment on the saying: 'The last shall be first, and the first last' (Mt 20$^{16}$; cf. Mk10$^{31}$ and parallels). Further, the picture of the payment of wages at the end of the day suggests the Last Judgement, the handing out of rewards in the kingdom of heaven. In this interpretation the brief word to those who grumbled can easily be taken as the final dismissal from the presence of God—'take your own and go' (Mt 20$^{14}$).

The parable remains an enigma, which is made no easier because there is no parallel account of it in the other gospels. There is, however, a parallel to the saying: 'Many shall be first who are last, and the last first' (Mk 10$^{31}$, Mt 19$^{30}$). This seems to have been an independent logion (cf. Lk 13$^{30}$, Mk 9$^{35}$).[40] It is asserted by Bultmann and Jeremias that the story does not, in fact, illustrate this saying. The idea that it does is mainly based on the order of payment, in which the steward was instructed to pay the labourers their wages 'beginning from the last'. In fact this seems to be an incidental detail in the original story, and it may well mean, 'including the last'.[41] We are left wondering what the original story did mean.

The suggestion that there are two parts to the parable, and that the emphasis falls on the second part, seems helpful. The first part of the story tells of the hiring of the labourers at different times, in circumstances which could well have been realistic, in view of the widespread unemployment and seasonal fluctuations of work. The second part tells of the grumbling of the early

[40] Jeremias, *Parables of Jesus*, p. 26, quoting Bultmann, *Die Geschichte der synoptischen Tradition* (1931), p. 191.
[41] Ibid. p. 25, especially note 17.

workers on account of the equal treatment of those who had only
worked a short time. The emphasis of the story may be intended
to show up the grudging and grumbling attitude of the Pharisees
in particular. In this case Jesus is again vindicating the offer of
the gospel by reference to 'the behaviour of a large hearted man
who is compassionate and full of sympathy for the poor'.[42] The
action of the owner of the vineyard is neither capricious nor over-
generous, for the amount he gives is only a bare subsistence to all,
and in any case, no more than he had agreed to give to those first
hired. Those who reject the view that this parable speaks of
reward being of grace, not merit, point out that the early workers
were rewarded according to merit, so 'all is not of grace'.[43] But
this seems to give too much weight to details in the story and it
may be that underlying the emphasis which criticizes the attitude
of the Pharisees is the conviction that the dealings of God with
men are not explicable on the basis of merit and reward but only
as undeserved generosity.[44]

It is clear from these considerations that the parable does not
refer to what God will do at the last Judgement, but to what He
is doing now. God is now dealing with people in this generous and
compassionate way. This, no doubt, implies that God will in
future deal in the same way at the last Judgement, but we have
to admit that the parable does not say this, being only concerned with the present saving activity of God revealed and
operating in Christ.

### THE PARABLE OF THE IMPORTUNATE WIDOW (Lk 18$^{1-8}$).

This is presented as an illustration of the value and efficacy of
prayer. It is interesting from the point of view of this study,
not only because it uses κριτής ('judge') in verse 2, but also
because it speaks of 'vindicating the elect speedily' (verse 8).
This last point is connected even more closely with the coming of
the Son of Man by the conclusion of verse 8. But there are difficulties in the view that this is an exhortation to prayer. Especially
the story tends to imply that prayer 'works' because like the

---

[42] Ibid. p. 26.
[43] Ibid. p. 25.
[44] K. L. Schmidt, *Basileia*, p. 45, makes this point: 'The object of all these parables
is to make clear that the ordering of God's kingdom is different from ordinary human
order.'

unjust judge, God will answer prayer in order to stop the continual pestering which otherwise he will get. Indeed, any comparison between God and the judge who 'neither feared God nor
regarded men' seems difficult to maintain. If the editorial setting
is disregarded; that is, if verses 1 and 8[b] are taken as not necessarily connected with the parable, we find a story which points a
lesson by contrast. Even an unjust judge will do justice to the
poor widow, although his motives are far from satisfactory. How
much more will God, the perfectly righteous One, do justice to
the poor and needy? He will certainly help them in their distress;
this is, in fact, what He is doing, and it ought to occasion no
surprise that this is happening. The time is NOW! The people
addressed are the critics of Jesus who cannot believe that God will
defend the cause of those normally regarded as beyond hope.
Again, we have to conclude that in spite of appearances, this
parable does not tell us anything about future judgement.

Two parables which remain to be discussed are closely concerned
with judgement and therefore of particular interest to us.

### THE PARABLE OF THE UNFORGIVING SERVANT (Mt 18[23-5]).

This is introduced by the question of Peter concerning how
often forgiveness should be extended to an offender. The answer
Jesus gave was that forgiveness must be continually repeated—
'until seventy times seven': which means 'without limit'. Although
the story of the unforgiving servant concerns forgiveness, it does
not say anything about unlimited, repeated forgiveness. We
therefore conclude that in its original form the parable does not
belong to the answer to Peter's question. But it is a parable about
forgiveness, very forcibly illustrating the point made in the Lord's
Prayer: 'Forgive us our debts, as we also have forgiven our
debtors' (Mt 6[12], cf. Lk 11[4]). The situation depicted is unusual; in
fact unique; for the unforgiving servant is said to owe a debt
which was fifty times as much as the total annual tribute for
Galilee and Peraea.[45] The enormity of the debt draws attention
to the story, and also points to the nature of the debt man owes
to God, and which by divine love, man is forgiven. Compared
with the debt owed by the servant, the debt owed to him by a

---

[45] Jeremias, *The Parables of Jesus*, pp. 22-3.

subordinate is trifling. There are details in the story which suggest that a Gentile setting is in mind; under Jewish law it was
forbidden to sell wife and family; and 'tormentors' (οἱ βασανισταί)
indicates a Gentile system of punishment.[46] These unusual features do not mean that the parable is not a genuine utterance of
Jesus; we often find unusual circumstances included in our Lord's
stories which indicate his skill as a story-teller.

This is without any question a judgement parable.[47] It is
addressed to all who will hear, and sets out the conditions necessary for obtaining divine forgiveness. The details of the condemnation of the unforgiving servant must not be taken literally to
indicate what divine condemnation is like, but we cannot avoid
the implication of eternal condemnation involved in the statement
'till he should pay all his debt' (Mt 18[34]). This clearly must
mean 'for ever', for the debt was so enormous that there could
never be any hope of paying it. The parable perhaps indicates
also that not only does such an attitude not deserve forgiveness,
but also it is incapable of receiving forgiveness. It is perhaps
allowable to say that the anger of the king represents the divine
wrath against this unforgiving spirit. It is often supposed that a
God of love must be incapable of wrath, and therefore judgement
is thought to be an automatic, impersonal response of the universe,
to the wrong sort of behaviour. Whether it is easier to contemplate this rather than divine wrath is questionable. But in any
case Jesus spoke in personal terms of the reaction of God to this
spirit of non-forgiveness.

The most important feature of this significant parable is that
the emphasis falls upon the conditions of condemnation rather
than upon the details of it. This is in agreement with what we
have already seen of the teaching of Jesus. This parable does not
add very much to our knowledge of what condemnation is to be;
it does very forcibly indicate the reality of future judgement, and
the condition upon which partly that judgement will be based.
This condition is the practice of forgiveness among our fellow
men. It is also to be noted that this condition of forgiveness
links together the present life and future life. Forgiveness of other
people must be practised now, and it is also a necessary condition
for man's life on earth now. This means that it is not true
to the teaching of Christ to say that the responsibilities of this

[46] Ibid. pp. 146-7.        [47] Ibid. p. 147.

life are to be neglected in order to obtain bliss in the future. On the contrary, it is only by fulfilling our responsibilities to each other in this present life, that we can hope to receive the forgiveness of God both in the present and in life hereafter.

### THE STORY OF THE SHEEP AND GOATS (Mt 25[31-46]).

This is designated 'The Parable of World Judgement' by A. Huck.[48] Many scholars, however, point out the almost complete absence of parabolic features, and describe this passage as a short apocalypse.[49] However, the form of the narrative is not for us the foremost question. We have to consider firstly whether this can be regarded as an authentic utterance of Jesus; and secondly, if so, what is its teaching about judgement.

There is a strong tendency in modern discussions to regard the passage as authentic. It is pointed out that although there are similar stories in Jewish literature, this pictorial representation of the last judgement has distinctive features.[50] These include the surprise of both righteous and wicked at the judgement passed on them, and the designation of the Son of Man as judge, which is different from the usual Jewish view that the Judge is God. The change from the Son of Man to the king in Matthew 25[31, 34] is explained by Jeremias as probably due to the stereotyped form of the introduction in verse 31.[51] To the argument that the reference to 'being in prison' (25[36, 43]) indicates a late date, as no Christians had been imprisoned in the time of Jesus, it is replied that the reference to 'the least of my brethren' does not mean Christians, but the poor and needy. We shall return to this point in our consideration of the teaching of the story about the conditions of judgement. Again, while it is true that Jesus did not speak of himself as King, this conception is not far removed from the Messianic conception, and there is the enigmatic reply to Pilate's question: 'Are you the King of the Jews?'—'You have said so'—i.e. 'That is your word for it' (Mk 15[2]; cf. Jn 18[37]). The conclusion on the question of authenticity can never be final, but there seems no adequate ground for doubting that this is a genuine

---

[48] *Synopsis of the First Three Gospels*, p. 181 (German title).
[49] e.g. Dodd, *The Parables of the Kingdom*, p. 85.
[50] Jeremias, *The Parables of Jesus*, p. 144; Manson, *Sayings of Jesus*, p. 249; Kümmel, *Promise and Fulfilment*, p. 92.
[51] *The Parables of Jesus*, p. 142.

story told by Jesus.[52] While it undoubtedly displays features similar to those commonly found in Jewish Apocalypses, this does not
require its rejection as an authentic saying of Jesus. The apocalyptic characteristics however, do necessitate full account being
taken of the pictorial nature of the language. This must not be
interpreted as a literal account of the last judgement.

Regarding the question of the teaching of this passage concerning judgement, the first matter requiring discussion is what is
meant by πάντα τὰ ἔθνη (all the nations) (Mt 25[32])? The idea
that the judgement depicted is a community judgement and not
applicable to individuals, can hardly be supported in view of the
description of things done or left undone. All these, feeding the
hungry, giving drink to the thirsty, and so on, are acts of individuals, not nations. It is generally agreed among scholars that
the Gentiles are meant; to which Jeremias adds a very illuminating suggestion. He thinks that this story really answers the
question: 'How will those be judged who have not seen or heard
of the Christ?' The conditions under which disciples are to be
judged can be briefly stated. These are, confession of Christ
before men (Mt 10[32]); doing the will of his heavenly Father
(Mt 7[21-2]); readiness to forgive others (Mt 6[14-15]); the exercise of
mercy (Mt 5[7]); and enduring to the end (Mk 13[13]). 'At the last
judgement God will look for living faith.'[53] But in the case of the
heathen these standards cannot apply except with the result that
all will be condemned. Therefore this story sets out the conditions by which the heathen will be judged, as revealed in attitude
to the brethren of Christ, who are the poor and needy. This view
of Jeremias differs from that expressed by Manson, who argues
that the 'least of these my brethren' is a reference to the disciples
of Christ who together with him form the composite Son of Man.[54]
While Manson's view agrees with his general theory that 'Son of
Man' means Jesus plus disciples, it is difficult on this view to
escape the criticism that this makes the standard of judgement of
non-Christians very narrow; and many will feel that it raises
Christians to an altogether too high position if the fate of millions
of people depends on the attitude shown to them. We therefore

---

[52] So Jeremias, *The Parables of Jesus*, p. 144; Kümmel, *Promise and Fulfilment*, p. 95;
Manson, *Sayings of Jesus*, p. 249. The contrary view is expressed by Dodd, who thinks
that the judgement scene was composed to give a dramatic setting to the saying in
Matthew 25[40, 45]—*The Parables of the Kingdom*, p. 85.
[53] Jeremias, *The Parables of Jesus*, p. 145.     [54] Manson, *Sayings of Jesus*, pp. 249f.

conclude that the view of Jeremias seems more in accord with the total picture of Jesus presented in the gospels.

It must not be assumed that this means that the standard of judgement is easy. While nothing is said about those sins which are usually regarded as serious, we must recognize that the standard is very exacting. The list of acts of kindness to the needy is probably not to be regarded as complete and exhaustive, and it would be contrary to the intention of the story to suppose that this list includes all acts required of men if they are to be counted among the blessed. We certainly have to notice that the surprise of those who were commended inevitably excludes from the company of the blessed those who are vividly conscious of their good deeds. Both the accepted and the rejected show that it is by an unconscious attitude of helpfulness that men are judged— in other words, by what men really are, not by what they or other people think they are. Nor can it be thought that this standard of judgement is an easy alternative for those who have found the demands of discipleship too hard for them. For those who have thus turned from Christ, the condemnation is clear, according to the teaching of Jesus. In three of the five conditions mentioned above relating to the judgement of disciples, there are grim alternatives to being blessed of God. Those who deny Christ before men will be denied before God (Mt 10³³); not every one who talks of Jesus will enter into the kingdom of Heaven (Mt 7²¹); those who do not forgive others will themselves not be forgiven (Mt 6¹⁵).

If this is to be regarded as a description of the destiny of non-believers, the question arises in which category the large number of men are to be placed who are indifferent to the claims of Christ. Fortunately, it is not for any man to decide this question, but it would appear reasonable to say that those who have in any way rejected the claims of Christ, and by their actions have spurned the offer of God's forgiveness, and refused to acknowledge him by worship and service, are not of 'the nations' who are referred to here. It would seem clear that once having heard the gospel, and having been brought up in circumstances in which it is possible to respond to the gospel, any man who then rejects Christ has condemned himself. If this seems to place too much emphasis on our attitude to Christ, which may indeed be very difficult to evaluate, we must notice that this story places the emphasis on this point. Those who are blessed and belong to God are so because through their attitude to the poor and needy they have 'done it unto me'. This means that even in the case of non-believers, their attitude is acceptable because through serving the poor and needy, they have, in fact, served Christ. It is not on the basis of the inherent value of human life that the blessing is pronounced. The value of human life is indeed safe-guarded by the standard of service to Christ, and there is never any danger of people being regarded merely as means to an end of serving Christ. But it is an undeniable feature of the Christian view that the standard by which all will be judged, is in the fullest sense, the way men in their lives accept or reject the One whom God has sent.

The two verses which describe the destiny of the blessed and accursed respectively can be seen to contain striking parallels and also significant divergencies when placed side by side:

Matthew 25[34]: Then the King will say to those on his right hand, 'Come you blessed ones who belong to my Father; inherit the kingdom which has been prepared for you from the foundation of the world'.

Matthew 25[41]: Then He will say to those on his left hand, 'Depart from me, you accursed ones, into the eternal fire which has been prepared for the devil and his angels.'

The parallels are as follows: 'Right hand' is contrasted with 'left hand'—one is the place of honour,[55] the other the position of less honour, but apparently, when $εὐώνυμος$ is used as here, not implying dishonour.[56] It is perhaps some indication of faith-fulness to the original that the phrase translated 'on the left' is not the one which would most readily imply dishonour and doom. 'Come' is sharply contrasted with 'depart from me'; 'you blessed ones' with 'you accursed ones'. The phrase 'which belong to my father' is a literal rendering of the Greek genitive, the significance

[55] 1 Kings 2[19], Psalm 110[1]. Quoted of the Messiah—Matthew 22[44], Mark 14[62], Acts 2[34], 7[55-6], Hebrews 1[13].

[56] $ἐξ$ $εὐωνύμων$ is used together with $ἐκ$ $δεξιῶν$, to signify left hand/right hand without any idea of inferiority, in Exodus 14[22,29] and Matthew 20[21,23], 27[38]. But Mark 10[37,40] implies that $ἐξ$ $εὐωνύμων$ and $ἐξ$ $ἀριστερῶν$ are synonyms, and there is an element of the ominous involved in $ἐξ$ $ἀριστερῶν$, evil being thought to come from the left. Cf. VTM, p. 440, and Arndt and Gingrich, *A Greek-English Lexicon of the New Testament*, p. 330.

of which is somewhat obscured by the English versions 'of my father', which seems to imply action rather than possession. It is noticeable that the word of condemnation does not say that those who are cursed belong to the devil, but that their destiny is the same as that prepared for the devil and his angels. Again, we notice that the kingdom which the blessed ones inherit[57] has been prepared for them from the foundation of the world, but nothing is said about the origin of the eternal fire. This may imply that the kingdom of the blessed belongs to the original order of creation, while the destiny of the wicked does not. This kingdom of the blessed has been prepared for those who now inherit it; but the eternal fire has been prepared for the devil and his retinue. This seems to imply that the happy destiny of the blessed is what God intended for man, while those who are condemned enter a state which they were not intended to occupy.

The chief problem of the words addressed to the unrighteous is the suitability of anyone being designated 'accursed' by Jesus. This is the only occurrence of καταράομαι ('curse', 'doom', 'imprecate evil upon') in which Jesus as subject applies the word to people. The other instance in the gospels is Mark 11[21], in which Peter refers to the fig tree which Jesus had 'cursed' on the previous day. The stronger Christian tradition springs from Luke 6[28], in which the disciples are instructed 'to bless them who curse you' (cf. Rom 12[14]). Can we believe that Jesus would call anyone 'accursed'? Some understanding of the significance of 'accursed' can be gained from noticing that it is frequently used in conjunction with 'blessed'. An early instance of this connexion is in Genesis 9[20-7], in which Ham, the father of Canaan, is cursed for looking upon his father's nakedness, and at the same time Shem and Japheth are counted blessed for their action in covering their sleeping, drunken father. This curse upon Canaan is referred to in Wisdom 12[3, 11]—'Those who dwelt of old in thy holy land . . . were an accursed race from the beginning'. Blessing and cursing go together in contrast in the story of Jacob being blessed by his father in mistake for Esau (Gen 27[29]). Cursed seems to be the opposite of blessed, possibly with the implication that to be cursed is to be deprived of blessing. We have to remember that the Hebrew way of describing the activity of God never employs

[57] For evidence that the kingdom was popularly used in the time of Jesus to describe the future state of the righteous, see C. Ryder Smith, *The Bible Doctrine of the Hereafter*, p. 224.

the convenient but confusing impersonal automatic idea of modern speech. God is one who can be angry, and in the same way, to be deprived of the blessing of God is to be cursed by Him. If this helps to soften the meaning of 'accursed' in this passage, it must not be thought to reduce its significance or its seriousness. The destiny of those who are condemned is terrible to contemplate; even when due allowance is made for the pictorial form of the language, there remains a clear impression of a dreadful doom awaiting those who do not fulfil the conditions required for blessedness.

Perhaps the most searching form of this condemnation is revealed in the simple command, 'Depart from me'; when this is set alongside the word to the blessed 'Come', we have in essence what is meant by hell and heaven. To be in hell is to be sent out from the presence of God; compared with the terrible deprivation it matters little into what condition or circumstances the cursed ones are sent. What really matters is that they are banished from the face of God. Equally, there is no description of 'heaven' more significant than that which is involved in the one word 'Come'—for to be with God is to be indeed in heaven. If we recognize the significance of this we can look on 25[46], the conclusion of the story, as no more than a figurative description of what has been already fully set out in these terms of 'come!' or 'depart!' 'Eternal punishment' is probably used as a well-known phrase descriptive of the fate of the wicked, without any attempt to face the question of the suitability of punishment which goes on for ever. It is interesting to note that the question of punishment being remedial is faced in the Book of Wisdom.[58] This shows that the question of punishment was a live issue in contemporary literature, but from this one reference we can only conclude that Jesus (or, more certainly, the author of the gospel) only repeated the current popular notion to indicate divine disapproval, without entering into any discussion of the matter.

This discussion of the teaching of Jesus about judgement can be briefly summed up as follows:

(1) The first emphasis in our Lord's teaching is upon the crisis which has arisen because he has brought the rule of God into operation. Many of the parables which seem to speak of future

[58] *A. & P.*, I.530-1.

judgement are seen on closer consideration to be parables of crisis.

(2) Jesus taught his disciples to expect a future judgement, and told them that the conditions upon which that judgement would operate for them are confession of himself before men, readiness to forgive, exercise of mercy, and endurance to the end.

(3) The condition of judgement for non-believers is attitude to the poor and needy, the least of Christ's brethren.

(4) In the two parables which certainly speak of future judgement (The Unforgiving Servant and The Sheep and Goats) the emphasis is on conditions of blessedness or condemnation, rather than on details of the future state.

# CHAPTER SEVEN

# THE FATE OF THE LOST

AS many of the difficulties in connexion with our subject arise in relation to the fate of those who do not 'get to heaven' we must look carefully at the teaching of the synoptic gospels about this. We have to consider at this point a list of formidable words—*Hades, Gehenna, fire*.

## I. HADES

This Greek word has passed into fairly common usage in English, often with the sense of 'Hell'.[1] The word is originally a proper noun, the name of the god of the underworld.[2] But the meaning of the word in biblical usage is determined by the fact that in LXX it is used to render the Hebrew Sheol. This is the real reason for the word appearing in the New Testament.[3] It follows from this that to understand the meaning of ᾅδης we must know the meaning of שְׁאוֹל. The matter is complicated by the fact that there is a discernible development of interpretation of the latter word, which can be very briefly stated as follows. In the early ideas of the Hebrew people, Sheol is the place to which all men go at death, irrespective of the quality of their life. Existence in Sheol can hardly be called 'life'; those who inhabit this cavern in the hollow of the earth have passed out of history. It is likely that the Hebrews thought that God could have acted in Sheol but that He chose not to do so; He is certainly not to be escaped, even in Sheol (Ps 139[8]). This idea that good and bad alike went down into Sheol gradually challenged the faith of pious men, who became increasingly dissatisfied with the view that the righteous merely went down to this shadowy, sub-existence. There are

---

[1] See footnote in *Methodist Book of Offices*, p. 23, explaining 'He descended into hell' in the Apostles' Creed—'That is, Hades, or the World of Spirits'.

[2] Arndt and Gingrich, *A Greek-English Lexicon of the New Testament*, p. 16.

[3] *The Vocabulary of the Greek Testament*, p. 9: 'Except for its appropriation from the literary language to represent Sheol in LXX, we should probably not find it in the New Testament.'

signs in the Apocryphal books of this discontent, and the criticism of the orthodox doctrine becomes open in the Book of Wisdom, which belongs to the first century B.C. Wisdom asserts that Sheol is the place of torment of the wicked, not simply a place of inactivity and sleep for all. At the same time this writer asserts that the righteous are in the hand of God and no torment shall touch them. They are delivered from Sheol, which is not a proper state for the righteous.

We have therefore to consider in which sense of Sheol, Hades is used in the gospels: and answer can be given only by considering the particular instances of the word. There are three passages in which Hades occurs in the gospels (Mt $11^{23}$; cf. Lk $10^{15}$; Mt $16^{18}$ and Lk $16^{23}$). As the last reference occurs in the story of Dives and Lazarus, which we treat separately below, it is necessary here to consider only the first two occurrences.

(a)  Matthew $11^{23}$, parallel Luke $10^{15}$: '*And you, Capernaum, will you be exalted to heaven? You shall be brought down to Hades.*'

According to Manson[4] this is a Q passage, reporting the words of condemnation Jesus spoke against the towns of Galilee; Chorazin, Bethsaida, and Capernaum. The Matthean version is fuller and is regarded by Manson as closer to the original. There is a clear reference to a passage in Isaiah, in which the king of Babylon is taunted for thinking that he can escape the lot of all other men, which is to go down to Sheol. 'All of them (the leaders of the earth and the kings of the nations), will speak, and say to you, "You too have become as weak as we! You have become like us!" ' (Isa $14^{10}$). 'You said in your heart, "I will ascend to heaven; above the stars of God, I will set my throne on high. . . . I will make myself like the Most High." But you are brought down to Sheol, to the depths of the Pit' (Isa $14^{13-15}$). The main import of this passage is that the king of Babylon, like all other men, is mortal; there is no suggestion that his going to Sheol is a punishment for his arrogant dealing with Israel. He is taunted only because in his arrogance he has thought himself to be above other men. There is a similar passage in Ezekiel $32^{17-32}$, which is a lamentation over the king of Egypt, who also has arrogantly set himself above all others. This passage illustrates the point that Sheol is the great leveller, for all the great ones of the earth, kings

4  *The Sayings of Jesus*, p. 77.

of Assyria, Elam, Edom, Sidon, are among those who go down to Sheol.

Consideration of these Old Testament references in regard to Matthew 11²³, shows that although the language is basically the same, and there are parallel ideas, there are also significant differences. Especially we notice the element of condemnation involved. Capernaum, the centre of our Lord's Galilean ministry, is condemned for its refusal to hear the message of Jesus. Plenty of opportunities had been given, which even notoriously wicked cities like Sodom would have taken. But Capernaum, with all its opportunities, remained unresponsive. In view of this condemnation, we are bound to interpret Hades in this passage in the later sense of the Book of Wisdom, rather than the early sense of Isaiah 14. Hades is a place of punishment for the wicked, not a general state of inactivity for all and sundry. As McNeile puts it: 'Hades expresses the lowest shame.'[5] The emphasis is on the contrast between pride of place on earth and lowest shame in Sheol. It is because Capernaum has indicated its self-sufficiency by ignoring Jesus, that its fall to Sheol will be the more grievous and tragic.

We should also notice that these words of Jesus are addressed to a town, not to an individual. From this it is permissible to draw one or two tentative conclusions. While necessarily individuals must respond if there is to be any real response to the claims of Jesus, in the response or refusal a whole community is involved. This may be a reminder to us that in these critical matters no one acts entirely on his own. He is influenced by others, and in turn influences them. Capernaum as a community did not respond because individuals did not respond. Equally, the failure of all to respond made it more difficult for any to do so. It looks as if we have here a hint of the fact that men are bound together, not only in life but also in what happens to them when they die.

The other important fact is that the ground for this condemnation is Capernaum's refusal of Christ. This is all the more serious because mighty works (δυνάμεις) which are signs of the activity of God, have been done and have been disregarded. Apparently this counts far more in relation to eternal destiny than good or bad behaviour. No doubt in Capernaum were some who

[5] *The Gospel according to St Matthew*, p. 161.

K

lived good lives and some who did not. But what stood out in our Lord's estimation was their attitude to him. This is a position which many sensitive people find difficult to accept; it seems unreasonable that so much should depend upon the response a man makes to the claims of Jesus. It has indeed to be admitted that this is a 'hard saying', but there are some things which must be noted if we are to appreciate it.

Firstly, this is not a case of people being condemned to Sheol who had no chance of responding to Christ. It may well be argued that it is unjust to condemn anyone who has never had a chance of responding to Jesus, and the Christian faith must take this into account. But the people of Capernaum do not fall into this category, for they had witnessed the mighty works of the Lord; they had heard for themselves his wonderful words. Their attitude therefore can only be described as deliberate and active unbelief. Involved in this unbelief is a more general refusal to be honest in face of the facts; they certainly had not acted according to the best truth they knew. So whatever we say about those who have not had a chance to hear and believe, cannot apply to the people of Capernaum.

Secondly, there is the question whether it is possible to justify this standard of judgement as a basis for determining a man's eternal destiny. Surely, we may say, there are other things more important than response to a man's claims about himself? Especially, we have a touching confidence in the efficacy of 'doing good' and 'not doing any harm'. But these vague standards are of little account when placed alongside the claims of Jesus. Certainly it would be an impertinent claim for an ordinary man to make if he were to say that a town will go to the lowest shame because it has not listened to him. We should rightly use the expression 'petulant' of such an attitude, and conclude that it arises out of disappointment at lack of success. But all this becomes irrelevant when we realize who Jesus is. He is the one through whom the mighty works of God are being wrought. He is the one who claims to have the words of life from God. It is true that all these claims can be, indeed have been, rejected by many. Yet these are the undoubted claims of Christ. If we apply our own standards of reference, and say that Christ's standards are unreasonable or unfair, we at least know where we stand. For either we accept Christ's standards and apply them to our own judgements or we judge Christ by our own standards. In these alternatives lies the difference between a Christian and a non-Christian. Inevitably many problems remain, when we accept Christ's standards as authoritative. But we cannot be true to the witness of the gospels unless we see that it is by attitude to Christ that a man's or a community's eternal destiny is to be determined.

(*b*) Matthew 16[18]: '*Upon this rock I will build my church; and the gates of Hades shall not prevail against it.*'

In addition to the main assertion of the power of the Ecclesia over Hades, this saying is interesting on account of the phrase 'the gates of Hades'. 'Gates' properly belong to a city (Lk 7[12], Acts 9[24], 16[13], Heb 13[12]), but also apply in the New Testament to the temple (Acts 3[10]) and to a prison (Acts 12[10]). The particular phrase 'gates of Hades' is used in the Old Testament and the Apocrypha in two main senses:

(1) *The boundary of Sheol*, which can be approached without being passed. Wisdom 16[13] reads: 'For thou hast power over life and death; thou dost lead men down to the gates of Hades and back again.' Again, in the very moving account in 3 Maccabees of the persecution of Jews, we are told that these unfortunate people, imminently expecting to be trampled to death by elephants, besought God 'to show pity on them now that they were come to the gates of Hades' (πρὸς πύλαις ᾅδου καθεστῶτας— 3 Mac 5[51]). Another very interesting use of the same phrase is in Psalms of Solomon 16[1-2]:

When my soul slumbered being afar from the Lord,
I had all but slipped down to the pit,
When I was far from God, my soul had been well nigh
    poured out unto death,
I had been nigh unto the gates of Sheol with the sinner.

(2) *The means whereby Sheol is 'the land of no return'*. This conception uses the idea of gates as preventing any exit from Sheol once they are passed. Especially this is connected with the hopelessness and purposelessness of existence in Sheol. After he had recovered from his illness, Hezekiah looked back upon his experience and said he thought: 'In the noontide of my days I must depart. I am consigned to the gates of Sheol for the rest of my

years' (Isa 38¹⁰). This usage seems to develop into a blurring of the distinction between death and Hades, with the result that the phrase 'the gates of death' seems to mean approximately the same as 'the gates of Sheol'. The implication is that death, or Hades, is a state from which there is no return, which is indeed a mystery not revealed to the wisdom of man (Job 38¹⁷). It is this latter usage which seems most relevant in our Lord's saying to Peter. McNeile argues that the promise that the gates of Hades shall not prevail against the Ecclesia is a reference to our Lord's coming Resurrection. 'The Ecclesia is built upon the Messiahship of her Master, and death, the gates of Hades, will not prevail against her by keeping him imprisoned.'⁶ This interpretation seems supported by the fact that immediately following the promise to Peter, Jesus went on to tell the disciples of the approaching Passion, Crucifixion, and Resurrection (Mt 16²¹).

If we accept this view, we have in this use of 'the gates of Hades' an entirely new and distinctive Christian attitude to Hades. Whether 'the gates of Hades' refers to its boundary, the difference between life and death, or to its power of retaining for ever those who are in it, in both cases Jesus is here affirming that these powers are now limited; the gates are broken down. The Church, because it is the Church of Christ, has in him the victory over the restricting and delimiting powers of Hades. This view certainly accords with Acts 2²⁷,³¹: 'Thou wilt not abandon my soul to Hades . . . he foresaw and spoke of the resurrection of Christ that he was not abandoned to Hades, nor did his flesh see corruption.' Philip Doddridge has expressed the same idea of Christ's victory over the restricting power of the gates of Hades:

> *Not all the bolts and bars of death*
> *The Conqueror could detain.*⁷

Without pressing the thought too far, we can also conclude that Hades is here regarded in an active sense, retaining in its grip those who have died. A comparison with the Church, founded by Christ himself, suggests an active enmity between Hades and the Church. We have travelled far from the old idea of Sheol as a place of endless inactivity. Here Hades is perhaps nearly equivalent to death (cf. *RSV*, Mt 16¹⁸, 'the powers of death'), and is

⁶ *The Gospel according to St Matthew*, p. 242.    ⁷ *Methodist Hymn-book*, No. 217³.

regarded as being overcome by Christ, who passes on the fruits of his victory to the Church.[8]

We can sum up this discussion of Hades in the synoptic gospels by pointing out that in neither case under consideration have we discovered any emphasis upon the ideas usually associated with hell. In fact, the equation of Hades and hell seems unfortunate. It is better to think of Hades as closely associated with death rather than with hell. It must be admitted that the early notion of Sheol as the place of all departed spirits is superseded by the view of Hades as applying to the destiny of the wicked. But we have not found any emphasis on those ideas of punishment which are usually associated with hell. Hades seems to retain something of the idea of a destiny which applies to all, with the glorious assertion that from the powers of Hades, or death, Christ has wrought a great deliverance for his Church.

## II. GEHENNA

This is the Greek and Latin form of a word in Hebrew and Aramaic which is translated 'hell' in the English versions. The derivation of the word is not difficult to determine; it arises out of the name of a valley to the west of Jerusalem in which the city's garbage was thrown, which, understandably, became associated with the idea of destruction, both by worms and by fire (see Isa 66[24]).[9] It is well to keep in mind the fact that there was an actual place called Gehenna in the time of Jesus, for this helps in the extremely difficult task of interpreting our Lord's words on this subject. That this task of interpretation is difficult is apparent as soon as we consider the occurrences of Gehenna in the gospels, for we find that we face the great problem of our Lord's teaching about future punishment. It must be admitted at the outset that we are considering one of the most intractable problems of New Testament study, in trying to determine what Jesus himself said about hell, and how his words are now to be interpreted.

It will help to state firstly what are the facts upon which our study must be based. The word 'Gehenna' ($\gamma\acute{\epsilon}\epsilon\nu\nu\alpha$) occurs twelve times in the New Testament; apart from James 3[6] all these

---

[8] Note that in his quotation of Hosea 13[14], St Paul in 1 Corinthians 15[55] substitutes death for Hades, thus indicating the close approximation between the two words in New Testament times.

[9] *The Bible Doctrine of the Hereafter*, p. 129.

instances are in the synoptic gospels; and all are recorded as used by Jesus himself. There are two clear groups of these sayings which use 'Gehenna':

(1) *Warnings addressed to disciples* about hindrances and stumbling blocks, and about the conditions governing personal destiny (Mt 5²², ²⁹, ³⁰, 10²⁸, 18⁹, Mk 9⁴³, ⁴⁵, ⁴⁷, Lk 12⁵).

(2) *Condemnation of the scribes and Pharisees* (Mt 23¹⁵, ³³).

(1) The words addressed to the disciples are in the form of stern warnings about the necessity of fulfilling the conditions for avoiding destruction. The sayings about stumbling-blocks are in two passages in Matthew and one in Mark. Matthew 5²⁹⁻³⁰ is part of our Lord's warning against adultery, in which 'the offence of the eye' appears to be a reference to lust—'if your right eye cause you to sin, pluck it out and throw it away; it is better that you lose one of your members than that your whole body be thrown into hell'. Verse 30 repeats the same thought, substituting 'hand' for 'eye'. The other group of sayings about stumbling-blocks is in Matthew 18⁸⁻¹⁰, Mark 9⁴³⁻⁸. These words about things which cause oneself to stumble follow the warning against causing occasions of stumbling to the least of those who believe (Mk 9⁴²). Mark's account of personal stumbling-blocks is fuller than Matthew's and is to be preferred as nearer the original.[10] Mark at this point preserves a comment based on Isaiah 66²⁴, following εἰς τὴν γέενναν: 'Where their worm does not die, and the fire is not quenched.' The reference to fire is preserved by Matthew with the phrase 'the Gehenna of fire'.

The sayings in which 'Gehenna' is used in connexion with personal destiny are (*a*) Matthew 5²²: 'But I say unto you that everyone who is angry with his brother shall be liable to judgement; whoever insults his brother shall be liable to the council, and whoever says, "You fool" shall be liable to the hell of fire.' (*b*) Matthew 10²⁸ (cf. Lk 12⁴, ⁵): 'And do not fear those who kill the body but cannot kill the soul; rather fear him who can destroy both soul and body in hell.' Luke's version reads: 'I tell you my friends, do not fear those who kill the body and after that have no more that they can do. But I will warn you whom to fear; fear him who, after he has killed has power to cast into hell; I tell you, fear him!'

[10] VTM, p. 412.

There are a few comments which must be made about these sayings. Firstly, we should note the frequent use of 'if'. In none of these sayings does Jesus tell anyone, 'You are going to hell'; but, 'if you do this, or fail to do that, you will go to hell'. This fact is very important in helping to decide to what extent Jesus was just using popular terminology, without necessarily committing himself to every detail of it. The warnings were all the more effective for being framed in contemporary language. Also, the plain intention of Jesus is not to consign people to hell, but to encourage them to take steps to avoid it. Secondly, we should notice the physical aspect involved in these warnings. There are references to the whole body, and also to the various parts of it— eyes, hands, feet. This fact tends to support the view that Jesus has in mind and wishes his hearers to have in mind, the physical fact of the valley of Hinnom. This emphasizes the figurative nature of these sayings, which is not to say that they mean nothing, but that what they mean is not necessarily the literal sense of the words used. This point is further supported if we interpret Matthew 5[22] as an ascending scale of offence and punishment. The 'judgement' and 'the council' are respectively the local and national courts before which offenders were brought, according to the seriousness of their offence. Then it seems natural to interpret Gehenna also in some well-known sense, such as a figure of speech describing destruction. Against this view, however, is the attractive idea that this verse, linked with the previous verse, provides two comparisons between the common interpretation and that of Jesus. 'Tradition says those who kill are in danger of judgement; I say, whoever is angry is in danger of divine judgement. Tradition says he who insults his brother is in danger before the council; I say, he who insults his brother is in danger of Gehenna.'[11]

Even if this latter interpretation is accepted, we are still moving in the realm of terminology which would be well understood by those who heard, and we can assume that Jesus used Gehenna in the popular contemporary sense in order to express these warnings.

(2) The other group of sayings in which 'Gehenna' is used involve our Lord's condemnation of the scribes and Pharisees. Matthew 23[15]: 'Woe to you, scribes and Pharisees, hypocrites! for you traverse sea and land to make a single proselyte, and

[11] McNeile, *The Gospel according to St Matthew*, p. 62.

when he becomes a proselyte, you make him twice as much a child of hell as yourselves.' Matthew 23³³: 'You serpents, you brood of vipers, how are you to escape being sentenced to hell?' There can be few Christians who do not wonder whether Jesus could possibly have spoken such bitter words, and who would be profoundly relieved if they could be satisfied that he did not. It helps our understanding of the matter if we remind ourselves of the offences and failings for which Jesus condemned these men. These are set out in Matthew 23³⁻³². They say something and fail to do it; they bind heavy burdens on men and refuse to help them to carry them; they do all their pious works with the hope that others will see and applaud them; they have a 'dog in the manger' attitude to the Kingdom of heaven, not going in themselves and trying to prevent others entering; they give misleading teaching about oaths, fuss over little things in religion and neglect judgement, mercy, and faith; they clean the outside of vessels and leave the inside filthy, and they condemn those who killed the prophets, yet do the same things themselves. The outstanding fact about this indictment is our Lord's concern for those who ought to have been able to look to these men for guidance and help. It seems to have been this failure as guides to the people which chiefly angered Jesus.

We shall perhaps appreciate more accurately the underlying feeling of these words of Jesus if we notice the way in which 'Gehenna' is used in contemporary Jewish literature. This is not to assume that Jesus must have used the words in exactly the same sense as his contemporaries. In fact we need to notice the differences of usage. Yet contemporary use will help us to appreciate the implications of the idea to our Lord's hearers. In the Jewish literature approximately contemporary with the gospels, there are several interesting uses of this notion of Gehenna. In the *Assumption of Moses*, which Charles dates in the first century A.D., we have the view that the sight of his enemies in Gehenna will make the righteous man rejoice—'Thou shalt look from on high and shalt see thy enemies in Gehenna, And thou shalt recognize them and rejoice, And thou shalt give thanks and confess thy Creator' (*Ass.Mos.*10¹⁰). Again, this literature often contrasts the delights of heaven with the torments of Gehenna, with the clear indication that the former are increased by comparison with the latter. In 2 Baruch, which also belongs to the

first century A.D., and expresses views which are representative of
the Jews against whom the Pauline dialectic was directed[12] we
find this in the description of Moses' apocalyptic vision: 'He
showed to him . . . the mouth of Gehenna, and the station of
vengeance, and the place of faith, and the region of hope' (2 Bar
59[5,10]). Similarly in the composite work known as the fourth
book of *Ezra* (or 2 Esdras), which was current in its component
parts at the beginning of the Christian era, there is a contrast
between the pit of torment and the place of refreshment, and
between the furnace of Gehenna and the Paradise of delight
(4 Ezra 7[36]).[13]

The first book of *Enoch* refers to Gehenna as 'this accursed
valley (which) is for those who are accursed for ever: here shall
all the accursed be gathered together who utter with their lips
against the Lord unseemly words and of his glory speak hard
things' (27[2-3]).

In contrast with these severe expressions, basing condemnation
to Gehenna upon obviously serious faults, there are some expressions which it is difficult to take so seriously at their face value—
*Pirke Aboth*, which is a composite collection of sayings, originating
throughout the period third century B.C. to third century A.D.,
says: 'So long as a man talks much with the wife he causes evil to
himself, and desists from words of Torah, and his end is that he
inherits Gehenna' (1[5a]). Hardly less insubstantial are the offence
and virtue mentioned in *Pirke Aboth* 5[24]: 'The bold-faced man is
for Gehenna, and the shame-faced man is for the Garden of
Eden.'

Now if we compare these references from contemporary Jewish
literature to the references to Gehenna in the sayings of Jesus,
certain conclusions are inescapable. In the sayings of Jesus there
is no suggestion that the righteous will gloat over the wicked when
they see them in Gehenna. Nor is there the idea that the delights
of heaven are increased by contrast with the torments of hell.
Equally, Gehenna is not treated with the levity which seems
apparent in some of the references we have adduced. On the
other hand, there are emphases in our Lord's words which are
significantly absent from these Jewish statements. Jesus uses the

---

[12] *A. & P.*, II.470.

[13] C. Ryder Smith, *The Bible Doctrine of the Hereafter*, p. 129, has some interesting
suggestions about the translation of this passage.

concept of Gehenna to reinforce his appeal for personal self-discipline. His object on all the occasions when he uses the concept in conversation with his disciples is to convince them of their need of care and self-denial if they are to avoid the condemnation of hell. Again, Jesus addresses all his references to Gehenna directly to the persons concerned. It is significant that he never talks about other people's danger of hell; it is always 'you'—whether disciple, scribe, or Pharisee. This contrasts vividly with the way Jewish literature uses Gehenna as an idea applied more often than not to people other than those being addressed.

This contrast becomes more marked if we look at the later development of Jewish literature. According to Charles, Gehenna in later Jewish writings applied particularly to apostate Jews; in some passages they are regarded as being punished spiritually and corporally for ever. Some references indicate that after a while the wicked are entirely swept away. Other passages indicate that apostate Jews receive spiritual punishment, but not corporal, in Gehenna. Later literature says that Gehenna is the purgatory of faithless Jews and eternal perdition for Gentiles.[14]

While later Christian literature painted the torments of hell in glowing colours, we note that all we can justifiably say of the teaching of Jesus in this regard is that he used the conception, without giving details or emphasizing minute aspects of the matter.

There is a further passage in Jewish literature which may help us to understand the significance of Jesus' restraint in the use he made of the concept of Gehenna. The fourth book of Maccabees sets out to extol the power of reason over the passions, and to illustrate the point tells the dreadful story of Eleazar, the seven Brethren and their mother. These were all threatened with torture and death by 'the overweening, terrible Antiochus Epiphanes' if they did not deny their allegiance to the law by eating swine's flesh. The book describes in graphic and gruesome detail the tortures endured by the old priest Eleazar, by the seven youths, and by their mother; who although forced to witness the terrible torture and death of seven sons in turn, did not urge them to escape by being unfaithful. Although Gehenna does not occur in this writing, the details of this story help us to understand the

[14] *A. & P.*, II.205, note on *Enoch* 27[1].

background of thought against which we must try to understand
our Lord's words. It is an understatement to say that those were
cruel and bloodthirsty days. It matters not whether the events
described in 4 Maccabees ever took place; this was the sort of
literature our Lord's contemporaries were used to reading. And
to anyone at all versed in these apocalypses, the words of Jesus
against the scribes and Pharisees must have seemed excessively
mild. There is no dwelling upon torture, no stirring up nationalist
feeling against the Romans, who were sometimes exceedingly
cruel to the Jews. There is significantly no mention of foreigners
being consigned to hell.

How then can we answer the question: 'What is the present-
day significance of our Lord's teaching about hell?' We cannot
remove entirely this element from the words of Jesus, for that
would be to alter his teaching to suit our own circumscribed
notions. But in view of the Jewish background which we have
considered, the following assertions seem well founded.

(1) In the contemporary setting the teaching of Jesus about
hell must be regarded as mild, without emphasis on details, and
restricted in its application.

(2) The teaching is always directed to the persons addressed,
and never encourages the idea that others can be thought of as
consigned to hell.

(3) The terminology is undoubtedly influenced by our Lord's
obligation to use language which his contemporaries would
understand. It is no exaggeration to say that if he were to use
the idea of Gehenna at all, he could scarcely have used it with less
controversial or objectionable meaning. To say that he need not
have employed the idea at all is to forget that Jesus had to use the
ways into the human understanding which contemporary thought
made possible. Most of all, we must not assume that Jesus did
not really believe in hell, for there is abundant evidence that
he did.

(4) A factor which should also be considered is to what extent
the gospel writers coloured the words of Jesus with the ideas of
the time. This is always a difficult question to answer. Some
would point out that out of the eleven references to Gehenna in
the gospels, seven appear in St Matthew, which is recognized
as the most Jewish of the gospels. But we have seen that the
thought is also firmly embedded in Mark, and we cannot

remove the sayings as expressions of a Jewish interpretation.[15]

(5) That Jesus did teach the reality of future condemnation seems inescapable. Using the thought-form of his day he was not, however, tied to it. His words leave us with a firm impression of his belief in hell, and a constant reminder that his chief concern was not to tell people they were going there, but to warn of its dangers so that they might escape them.

### III. FIRE

The connexion between hell and fire is still maintained in popular thought, though many who talk of 'the flames of hell' seem to be very lighthearted about it. Our purpose in considering the occurrences of this idea in the synoptic gospels must be to discover what light, if any, this idea sheds upon the view of the destiny of the wicked.

We can first notice briefly the few instances of the phrase 'the Gehenna of fire' (Mt 5[22], 18[9]). These instances do not add anything to our knowledge of Gehenna, for as we have seen, the continually burning fires in the valley of Hinnom made a connexion between Gehenna and fire very natural. 'Gehenna of fire' is therefore only another way, perhaps a little more forcible and expressive, of speaking of Gehenna.

The phrase 'eternal fire' is found in Matthew only (18[8], 25[41]). This seems to mean the same as 'unquenchable fire', for Mark uses the latter phrase in the passage parallel to Matthew 18[8], and this term also appears in the report of the preaching of the Baptist (Mt 3[12], Lk 3[17]). The use of 'eternal fire' in Matthew 18[8] raises the very important question of the meaning of 'eternal'. The word derives from $\alpha i \acute{\omega} \nu$ which means 'age', with reference especially to history. In biblical thought there are three ages— before Creation, in which God is at work in predestination and through the Logos; the 'present age' which begins with Creation and ends in the future with the Age which is to come, which is the third age.[16] In the New Testament the Age to come overlaps with the present Age; the life of the Age to come is possible in the

---

[15] Dalman, *Words*, p. 161: '$\gamma \acute{\epsilon} \epsilon \nu \nu \alpha$ is the one term whose use by Jesus is assured, since all three synoptists record it among the words of Jesus' (Dalman is writing of the terms applied to eternal perdition).

[16] O. Cullmann, *Christ and Time*, p. 67. Cf. p. 181 below, for fuller details of Cullmann's exposition.

present Age. Cullmann insists that eternity is a 'temporal conception', i.e. it belongs to time; it is not set over against time in opposition to it. 'Eternity is the endless succession of the ages.'[17] Thus 'eternal' means that which belongs to the ages—to this present age and to the coming age. In effect, it means 'everlasting' when applied to 'fire'. It is fire which lasts as long as matters, and beyond then, without any question being raised whether in a philosophical sense any 'thing' can be strictly 'eternal'. The value of this conception lies in the fact that to think of 'eternal fire' is not necessarily to suppose a predestination view. 'Eternal' does not mean in this context something that 'always has been'; it does mean that which continues into the future, which appears to man to be limitless, but is in the divine view belonging to the future age, which is as much 'in time' as the present age.

If we thus regard 'eternal fire' as equivalent in meaning to Mark's 'unquenchable fire' (Mk 9[43]), we have still to consider the relation of these phrases to the teaching of Jesus. As we have already noted above, the Marcan account is preferable here.[18] This means that Matthew's 'eternal fire' is a synonym for Gehenna (Mk 9[43], Mt 18[8]). The origin of Matthew's phrase may very well be the additional phrase used by Mark—'the unquenchable fire'. But, as Taylor points out,[19] this phrase is likely to be Mark's own comment, based on Isaiah 66[24]. The phrase does not add anything to our understanding of the mind of Jesus on this subject.

Apart from Matthew 25[41], which is from the Parable of the Sheep and Goats, and Luke 16[24], from the story of Dives and Lazarus,[20] which are both dealt with more fully elsewhere, the only other relevant references are Matthew 13[42, 50], and also 7[19]. The first two references are from two parables, the Wheat and Tares and the Drag Net, which Jeremias insists should be taken together.[21] Both verses read 'and throw them into the furnace of fire; there men will weep and gnash their teeth'. Matthew 13[42] is part of the explanation of the parable of the Wheat and Tares, which allegorizes the details of the parable, and seems to obscure the main point of the original story; namely, that good and bad must continue together until God brings the end, which will provide occasion of separating good from bad.

---

[17] Ibid. p. 62.     [18] See above, p. 144.     [19] VTM, p. 412.
[20] The word here (Lk 16[24]) is φλόξ ('flame').     [21] *The Parables of Jesus*, p. 155.

In view of this, and the general suspicion of esoteric explanations of the parables, it seems necessary to agree with Dodd in regarding both these verses as secondary and not part of the authentic teaching of Jesus.[22]

Matthew 7[19]: 'Every tree that does not bear good fruit is cut down and thrown into the fire.' This word of Jesus in connexion with unfruitful trees is apparently an echo of the teaching of John the Baptist (Mt 3[10]). In both cases the obvious implication is that people are being referred to under the picture of trees. But it would be wrong to press the analogy to the extent of saying that unfruitful people will suffer the fires of destruction. The point is perfectly natural when made in reference to fruit trees—for in fact they are burned when cut down. But it is no more reasonable to say that a bad man's destiny is that he will be consumed in the fires of hell, than it would be to say that a bad man will be literally 'cut down', as the unfruitful tree is.

The outcome of our discussion leaves little doubt that the concept of eternal fire and the idea of the flames of hell have been much emphasized by the Jewish element in the presentation of St Matthew's gospel. The idea of the punishment of fire in Gehenna was certainly a common one in Jewish literature, and undoubtedly this has influenced the way in which the matter is presented in the Gospels. But it is not adequate merely to dismiss the notion as 'Jewish' and be done with it. If it is an over-emphasis imposed on the teaching of Jesus, nevertheless the germ of the idea is present in his teaching; and we cannot just dismiss the Jewish tradition as of no importance whatever. Because of this, it may prove valuable to look a little more closely at the Jewish use of the concept of fire in connexion with hell or Gehenna.

There appear to be four influences at work in making this connexion. Firstly, as we saw when considering Gehenna, there is the obvious connexion through the continual burning of rubbish in the valley of Hinnom. Secondly, as Ryder Smith points out,[23] there is probably a connexion through volcanic phenomena. It appears from references in the *Book of Enoch* that notice is taken of the lava flowing into the sea in the volcanic area of the

---

[22] *The Parables of the Kingdom*, pp. 184, 187. Dodd puts the point very clearly: 'This is the developed eschatology of the Church . . . we shall do well to forget this interpretation as completely as possible'. Jeremias, *The Parables of Jesus*, pp. 155-7 substantially agrees with this judgement.

[23] *The Bible Doctrine of the Hereafter*, pp. 129-30.

Mediterranean. This may explain the otherwise obscure references in 2 Esdras 7³⁶ to the lake of torment and the oven of
Gehenna, for these terms do naturally apply to volcanic lava,
although not at all to garbage heaps. There is also the tradition
that Sinai was volcanic (see Ex 20¹⁸), to lend support to the idea
that volcanic phenomena were not unknown in Hebrew thought.
In view of the cosmology generally accepted, in which the place
of departed spirits is a cavern in the bowels of the earth, it would
be natural for fire to be connected with Gehenna, for volcanoes
were thought to indicate that the bowels of the earth were continually on fire.

A third reason for the connexion between fire and hell can be
found in the use made of fire in torture and persecution. Many of
the Jewish Apocalypses give graphic accounts of the persecutions
of faithful Jews. Among the terrible sufferings described, ordeal
by fire takes a very prominent place. We cannot understand or
appreciate Jewish views on eternal punishment unless we remember the background of the sufferings they had to endure. Fire is,
after all, a most terrible means of causing pain, and because of
this the Jewish view of the punishment of the wicked included the
fire of hell. It is not surprising that the persecutors were regarded
as destined to suffer a greater punishment than they had inflicted
on the innocent; and that it should include the same methods,
made infinitely worse by divine power. So we read of the youngest
of the seven brothers replying thus to the tyrant who had already
tortured and killed all his brothers. 'O impious tyrant, and most
ungodly of all sinners, art thou not ashamed to take thy blessings
and thy kingship at the hands of God, and to slay his servants and
torture the followers of righteousness? For which things the divine
justice delivers thee unto a more rapid and an eternal fire and torments which shall not leave hold on thee to all eternity' (4 Mac
12¹¹⁻¹²). It is very much to the credit of the writers of this Jewish
literature that they did not limit the fires of hell to their persecutors, but asserted that the unfaithful among their own nation
would suffer the same fate.

The fourth, and most significant, source of the connexion
between fire and hell is to be found in the connexion between
God and fire. God had appeared to Moses in a flame of fire in
the midst of a bush (Ex 3²); he rained brimstone and fire upon
Sodom and Gomorrah (Gen 19²⁴; cf. Lk 17²⁹); his ministers are

a flame of fire (Ps 104⁴). In *Sirach* 45¹⁹ we read of the way God uses the fiery flame to devour the wicked.

> Jahveh saw it and was angered,
>     And consumed them in His fierce wrath:
> And He brought a sign to pass upon them
>     And devoured them with His fiery flame.

Now the implication of all this is plain. When fire is mentioned the thought of God is never far away. And as always, the divine presence and power are the most significant factors with whatever they are joined. The significant fact about the visitation of Sodom and Gomorrah is that it was a divine visitation; compared with this, the question what is fire and brimstone is definitely of seccndary importance. The Jewish concept of the fire of hell means that this is a divine visitation. It is not the work of the devil, but of God. The Jews did not, perhaps, see the inner contradiction between a God who creates and a God who utterly destroys what he has created. Even in the New Testament this contradiction is not really faced, but the emphasis of this teaching means religious men have had to face it. But the problem of divine activity in the face of rampant evil would not exist at all if hell were to be regarded as merely the province of the devil.

The further point which can be made on the basis of this consideration of the origin of the idea of hell-fire, is that men's views on eternal subjects are very much influenced by their views of temporal things and by their experiences in their earthly existence. We have seen the connexion between ideas of hell and garbage disposal, between contemporary cosmology and persecutions. This may well encourage us to think that in a different age, different views and experiences may contribute to the view of eternal destiny. Yet beneath all the terminology, which because it is figurative is necessarily temporary, there lies the unalterable fact of the divine lordship over the destiny of men.

We can now sum up the results of this part of our study, with the hope of answering some of the questions raised in contemporary thought.

(1) There is a definite place in the teaching of Jesus given to the idea of the destiny of the lost. Although figurative language is used, beneath this terminology there is an inescapable reality.

(2) The term Hades is used in the sense of the later understanding

of Sheol. That is, as a separation of the bad from the good. This separation is connected with death, for death and Hades are almost synonymous. Two implications arise out of this connexion.

(*a*) Christ has conquered death and made his Church share his victory over death. Those who are condemned to Hades are condemned by their own refusal to respond to the offer of God's grace in Christ. They are not condemned by any prior decision or fiat of God.

(*b*) While the destiny of the lost is not described in detail, it is possible to infer that, like shadowy existence in Sheol was conceived to be, this existence is hardly worth calling 'life'. The idea of extinction rather than that of eternal punishment arises out of the relation between death and Hades.

(3) Gehenna is the term most closely associated with the modern notion of hell. This state is on every count a tragic and unwelcome destiny, but the emphasis still rests more upon the idea of destruction than upon the idea of punishment. This arises partly through the association with the valley of Hinnom, which was primarily a place of destruction; and also through the subsidiary idea of fire. Although fire gives rise to the thought of torture in contemporary Jewish thought, the more prominent notions connected with fire are of the sovereignty of God and the possibility of destruction. The sovereignty of God can be expressed in destruction as well as in creation.

(4) Although the connexion between the destruction of the lost and the gift of eternal life to the saved is not worked out in the gospels, it is possible to argue that the one view necessitates the other. If man is not naturally immortal, but can receive from God the gift of eternal life, the question of the refusal of that gift must arise.

What happens to the man who refuses the gift? According to these hints in the gospels, he is lost; he ceases to be. This must not be regarded as a pleasant alternative to the pains of punishment in hell. To cease to be is the final tragedy which can befall a living soul who is able to receive the gift of eternal life. Compared with this, punishment which leads to eventual restoration would be infinitely preferable. But of such remedial punishment there appears to be no sign in the words of our Lord. If the idea of annihilation is only dimly perceived in that teaching, there are grounds for saying that such an idea can be inferred from our Lord's words on Hades and Gehenna.

L

# CHAPTER EIGHT

# THE DESTINY OF THE SAVED

W E have already noticed in our earlier discussion that the promise of future life is not described in terms of being in heaven or going to heaven. When we come to consider in what ways this future life is described, we find a rich collection of words and phrases which serve to present a very wonderful picture of that life beyond death. These terms and phrases must now be studied in detail.

## I. THE KINGDOM

While the phrase 'Kingdom of heaven' (*malkuth shamayim*) is rare in rabbinic literature[1] there is enough evidence of the use of it to justify the assertion that the contemporaries of Jesus thought of the future in these terms. That this conception was also concerned with the present life is shown by the fact that one point emphasized was that it is necessary for men to accept the yoke of the kingdom of heaven now, in this present life. This means deciding to accept God as Lord, which was a necessary part of sincere Jewish religion. The daily recital of the *Shema* (Deut 6[4]) was to some degree regarded as accepting the yoke of the Kingdom; and equally there is the real possibility of rejecting the rule of God—i.e. of 'casting off his yoke'. It is noteworthy that in this respect the Jewish conception of the Kingdom of heaven involved real decisions and actions in this present life.

But the future idea is also expressed as follows. This period of decision will be eventually terminated, and the end will come. This was the subject of the prayers of the Jewish people, e.g. *Tractate Sŏpherîm* 14[12]: 'May it be possible for thy royalty to be revealed and to shine over us speedily in the near future'; 19[7]: 'Reveal the majesty of thy kingly rule over us.'[2] In this particular meaning the phrase *malkuth shamayim* is thoroughly eschatological,

[1] K. G. Kuhn, *Basileia*, p. 17.
[2] Strack-Billerbeck, *Kommentar zum Neuen Testament*, I.179.

looking forward to the end of this present time of choice and decision.[3]

All this, of course, has repercussions on the view of personal destiny in Jewish teaching; indeed, Kuhn asserts that 'here man stands before God as an individual (who must make a decision) just as "man", not as a citizen of some country'.[4] Yet at the same time the thought of God as the God of Israel, and of His people as the object of His future salvation, was never far away. There seems in fact to be a wonderful combination of the concept of individual responsibility with that of a future destiny linked with the community of the people of God. It is also noteworthy that while the idea of the future Kingdom of Messiah exists alongside that of the Kingdom of heaven, the two are by no means synonymous. Especially the Messianic Kingdom idea grew out of, and continued to express, the idea of the nation under its king to whom all other nations are subject. On the other hand the notion of the Kingdom of heaven was always expressive of the purely religious concept of the 'end', in which the nation of Israel has no special place but God 'is all in all'.[5]

There are interesting indications in the gospels of the extent to which the idea of the future was popularly expressed in terms of 'kingdom'. The fact that these are incidental references, not emphasizing the distinctive Christian usage of 'kingdom', makes them all the more helpful in revealing contemporary thought. 'He will reign over the house of Jacob for ever, and of his kingdom there will be no end' (Lk 1[33]), is regarded by Easton as 'a typical expression of the Messianic hope of the period'.[6] When the crowds enthusiastically welcomed Jesus into Jerusalem they sang 'Blessed is the Kingdom that cometh, the Kingdom of our father David' (Mk 11[10]). Even if this greeting was not fully Messianic[7] it seems undoubtedly to indicate the way in which popular expectation was expressed in terms of a coming Kingdom. Again, one of our Lord's companions at dinner said, 'Blessed is he who shall eat bread in the Kingdom of God' (Lk 14[15]), and the penitent thief used the terminology of the Kingdom in his request to Christ: 'Jesus, remember me when you come into your Kingdom' (Lk 23[42]).

These instances remind us that when he spoke of the Kingdom

[3] Kuhn, *Basileia*, pp. 17-19.     [4] Ibid. p. 19.     [5] Ibid. p. 21.
[6] *The Gospel according to St Luke*, p. 9.     [7] VTM, p. 452.

of God, Jesus was using words which had considerable currency among his hearers. While undoubtedly Jesus spoke of the Kingdom as a present fact, he also used the expression in something like the popular contemporary sense which also applied to the future. One of the great contributions of the recent study by W. G. Kümmel (*Promise and Fulfilment*) is to show that both the present and the future implications of the teaching of Jesus about the Kingdom of God must be taken seriously. The problem which has been the core of most of the recent discussions of the eschatological teaching of Jesus is concerned with the apparent misunderstanding of the disciples or the possible mistake of our Lord in promising the *imminent* fulfilment of the expectation of the reign of God. Kümmel believes that the reality of the future expectation must not be minimized, even if we have to regard the expectation of its imminence as a contemporary expression: 'If therefore the *imminent* expectation, being a necessarily contemporary form of expression, can be entirely detached from Jesus' message, the *future* expectation is essential and indispensable, because in this form alone can the nature of God's redemptive action *in history* be held fast.'[8] This means that far from being an embarrassment, as some have thought it, the future element in our Lord's eschatology is essential to an understanding of the full meaning of the Kingdom of God. It is equally true of course that an understanding of the present fact of the rule of God breaking into human life is essential to a full appreciation of the future meaning of the Kingdom. It is only when we see the intimate connexion between the One who now brings the rule of God, and the future completion of that Rule, that we can appreciate the significance of Jesus' reference to future destiny in terms of the Kingdom of God.

While all references to the future consummation of the rule of God obviously bear on our subject, there are some passages which have a special significance. In particular two groups of sayings about the Kingdom are especially important: (*a*) Passages in which the Kingdom is described as a gift; (*b*) passages in which the Kingdom is to be entered.

We shall consider these groups of sayings in turn, seeking to discover what light they shed on the meaning of the Kingdom as a description of the future life.

[8] Kümmel, *Promise and Fulfilment*, pp. 152-3.

## (a) The Kingdom as a Gift of God

The relevant passages are:

(1) Luke 12³²: '*Fear not little flock, for it is your Father's good pleasure to give you the Kingdom.*'

(2) Luke 22²⁸⁻³⁰: '*You are those who have continued with me in my trials; as my Father appointed a Kingdom for me, so do I appoint for you that you may eat and drink at my table in my Kingdom, and sit on thrones judging the twelve tribes of Israel.*'

(3) Matthew 26²⁹: '*I tell you I shall not drink again of this fruit of the vine until that day when I drink it new with you in my Father's Kingdom.*'

(4) Matthew 21⁴³: '*The Kingdom of God will be taken from you and given to a nation producing the fruits of it.*'

This concept of the Kingdom being given to particular people is found only rarely in Jewish literature. In Wisdom 5¹⁶, the righteous are described as those who 'shall receive a glorious Kingdom'.[9] Also Daniel 7¹⁸ and 7²² need to be noticed. Both verses describe how 'the saints of the most High shall receive the Kingdom and possess the Kingdom for ever and ever'. Apart from these instances, there is little reference in Jewish writings to the Kingdom being promised to anyone.

Thus we notice immediately that this is one of the distinctive features of our Lord's teaching about the Kingdom. He promised it in the future, to those who were joined to him in the community of his disciples. Clearly this is one of the important expressions used by Jesus to describe the life of believers after death. They will share with him the triumphs of his Kingdom. We can draw out the implication of this if we look a little more closely at these particular passages.

(1) Luke 12³² ('*Fear not little flock, for it is your Father's good pleasure to give you the Kingdom*') has no parallel in either Matthew or Mark and for that reason is regarded as a detached saying, the meaning of which cannot be determined from its context.[10] Kümmel thinks that it is included at this point because

---

[9] *RSV* translates 'glorious crown'. The Greek is τὸ βασίλειον τῆς εὐπρεπίας, which seems perhaps to justify this rendering. But S. Holmes, *A. & P.*, I.543, argues that here and in Wisdom 1¹⁴ 'Kingdom' must be the meaning. In any case, the word is clearly cognate with βασιλεία ('kingdom').

[10] Kümmel, *Promise and Fulfilment*, p. 53.

of the 'catchword' βασιλεία, which also occurs in the preceding
verse. On the other hand Easton asserts that this verse ($12^{32}$)
is connected with the first part of the following verse, to form a
compact logion.[11] Thus the verse may not be as isolated as Jeremias claims, and it is noticable that even if the connexion with
the preceding verse depends upon a catchword, the continuity of
thought is remarkable. The passage from Luke beginning at $12^{22}$
is concerned with our Lord's teaching about avoiding anxious
care. The main emphasis in this passage is not that Christians
should care nothing about food and clothing, but that they
should put things in the right order. 'Life is more important than
food; but there is something more important than life itself—the
Kingdom of God.'[12] The Kingdom of God is to be sought; this
is not regarded as an easy thing. As lambs among wolves seem
to be in a hopeless position, so it seems a hopeless search to
look for the Kingdom. Yet because it is a gift of God, it will be
found. In view of the pressing claims of daily life, the need to
provide food and clothing for oneself and one's dependants,
even the argument of Jesus that anxious care doesn't make
any difference, is not really adequate to meet the problem of
anxiety.

Consequently Jesus adds two more statements which are a
complete answer to human needs; on the one hand, positively
seek the rule of God in your present life; on the other hand, realize
that God is promising the gift of His rule both now and in the
future. Both these statements belong to, and indeed complete,
the argument of verses 22-30. The seeking of something positive
which is worth while is a practical and effective answer to the
problem of worrying about everyday things, to which everyone is
prone at some time or other. Allied to this is the comforting
assurance that the rule of God which we thus seek will be given to
us, by the good pleasure of our Father. The whole discussion is
completed with a practical injunction to almsgiving ($12^{33}$) which
is also vital, because in all these things, it is not only right thoughts
and attitudes, but also right actions which really meet the need of
our anxiety. Thus it seems reasonable to argue that even if this
passage is composite, in its present form it presents a whole truth,
in which the several parts cohere and add to the meaning of the
truth being expressed.

[11] *The Gospel according to St Luke*, p. 204.    [12] Manson, *The Sayings of Jesus*, p. 113.

Looking more closely at the future promise expressed in 12³², we find several points of significance to our consideration of the teaching of Jesus about future life. Firstly, we note that these words of encouragement are addressed to a community; to the 'little flock'. Plummer (*ICC*, ad loc.) comments that the phrase 'little flock' is not so much an expression of endearment as of a matter of fact. Jesus had sent forth his disciples as lambs in the midst of wolves (Lk 10³; cf. Mt 10¹⁶). Their position was always one of apparent hopelessness and real danger. But they were the flock of Christ, and in him God has promised that they will receive the victory of the rule of God. This promise is made to a company of men who are truly a community because of their relationship to Christ the good Shepherd. It is not a promise made to individuals, nor to all who may indeed be burdened with the cares of life. It is to those who have entered a new relationship with one another through their relationship with Jesus; those who have proved their faith in him by seeking his rule now in this present life.

Secondly, there is the implication of a persecuted minority in this saying. The flock was indeed in the midst of wolves, and this situation has often been repeated in the history of the Christian Church. We shall notice below that in the Supper sayings this idea of the gift of the rule of God is much in evidence. Luke 22²⁸ is especially relevant: 'You are those who have continued with me in my trials.' While this line of thought does not imply that only those who have known persecution will be assured of the blessings of the future, it does place much emphasis upon the assurance of future life as a help in meeting persecution.

Thirdly, if we accept the argument outlined above about the inner connexion between the various parts of the teaching in 12²²⁻³⁴, we shall readily see the connexion between this life and the life hereafter in the teaching of Jesus. The statement about God's gift of the kingdom is in a context dealing with some of the urgent matters of everyday life. Worry about the means of livelihood or the standard of living is very much a matter of present existence. But the teaching of Jesus concerning future life in the Kingdom of God is not that the present can be ignored in view of the future promise. On the contrary he says that the present can be properly valued and kept in its place by man's search for the rule of God here and now, and by his conviction that God will reward that search with the gift of the Kingdom. This is further emphasized by 12[33], which advises the selling of goods and the giving of alms. This is not just a world-denying gesture, but a way of keeping the things of this life in their proper place.

This can be put another way by saying that Jesus did not command his disciples to ignore entirely the laying up of treasure, but advised them to lay up the right kind of treasure, that is, treasure in heaven. This may, of course, appear to mean that there is a system of strict reward in the future life, for which due payment has to be made in terms of self-sacrifice here and now. But however much we regard sacrifice as an essential part of Christian discipleship, there is always something wrong with sacrifice undertaken with the main idea of greater reward in the future. This reduces man's dealings with God to a sordid commercial level in which the 'religious' man is really the man with an eye to a bargain, who calculates the cost of discipleship and reckons that the great reward after death is worth the cost of the sacrifice necessary to obtain it. Such an attitude is not even moral, let alone religious, for the man who does good because he expects to be rewarded for it, is not to be compared with the truly moral man who does good because he loves the good, whether he is rewarded or not. And this attitude is a complete denial of true religion, which is fellowship with God, for it attempts to place a personal relationship on a commercial footing. This is impossible even between men who are equals; how can it be anything but gross impiety when made the basis of relationship between God the Creator and man his creature? One of the first lessons man must learn about his relationship with God is that it cannot be based on merit and reward, but only upon grace and forgiveness. This being so, it sometimes seems as if this idea of treasure in heaven is a flat contradiction of the basic truth of the Christian faith.

That this cannot be the right interpretation of this passage is evident when proper weight is given to the word 'give'. The Kingdom is promised as a gift, not as a reward. The treasure in heaven is not intended as a means of being able to purchase the reward of the Kingdom; this Kingdom is given, not purchased. So whatever may be the purpose of treasure in heaven it certainly cannot be a sort of heavenly bank balance to be used to purchase something. There is great help in this question if we look back to

Luke 12²¹, the conclusion and application of the story of the Rich Fool: 'So is he that lays up treasure for himself and is not rich toward God.' Here treasure is compared with a relationship —that of being rich toward God. This is indeed a proper way of looking at a relationship between persons. If it is a close and rewarding relationship it is aptly described as 'rich'. Thus interpreted 'treasure in heaven' is a 'rich relationship with God'. This is all the more tenable in view of the fact that, as we have seen, heaven is not a place, but in this instance a clear synonym for God. Thus we can interpret Luke 12³³ in the sense that by a proper attitude toward worldly possessions and especially by a certain detachment from them, there can be found a rich relationship with God. But lest this relationship be thought to arise merely out of self-renunciation, we are to remember that it is a gift of God, promised through His son Jesus Christ. In other passages we shall see more clearly this emphasis on the part played by Jesus in bringing about this relationship, which is described here as receiving the gift of the Kingdom. While this passage does not explicitly state that Jesus is instrumental in the giving of the gift, we should notice that he announces the gift and the people to whom he announces it are a real community, a little flock, only through their relationship to him. Equally we should note the title for God the giver of the Kingdom is Father—a name having a peculiar significance owing to its use by our Lord himself. Therefore, implicitly, if not explicitly, this promised gift is mediated through Christ.

It is typical of our Lord's attitude to future bliss that in this passage describing that bliss in terms of the Kingdom, we have practically no indication of what 'heaven' is like. Indeed there is possibly no term used by our Lord which means so much and yet is so hard to define as 'Kingdom'. We can at least conclude that by this phrase applied to the future, Jesus meant that his little flock would triumph, for the promised Kingdom cannot be thought of in terms of defeat. But the main emphasis, as we have seen, falls upon the conditions of receiving the Kingdom, rather than on the description of the Kingdom itself.

(2) Luke 22²⁸⁻³⁰ (*'You are those who have continued with me in my trials; as my Father appointed a Kingdom for me, so do I appoint for you that you may eat and drink at my table in my Kingdom, and sit on thrones*

*judging the twelve tribes of Israel'*). These verses are peculiar to Luke although there are near parallels in Matthew and Mark. The differences between Luke and the other synoptics are not only in details of expression but more significantly in the occasion of the saying. Luke records that after the Supper there arose a contention among the twelve who should be the foremost. Jesus rebuked them by showing that the standards of judgement among themselves must be on a different basis from that accepted by the world. The greatest among them will be the chief servant, even as Christ himself was among them as servant. Then follows what appears to be an affirmation of the authority granted to the twelve, who have continued with Jesus in his trials. To them Christ appoints a Kingdom, as his Father has appointed him a Kingdom: this is further clarified as eating and drinking with him in his Kingdom and judging the twelve tribes of Israel.

Matthew 19²⁷⁻⁸ and Mark 10²⁸ record a similar saying in very different circumstances. After the reply to the Young Man who asked about the way to eternal life, Peter rather ungraciously reminded Jesus that they had left all to follow him; what reward would they get? Matthew (not Mark) reports that Jesus replied in terms similar to our passage in Luke, with the difference that Matthew refers to παλινγενεσία (regeneration or re-creation), but makes no reference to 'Kingdom'.

If the saying is interpreted in terms of 'realized eschatology', it is important to try to determine when these words were spoken. If they belong to the Galilean ministry they will seem to refer to the priority given to the twelve during the earthly ministry of Jesus. If, on the other hand, they belong to the end of our Lord's ministry they appear to refer to the period between the death and the Parousia of Christ.[13] But if the passage is really intended to apply to the future, these questions of the circumstances in which the words are spoken are not so important. Thus the necessary issue to be faced is whether this is a passage referring to the future or to the present. This question is affected to some extent by the comparison between the Lucan passage and Matthew 19²⁸, for Matthew speaks of the Parousia more specifically than Luke. (Note 'the Son of Man shall sit upon the throne of his glory' Mt 19²⁸.) Scholars are divided concerning which account of the saying should be accepted, and no definite

13 VTM, p. 622.

judgement seems possible.[14] The fact that Luke omits the reference to 'twelve' thrones suggests that he realized the difficulty of including Judas in this promise, at this stage in the ministry,[15] and this may weigh the balance in favour of the view that Matthew represents both the occasion and the form of the saying more accurately than Luke.

If then we accept the superiority of Matthew here, we have a saying which is more clearly eschatological, but at the same time one which does not contain any explicit reference to the Kingdom. But it may be argued that Luke correctly interprets the mind of Jesus with the reference to the Kingdom, which then must be taken to refer to the future. On the whole this conclusion seems most acceptable. The promise is one referring to the future, in which Jesus was understood to mean that he would give to the twelve a rule dependent upon that given to him by God. As Kümmel shows, this does not remove every thought of the rule of God now being operative in Christ; for it is precisely and only on the basis of the rule of God now present in him that Jesus can offer a kingdom to his disciples.[16] This also points to the significance of this saying to the Church as a whole. While this promise is clearly made to the twelve disciples, it is made to them as close companions of the Lord. It is not by virtue of their own powers or capabilities that they are given the promise, but only because they belong to Christ—they have continued *with him* in *his* trials. They are the nucleus of the community of Christian people, and through them this eschatological promise is made to all.

What then does this promise indicate about the future bliss of the redeemed? It uses the two connected ideas of a banquet and a judgement to express the thought of the exalted position to which believers are elevated by the appointment of Christ. To sit at table with anyone implies fellowship, and to some degree equality. This exalted position is connected with the idea that the disciples and, if Paul understands the position correctly,[17] all Christians as well have a place in the judgement of the world. Manson sums up the teaching of this passage as follows: 'God has

[14] Taylor regards Luke as more authentic (VTM, p. 622). So also Glasson, *The Second Advent*, p. 142. Kümmel (*Promise and Fulfilment*, p. 47) writes: 'The saying which undoubtedly in this version of Matthew represents the more original form.'

[15] Manson, *The Sayings of Jesus*, p. 339.

[16] Kümmel, *Promise and Fulfilment*, pp. 47-8.

[17] 1 Corinthians 6².

assigned the Kingdom to Jesus: and He assigns a share in it to his disciples. This share includes both the joy of the Kingdom—represented under the figure of feasting at the table of the Messiah—and its privileges and responsibilities—represented by the sitting upon thrones and judging.'[18] Even allowing for the figurative language used, which certainly must not be interpreted literally, we have here a clear denial of the notion that the future life is an unending succession of inactivity. It is rather a state of dynamic activity, not only concerned with the 'final judgement', but also with 'ruling' with which judges were closely associated in Jewish thought (cf. Ps 122[4-5]).

(3) Matthew 26[29] ('*I tell you I shall not drink again of this fruit of the vine until that day when I drink it new with you in my Father's Kingdom*'; cf. Mk 14[25]). Both accounts use the expression 'the Kingdom' in this prophecy of our Lord, but Matthew's account relates the promise more closely to the disciples by the additional words 'with you'. Luke 22[18] places a similar saying before the breaking of bread after the distribution of the first cup, which is a peculiarity of Luke's account. 'I tell you that from now on I shall not drink of the fruit of the vine until the Kingdom of God comes.'

In whichever version this saying is considered, it seems clearly to state that Jesus looked forward to a future coming of the Kingdom of God. The question of the interval that is assumed is an important one, but not of the first importance to our present study. The same may be said of the discussion concerning the possible priority of the Lucan account.[19] The question on which we must concentrate is the meaning this saying has for the future destiny of the disciples, and through them for ordinary Christians. Jesus spoke of his own abstinence from 'the fruit of the vine' until he should share it with his disciples in the Kingdom of God. While Matthew's $\mu\epsilon\theta$'$\dot{\nu}\mu\hat{\omega}\nu$ ('with you'), which makes this sharing explicit, is not included in Mark's account, it seems to draw out the inescapable implications of that account. Thus Kümmel, referring to Mark 14[25], writes: 'Jesus declares that he will not drink wine any more until he can partake of the Messianic

---

[18] *The Sayings of Jesus*, p. 339.

[19] The discussion is conveniently summarized in Kümmel, *Promise and Fulfilment*, pp. 30-2.

meal *with his disciples.*'[20] This is indeed inescapable, unless we are to suppose that Jesus looked forward to a lonely Messianic feast, which can hardly be described as a banquet.

Therefore, even on the basis of Mark's account, we can see that this saying, which is surely as authentic as any in the gospels, has important implications about the future destiny of the disciples. They are to share the fellowship of the coming Kingdom. This obviously is an idea that arises in the circumstances of the Last Supper when Jesus shared with his disciples this meal of fellowship which became an occasion of looking forward to the death of Jesus, and beyond his death to his coming triumph. Because the shadow of the Cross falls so clearly over this meal, we can assert that this future destiny is bound up with the death and resurrection of Christ. It is a very strong indication of the historical trustworthiness of these accounts of the Last Supper, and the promise of the coming Kingdom, that the connexion between Christ's death and resurrection, and human destiny, is not explicitly stated. We find nothing, for instance, comparable with St Paul's argument about resurrection in 1 Corinthians 15 nor with the Johannine account of the raising of Lazarus and the conversation with Martha, which link so closely the hope of eternal life with the resurrection of Christ (Jn 11[25-7]). But what is not explicitly stated in the synoptic accounts is involved implicitly. It was at the time when Jesus was most vividly aware of his coming death that he made this clear statement of the coming Kingdom in which he would share another fellowship meal with his disciples. This means that the later teaching expressed by Paul and John is completely in accord with the implications of the teaching of Jesus and the veracity of both original and derived traditions is increased by the absence of confusion or collation between them.

Another point which equally arises in connexion with this Supper saying is that the sense of community is very strong in this context. There is, in fact, no incident in the gospels which so clearly exhibits the sense of the disciples with Jesus forming a living community, as the account of the Last Supper. It does not need much imagination to picture the scene and to speculate on the impression it must have made on the disciples. If any one of

[20] Ibid. p. 31 (italics mine); cf. VTM, p. 547: 'The saying shows that at the Supper Jesus looked forward beyond death to the perfect fellowship of the consummated kingdom.'

them had asked himself that night 'Why am I here?' there could have been only one answer. It was because each one had been called and chosen by Jesus that they were together. They belonged together because they all belonged to the Lord. This sense of belonging together and belonging to the Lord must surely be carried over into the promise of the future. It is not a purely individual survival, depending on any inherent quality of immortality in human beings, that is the ground of the hope implied in this saying. It is as a community that they have hope for the future, and as belonging to Christ in a redeemed relationship, not in their own strength or worth. Whether or not they believed in a 'future life' before they met Jesus (the probability is that they did, like most of their contemporaries) they now had a promise of something far more significant than survival until a final judgement. This was the promise of sharing with their Lord the joys of the Messianic banquet. This is not to say that all this was immediately apparent to the disciples at the actual time of the Lord's Supper. Indeed, they could scarcely know how the the death of Jesus would make certain for them the sharing in future bliss, since they did not realize that Jesus was so soon to die on the Cross. But Jesus knew, and communicated his knowledge in words which were faithfully recorded, although at the time by no means fully understood.

One of the most interesting facts about the Marcan and Matthean accounts of the Last Supper is that they contain no command for the rite to be perpetuated. Luke 22[19] ('Do this in memory of me') might lend itself to such an interpretation, but there is a strong possibility that this phrase was not part of Luke's original account. The Christian tradition that Jesus commanded his followers to repeat the rite depends partly on St Paul's account in 1 Corinthians 11[23-6], and equally upon the tradition of breaking of bread which the disciples practised from the beginning. In view of this it is not possible, on the basis of the accounts in Mark, Luke, and Matthew which have been under consideration, to assert that through the continuance of this rite, Jesus meant his disciples to maintain that fellowship with himself which would come to perfection in the final Kingdom of God. This is not to deny that to the primitive Church the Eucharist was an eschatological sacrament. It did, indeed, in the words of Paul, 'proclaim the Lord's death until he comes'. But in the teaching of Jesus, which is our immediate concern, there is no explicit statement that in the rite of the Eucharist is both a foretaste and a guarantee of the joys of the bliss of the redeemed. Again, it is to be noted that this does not mean that the Church was wrong in making this connexion between Eucharist and the future life. But this connexion is read into the Eucharist through the experience of the Church, rather than found in it as it appears in the synoptic records.

(4) Matthew 21⁴³ (*'Therefore I tell you, the Kingdom of God will be taken away from you and given to a nation producing the fruits of it'*). This is found in Matthew only. It is the end of the allegorical interpretation of the Parable of the Wicked Husbandmen. As we have argued above,[21] Matthew seems to have added very considerable allegorical material to the original parable, which was in its original form a vindication of the divine activity in offering the gospel to the poor and needy. This verse is part of the allegorical interpretation which makes the parable an account of salvation history culminating in the offer of the gospel to the Gentiles. Because of this insight into the structure of this parable, it does not seem possible to conclude anything from this verse about the view of Jesus on the meaning of the future life.

We can sum up as follows the results of this study of the meaning of the future life as it is expressed in the idea of the Kingdom as a gift:

(1) Life hereafter involves the idea of a community, centred on Christ himself; while persecution is not an essential factor in obtaining the gift it is significantly related to it.

(2) Present life and future life are closely related.

(3) Life hereafter is not endless inactivity; it involves the activity of judging.

### (b) *The Kingdom as that which can be Entered*

The sayings which speak of the Kingdom of God or heaven as that which can be entered are usually regarded as references to the future[22] and are therefore specially relevant to our present discussion. We shall consider these sayings, as we have considered

---

[21] See pp. 114-16.   [22] Kümmel, *Promise and Fulfilment*, p. 52.

those referring to the Kingdom as a gift, with a view to discovering their teaching about the nature of the future life. The sayings can be grouped conveniently according to their teaching about the conditions which have to be fulfilled if men are to enter into the Kingdom of God.

(1) *Faithful obedience to the commands of God in intention as well as outward act*

Matthew 5²⁰: 'For I tell you, unless your righteousness exceeds that of the scribes and Pharisees, you will never enter the Kingdom of heaven.' The explanatory context of the saying is twofold. As an introduction to this demand for more righteousness than is practised by the scribes and Pharisees, Jesus has made clear that far from abrogating the law of Moses, he has come to fulfil it. As a further explanation of this demanding condition of entry into the Kingdom of heaven, Jesus insists that it is the inner attitude which is judged. To be angry with one's brother is the root from which murder grows (5²¹⁻²); reconciliation with one's fellow men is a necessary preliminary to offering acceptable service to God (5²³⁻⁴). The lustful intention not only leads to adultery; it *is* adultery (5²⁷⁻⁸). In the same way, Jesus announces new principles of conduct regarding divorce, the taking of oaths, revenge, love of enemies, and so on.

There is no need in this discussion to attempt to draw out the many implications of this teaching. For our purpose it is sufficient to notice that these are intensely practical directions, directly arising out of the situations of this life. In other words, the conditions for entering the Kingdom of heaven are very much concerned with man's responsibilities to his fellow men. When such a statement as this is taken into account, it seems very difficult to account for the fact that sometimes the reality of a future life has been so divorced from the realities of this life that it has seemed as if the best way to find bliss in heaven was to ignore completely the claims of this life. This attitude cannot flourish for an instant when we take into account these words of our Lord. Jesus never divorced this life and the future life, but always regarded them as complementary to each other.

(2) *The avoiding of occasions of stumbling, both to others and to oneself*

References to 'occasions of stumbling' (σκάνδαλα) occur in

Matthew 5²⁹⁻³⁰, 18⁶⁻⁹, and Mark 9⁴²⁻⁸. All these sayings occur in passages which are composed of separate logia linked together for various exegetical purposes²³ and it seems probable that all originate in one saying giving warning against stumbling-blocks. It is noticeable that all these sayings contain references to future life; either in the form of 'Kingdom of God' (Mk 9⁴⁷) or 'life' (ζωή—Mt 18⁸, ⁹, Mk 9⁴³, ⁴⁵).

There are two forms of stumbling referred to. In the first place there is the warning against causing 'one of these little ones to stumble' (Mk 9⁴², Mt 18⁶), and secondly, warnings against things which cause oneself to stumble (Mt 5²⁹⁻³⁰, 18⁸⁻⁹, Mk 9⁴³⁻⁷). We have already discussed these passages in connexion with Gehenna, but it can be added, in connexion with the idea of the conditions relative to future life, that there is an emphasis here on the stringency of those conditions. Especially with regard to the necessity of avoiding those things which cause destruction, a severe self-discipline is required. 'Actual self-mutilation is not counselled, but in the strongest possible manner the costliest sacrifice.'²⁴ For a generation like ours, which seeks fulfilment of life in the satisfaction of every desire, it is more necessary than ever to be reminded that there are desires which must be sacrificed if the greatest good is to be obtained. If it is good worldly wisdom to remember that 'You can't have everything', it is also sound Christian thinking to realize that 'You can't do everything'. It is by seeking the highest good we are capable of that we enter into life. Self-denial is never out of date for the Christian man.

The most difficult question in connexion with these 'stumbling passages' is to decide what precisely are the actions and attitudes to be avoided. It may be that this was much clearer to the hearers of Jesus' words than it is to us, because we cannot now be sure what were the surrounding circumstances. In Matthew 5²⁹⁻³⁰, it would appear that wrongful sexual desire is intended by 'your right eye causing you to stumble', as this follows the saying about adultery. It may be that 'right eye' is mentioned because of the reference to 'right hand'. The right hand, being the more useful, may be Matthew's way of emphasizing the need to give up even valuable things in order to avoid occasions of offence (cf. Mk 9⁴³).

In the sayings which warn against causing others to stumble, there appears to be a connexion of thought with our Lord's words

²³ E.g. catechetical needs; cf. VTM, p. 409.    ²⁴ VTM, p. 411.

M

about the right attitude to those who believe in Christ (Mt 18⁶; cf. Mk 9⁴²). The little ones are probably those young and weak in faith, toward whom more mature Christians have a serious responsibility. But this is vague at the best, and we can only interpret these warnings with reference to those things which, as we know only too well, do hinder true growth and progress; which make men slow to climb the heavenly hill, and divert their attention from the real service of God and man, which must engage our utmost efforts.

(3)  *The necessity for real obedience, contrasted with promises which are not kept*

There are two passages in Matthew which can be considered together under this head—7²¹: 'Not everyone who says to me, Lord, Lord, shall enter the Kingdom of heaven, but he who does the will of my Father who is in heaven'; and 21³¹: 'Truly I say to you, the tax collectors and the harlots go into the Kingdom of heaven before you.'

In the case of the first reference, there is a parallel saying in Luke 6⁴⁶: 'Why do you call me Lord and not do what I tell you?' Comparison of Matthew and Luke at this point shows that Matthew's account, which is fuller, is more openly eschatological. Not only is there this reference to entering the Kingdom of heaven; there is the obviously eschatological phrase 'in that day' in 7²², and the reference to the sending away of the 'workers of iniquity' in 7²³. Luke's parallel contains nothing of this obvious eschatological material, and many scholars regard Luke's shorter version of Matthew 7²¹ as the more original.[25] As McNeile points out: 'In Luke the character of the disciples in the present is dealt with, in Matthew that of the false teachers, which will be revealed at the last day.'[26]

This difference in emphasis between the two evangelists at this point affects the interpretation of the story of the two houses which follows (Mt 7²⁴⁻⁷, Lk 6⁴⁷⁻⁹). Although the differences in the two versions of this story do not seem to be based on an eschatological compared with a present sense, the way the story is introduced gives it a different emphasis. Thus it is easier to think that Matthew's version is referring to the Last Judgement,

[25] E.g. Kümmel, *Promise and Fulfilment*, p. 52, note 106; Manson, *The Sayings of Jesus*, p. 60.
[26] *The Gospel according to St Matthew*, p. 96.

while Luke's appears to be a lesson directed to this life. If, indeed, this story is really eschatological in intention, it may be that Matthew's introduction makes its true meaning clearer. In this case it is possible to argue that Matthew has rightly interpreted the inner meaning and implication of the more original Lucan saying. This means that although we have to regard Matthew 7²¹ as secondary and not necessarily to be accepted as an authentic word of Jesus, it can be interpreted as expressing a view closely connected with our Lord's teaching.

Thus the word about obedience to the will of God as a necessary condition for entry into the Kingdom of heaven is a further indication of this emphasis in our Lord's teaching. The thought is closely linked with the story of the two houses; it is both 'hearing' and 'doing' the words of Jesus which distinguishes the wise man. This is the good foundation upon which can be built a house that will withstand the storm. To say that these words apply to the future judgement is not to exclude from them all present implications. Indeed, it is true that the only satisfactory way to build for the present is to build for eternity. If this is particularly addressed to the company of disciples, who have to be sifted and purified,²⁷ then its warning must still apply to all Christians. Not by profession only, but by practice, shall the Kingdom of heaven be entered.

The context of our second saying about entering the Kingdom of heaven is the parable of the Two Sons (Mt 21²⁸⁻³¹). This is generally accepted as authentic; according to Jeremias it is addressed to members of the Sanhedrin²⁸ and vindicates the action of God in offering the good news to the poor and needy, seeing that those who profess to be obedient to the will of God have failed to carry out his commands. The lesson is the same as in the story of the two houses; not only profession but practice also is needed in those who are to enter the rule of God.

An interesting point arises in connexion with 'go before' ($\pi\rho o\acute{a}\gamma o\upsilon\sigma\iota\nu$). The verb $\pi\rho o\acute{a}\gamma\omega$ means 'to go before', in the sense of leading the way, and also to go before in respect of time. These two uses can be illustrated from the gospels; leading the way is illustrated in Mark 10³²: 'And they were on the road, going up to Jerusalem, and Jesus was walking ahead of them: and they were amazed, and those who followed were afraid.' This

---

²⁷ Jeremias, *The Parables of Jesus*, p. 157, note 92.　　²⁸ Ibid. p. 100.

means to walk ahead of those who are going slowly and with hesitation.[29] The meaning connected with time is illustrated in Matthew 14[22]: 'Then he made the disciples get into the boat and go before him to the other side while he dismissed the crowds.' The saying in Matthew 21[31] is usually interpreted in this sense— i.e. 'the tax collectors will get into the Kingdom of God before you'.[30] It is noticeable that whether the word is taken in the sense of preceding in time, or in the sense of leading the way, there is a strong suggestion that those addressed will also 'get into' the Kingdom of heaven. McNeile writes: 'The words neither imply nor deny that those addressed will finally reach the Kingdom',[31] but by the usage of $\pi \rho o \acute{a} \gamma \omega$ in the gospels, it is possible to argue that there is an implication that they will.[32] It is perhaps rash to build very much upon an implication, but it seems that here there is an inference that the Kingdom of God is regarded as eventually open to these leaders who at present oppose Jesus, and also that there is some sort of precedence in that Kingdom. Apparently it matters considerably who precedes whom into the Kingdom. It is also just possible that there might be a suggestion that the tax collectors and harlots will lead the Jews into that rule of God. This would be just the sort of reversal of common expectation which Jesus might use. The spectacle of tax collectors and harlots being guides to members of the Sanhedrin in matters of religion is certainly unusual. By this bold figure, Jesus may have emphasized that a repentant, believing tax collector or harlot might indeed be able to assist the staid members of the Jewish Council to a proper appreciation of the meaning of religion.

## (4) *The necessity for an attitude of childlike trust*

There are two occasions on which our Lord's relationship with children is recorded in the gospels. Matthew 18[1-5] tells how in answer to the disciples' question about who would be greatest in the Kingdom of heaven, Jesus said: 'Truly I say to you, unless you turn and become like children, you will never enter the Kingdom of heaven.' The Marcan and Lucan parallels to Matthew's saying occur in another context, in which the disciples tried to send

---

[29] Arndt and Gingrich, *A Greek-English Lexicon of the New Testament*, p. 709.
[30] Ibid.
[31] *The Gospel according to St Matthew*, p. 306.
[32] Jeremias on the contrary takes $\pi \rho o \acute{a} \gamma o \upsilon \sigma \iota \nu$ as not temporal, but exclusive—'the publicans . . . will enter the kingdom of God rather than you'—*The Parables of Jesus* pp. 100-1.

away children who had been brought to the Lord (Mk $10^{13-16}$, Lk $18^{15-17}$; cf. Mt $19^{13-15}$). 'Truly I say to you, whoever does not receive the Kingdom of God like a child shall not enter it' (Mk $10^{15}$, Lk $18^{17}$). Mark and Luke record that there was a dispute among the disciples who should be greatest, partly in reply to which Jesus placed a child in their midst and said: 'Whosoever receives one such child in my name receives me; and whosoever receives me receives not me, but him who sent me' (Mk $9^{37}$; cf. Lk $9^{48}$).

It seems reasonably clear that Mark $10^{15}$, Luke $18^{17}$, and Matthew $18^3$ contain an authentic word of Jesus[33] although the occasion of the saying is not agreed among the evangelists. The verbal differences between Matthew and the other two gospels do not affect the agreement in meaning, and for the purposes of our study we can concentrate on the Marcan version. This includes in $10^{14}$, the statement: 'Let the children come to me, do not hinder them; for to such belongs the Kingdom of God.' Together with the first part of $10^{15}$, this appears to stress the present reality of the Kingdom. Taylor allows the possibility that the distinction between receiving the Kingdom and entering it is 'the present Kingdom is received, the future Kingdom is entered'.[34] But there is also the possibility that the idea running through these words is: 'Men who do not receive the Kingdom as a gift cannot enter upon its blessings and responsibilities'.[35] In any case what is being required as necessary for receiving and entering the Kingdom is the attitude of a child. The qualities usually thought to be uppermost in our Lord's mind are humility and receptiveness. These are, in fact, the same qualities which are constituents of faith. So the condition of entering the Kingdom which is expressed here is an attitude of childlike trust. When account is taken of the references to Jesus himself in this passage, this attitude of trust can be interpreted as trust in Christ (note Mk $10^{14}$: 'Let the children come to *me*'; cf. Mk $9^{37}$ and parallels). If this condition can thus be fairly expounded as trust in Christ, a personal attitude to him, we ought to notice that in spite of the popularity of our Lord's attitude to children, this condition of entry into the Kingdom of God is neither widely known nor

---

[33] So VTM, p. 424. 'There can be no question about the genuineness of the saying.' Bultmann includes it in his (short) list of those sayings which are 'characteristic of the preaching of Jesus'.
[34] VTM, p. 423.     [35] Ibid. p. 424.

readily accepted. It seems that the 'ethical' conditions so far outlined are more easily accepted than the more distinctively 'religious' conditions brought out in this discourse about children. Yet
we have no warrant for choosing our own conditions out of the
list declared to be necessary by our Lord. It is just as necessary
that we should adopt this attitude of childlike trust to Christ, as
it is that we should fulfil the other conditions of sincere obedience
to the will of God.

(5) *The necessity of freedom from dependence on riches*

Mark $10^{23}$, Luke $18^{24}$, and Matthew $19^{23}$ record the words of
Jesus, following the rich young man's sorrowful turning away from
the Lord after he had been told to sell his possessions and follow him.
'And Jesus looked round, and said to his disciples, "How hard
it will be for those who have riches to enter the Kingdom of
God".' There is a difference among scholars concerning the
present or future meaning of Kingdom of God in this saying, but
if we accept the view that present and future meanings of Kingdom are complementary to each other, we may assume that often
it is not possible to say any particular reference means one or the
other; it is usually both. There seems no strong reason for regarding this as exclusively a present reference, especially in view
of the future tense used in this verse. Taken together with the
saying about a camel and a needle's eye, this is really an illustration of the general truth that entry into the Kingdom of God is
very difficult. This is made all the clearer if, with the Western
text, we take Mark $10^{24}$ after $10^{25}$. Then the two expressions, the
rich man and the camel, are summed up in the statement: 'How
hard it is to enter the Kingdom of God'. This concluding summary
may well be made the summary of our investigation of the conditions of entry into the future Kingdom of God. How hard it is!
The gospels do not in any way encourage us to think that it is
easy to enter the bliss of a satisfactory future life. Indeed the
attitude which says 'It must be so' is often based upon a very
scanty and superficial knowledge of God and man. The person
who is so assured of the natural immortality of the human species
that he can say 'of course there is a future life', may not necessarily be expressing the deepest faith. The One to whom all these
things are open has told us how difficult it is, and even a glimmer-
ing of self-knowledge will confirm this. We seem to have so little

about us that is worth continuing, we are so easily tied to the present, and death remains such a mystery, that we have humbly to agree with Jesus. How hard it is to enter the Kingdom of God!

But the matter is not left there. With man it is not only hard; it is impossible. Man cannot guarantee his own survival, any more than he can keep on living on this earth. But with God all things are possible. The emphasis in the end is not on man's powers but on the power of God. Life in the Kingdom of God is a gift from God. These sayings about the conditions of entry into the Kingdom do not state the way in which man can earn or merit the Kingdom of God. But they are the conditions on which the gift of the Kingdom will be given. Thus our Lord, in Mark $10^{27}$ and parallels, has brought us face to face with the greatest truth of all about the future life. It is given by God, not earned or naturally acquired by man.

The conclusions we can reach about the nature of the future life and the conditions of entering it, which can be derived from this consideration of the idea of entering the Kingdom of God, can be summarized as follows:

(1) The main emphasis is on the conditions of entry. These conditions concern our relations with God, with our neighbours and with ourselves.

(a) To God we must offer sincere obedience, in deed as well as thought. We must also receive the promised gift of God in childlike trust. This obedience and trust must also be offered to Christ.

(b) Toward our neighbour we must act in such a way as will not cause him to stumble. Our obedience to God requires that we treat our neighbour in the right way.

(c) To ourselves we must avoid occasions of stumbling. We must not depend on riches to ensure our future blessedness. Self-denial is necessary, for it is not easy to enter into the full life of the future.

(2) Little is said or implied about the nature of future life in these passages. We may possibly infer some degree of universalism in the Parable of the Two Sons, but this is questionable.

(3) The certainty of future life is assumed throughout these passages.

## II. ETERNAL LIFE

The phrase translated 'eternal life' (ζωή αἰώνιος) is comparatively rare in the synoptic gospels, and it is necessary to be on our guard against importing into these records ideas and interpretations which belong to a later stage of Christian thought. Especially there is the danger of being too much influenced by the use of this term in the Fourth gospel, which is, in the words of an eminent scholar, 'the classical treatment of the theme of eternal life'.[36] The value of limiting our present study to the synoptic gospels is well illustrated here. If we consider the teaching of these gospels separately from the development of this notion in the rest of the New Testament, we are in a better position to see the way in which Christian thought is a true development based upon the authentic original of the teaching of Jesus. This will perhaps reconcile us to the fact that we are to study the meaning of 'eternal life' without considering the literature in which this theme is most fully developed.

Although ζωή αἰώνιος is a unified expression, it will be helpful to take it apart and look at each component separately before we attempt to understand the meaning of the whole phrase. Ζωή is one of the words used in the New Testament to designate 'life', and it is well to remember that ζωή is no easier to define or delimit than is 'life'. Usually ζωή, as distinct from the other word for life (βίος), denotes 'the higher life of the soul in fellowship with God'.[37] It is helpful also to note that although ζωή bears this specialized 'religious' meaning, it is by derivation a perfectly ordinary 'secular' word. This can be seen if we consider the verb ζάω from which ζωή is derived. In the synoptic gospels this verb is used mainly to denote present existence—'living' in the ordinary sense of our word. Thus Anna the prophetess had lived with her husband seven years from her virginity (Lk 2[36]); in his temptation Jesus answered the devil in the words of Deuteronomy 8[3]; 'Man shall not live by bread alone' (Mt 4[4], Lk 4[4]). In the account of the raising of Jairus' daughter we read of the father's request: 'Come and lay your hands upon her, that she may be made well and live' (Mk 5[23]; cf. Mt 9[18]). It is said of the younger son that in the far country 'he wasted his substance in riotous living' (Lk 15[13]); the Jews said of Jesus after the crucifixion: 'That

---

[36] C. H. Dodd, *New Testament Studies*, p. 163.        [37] VTM, p. 411.

deceiver said while he was alive . . .' (Mt 27⁶³); and there are two
instances in the resurrection stories in which 'live' means basically
'real existence', even if new aspects are also added to it—Luke
24⁵, 'Why do you seek the living among the dead?' and Luke
24²³, in which the two men going to Emmaus reported that
'some women of our company said that he was alive'. These last
two instances indicate that the word 'to live' begins to take on
wider implications, and cannot be limited to physical life. Other
illustrations of the same widening process are Luke 10²⁸, the
answer to the lawyer: 'You have answered right: do this, and
you will live'; and Luke 15²⁴, ³²: 'This my son was dead and is
alive again; he was lost and is found.'

The other and more significant way in which this verb is used
is as a description of God, the 'Living God'. At Caesarea Philippi
Peter said: 'You are the Christ, the son of the living God' (Mt
16¹⁶); in the discussion with the Sadducees Jesus reminded them
that 'He is not God of the dead, but of the living' (Mk 12²⁷ and
par.); and at his trial the high priest said: 'I adjure you by the
living God, tell us if you are the Christ, the Son of God' (Mt 26⁶³).
These instances are exceedingly important because they show how
closely the thought of living is connected with God. This concept
is not to be regarded as an antithesis of the ordinary use of 'living',
for, as Dodd writes, concerning the Hebraic background of New
Testament thought: 'In Hebrew thought as represented by the
Old Testament, "life" stands for fullness of earthly welfare, for
health, vigour, activity and enjoyment unimpaired by the forces
of death which lie in wait for man. . . . He lives the best life on
earth when he has communion with God, for with Him is the
fountain of life, and in His presence is fullness of joy.'³⁸ In this
connexion between the 'living God' and the life of man is the
conviction that man's life is a gift from the living God, as well as
the knowledge that in conscious fellowship with the living God
man finds the true fullness of his life. So we can say that although
ζωή has a special meaning connected with future life, that meaning is not to be separated from the reality of this life, nor from
the essential relationship with God, in which alone any life worthy
of the name is to be found.

The second part of the phrase ζωὴ αἰώνιος is that which has
the meaning 'eternal'. We have to recognize that quite apart

---

³⁸ *New Testament Studies*, p. 161.

from any special considerations, with which we are to deal below, 'eternal' is a very difficult word to describe and understand. A moment's thought will reveal that this word cannot properly apply to any fact of present human existence. Whatever else can be said of the stuff of ordinary life, it can never be said to be eternal. We often use the word in a quite negative sense of that which is opposite to the temporary and transitory. Again, there is often the implication of inactivity involved in our use of the word 'eternal', for activity seems necessarily to involve movement and change, both of which seem completely contrary to 'the eternal'. These comments will help to remind us that although the New Testament use of αἰώνιος demands some thought if we are to understand it, this is not unusual when this kind of word is being considered.

The noun αἰών usually means 'period of time', 'age',[39] but it is an expression which embraces a wide variety of meanings. Especially interesting is the sense of 'world'; that is, a spatial rather than a temporal meaning. Instances of this usage in Jewish literature are gathered together by H. Sasse in Kittel's *Theologisches Wörterbuch*, Vol. I, p. 203. Examples which may be quoted are Assumption of Moses 12[4], which speaks of God having created all nations: 'He hath foreseen them and us from the beginning of the creation of the earth unto the end of the age [i.e. 'world'].' 4 Ezra 6[25] reads: 'Whosoever shall survive all these things that I have foretold unto thee, he shall be saved and shall see my salvation and the end of the world.' In 2 Baruch 54[21] we read: 'At the consummation of the world vengeance shall be upon those who have done wickedness, according to their wickedness.'[40]

There are some passages in the gospels in which αἰών is best interpreted in this sense of 'the world'. The clearest examples are those passages which refer to ἡ συντέλεια τοῦ αἰῶνος ('the end of the world')—see Matthew 13[39, 40, 49], 24[3], 28[20]. This is a clearly eschatological phrase, peculiar to Matthew, which refers to the coming end of the created order, 'the completion of the

---

[39] Cullmann, *Christ and Time*, p. 45.

[40] Other passages which illustrate this point are 2 Baruch 69[4], Tobit 14[5], Wisdom 18[4]. Of special interest to our modern technological civilization is Wisdom 13[9]:

'For if they had the power to know so much
That they could investigate the world
How did they fail to find sooner the Lord of these things?'

transitory course of the world'.[41] This eschatological influence on the word αἰών is to be noted, for this appears more clearly in the phrase ζωὴ αἰώνιος which is specially important in our present study.[42] The sense of 'world' applied to αἰών also appears in the phrase ἡ μέριμνα τοῦ αἰῶνος ('the cares of the world'—Mt 13[22], Mk 4[19], RSV). Dalman thinks this is a reference to that which is temporal, and hazards the opinion that the best rendering may be 'the troubles of their life'.[43] In any case αἰών in this passage refers to what we usually call 'the world', meaning the life of man in this universe, which, as we know only too well, can divert our attention from things which do not belong to our physical, earthly life. Αἰών is also used in the sense of 'world', i.e. 'present existence', in the phrase 'Sons of this αἰών' (Lk 16[8], 20[34]).

We have discussed this meaning of αἰών in some detail in order to emphasize that all occurrences of the word cannot be forced into the same mould. Yet we readily recognize that the meaning so far discussed is not the most usual. The characteristic usage of αἰών in Jewish literature and in the New Testament has a clear time reference.

In the New Testament, time is not a uniform succession of years, days, and moments, without any special significance attaching to each part. There are three distinct divisions of time. The first refers to the period before the Creation, and is expressed in such phrases as 'out of the age' (ἐκ τοῦ αἰῶνος), 'from the age' (ἀπ'αἰῶνος) 'from the ages' (ἀπὸ τῶν αἰώνων). The second division is the long, but definitely limited period of time between the Creation and the end of this present age, which is also the beginning of the coming age. This is described as the 'present age' (ὁ αἰὼν οὗτος, ὁ νῦν αἰών). The third and last division is 'the coming age' (ὁ αἰὼν ὁ μέλλων, ὁ ἐρχόμενος αἰών). This is 'the time that extends beyond the end of the present age'.[44] Not all the above terms occur in the synoptic gospels, but we can see the meanings outlined in other New Testament writings, and safely assume that the background of the synoptic teaching is substantially

---

[41] McNeile, *The Gospel according to St Matthew*, p. 201. Cf. Dalman, *Words*, p. 155—not an abbreviation but 'a designation of time as transitory, of the world's course'.

[42] Cf. *TWNT*, I.203.

[43] *Words*, pp. 154-5.

[44] O. Cullmann, *Christ and Time*, p. 48.

the same as that indicated in other New Testament passages.[45]

Cullmann insists that the implication of this usage in regard to the biblical concept of eternity is that the Bible conception is not the philosophical idea of eternity as timelessness. The biblical view of eternity is that it is unending time. The coming age, in particular, is not to be regarded as timeless. It differs from the age that is past and from the present age only in that it is unlimited in one direction. The present age especially is regarded as limited 'at both ends'; at its beginning by the Creation, at its conclusion by the beginning of the 'coming age'. But the coming age is only limited in its beginning. 'The coming age is limited on one side but unlimited on the other; its beginning is limited, inasmuch as it begins with the events that are pictorially described in the apocalypses, but no limit is set for its end. In other words, it is without end, but not without beginning, and only in this sense is it "eternal".'[46] The practical significance of this understanding of eternity as unending time rather than timelessness, needs to be noticed.

In the first place, the biblical view cannot accept the idea that God is apart from time, and that therefore time is without permanent significance. On the contrary, the Bible asserts that God is involved in time in a most significant way. He is the originator of time, which is made significant by His continuous activity. The distinctive Old Testament attitude to the power of God, for instance, is that He has acted 'in time' to deliver His people. Especially He brought His people out of the land of Egypt, out of the house of bondage. But the greatest significance of all is that in the fullness of time God sent forth His Son (Gal 4[4]). This mighty act of God for ever links him with man. The eternal God has acted in 'time'; no longer can man think of God as remote from the world, which is so closely involved in time, for God has involved Himself in time also.

Secondly, the biblical notion of eternity as endless time means

<hr>

[45] The terms considered occur as follows:
ἀπ' αἰῶνος (Lk 1[70]).
ὁ αἰὼν οὗτος (Mt 12[32], Lk 16[8], 20[34]).
ὁ αἰὼν ὁ μέλλων (Mt 12[32]).
ὁ αἰὼν ὁ ἐρχόμενος (Mk 10[30], Lk 18[30]).
ἐκ τοῦ αἰῶνος (Jn 9[32], Gal 1[4]).
ἀπὸ τῶν αἰώνων (Eph 3[9], Col 1[26]).
ὁ νῦν αἰών (1 Tim 6[17], 2 Tim 4[10]).
[46] Cullmann, *Christ and Time*, pp. 47-8.

that eternity cannot involve inactivity, for time has no significance unless it is filled with events. The biblical idea of eternity as endless time means that although man cannot conceive it, the future is absolutely unlimited. This limitless succession of time in the coming age is known only to God, but we can at least say that so long as there is time, there must be events, and so the concept of eternity must be concerned with a succession of events. What these events will be, the synoptic records do not say. We can only say that because Christ has come, the character of future events in the coming age is determined by him. Not only do we see the significance of the present from the revealing midpoint of history; that is the Incarnation. We also know by faith that that which is to be, into endless time in the future, is determined by the power of God, the Lord of time, who has revealed his purpose in Christ Jesus.

This fact of God's sovereignty over time is well illustrated in the synoptic uses of the phrase εἰς τὸν αἰῶνα ('for ever'). This always occurs in a context closely related to God and to His saving power and activity. The divine prerogative of forgiveness is said by Jesus to be withheld 'for ever' when anyone speaks blasphemously against the Holy Spirit (Mk 3[29]). In Mark 11[14] (par. Mt 21[19]) it is our Lord who 'curses' the barren fig tree with the words: 'Let there be no longer fruit on you for ever.' It is 'the Lord God who will give to the Son of the Most High the throne of his Father, David, and he will reign over the house of Jacob for ever' (Lk 1[32-3]); and in her song of exultation Mary says: 'He (God) has helped his servant Israel . . . to Abraham and his posterity for ever' (Lk 1[54-5]). It is noticeable that the phrase 'for ever' is not used in any context which would even remotely imply that anything man does or is can be 'for ever'. Man can only be thought of in connexion with eternity so far as he is thought of in connexion with God; for eternity is a divine concept, beyond the understanding of man to know and certainly beyond the power of man to achieve by his own efforts.

Having thus considered the two constituent parts of the phrase 'eternal life', we must now put together that which we have artificially sundered, and consider the uses of ζωὴ αἰώνιος in the gospels. This is clearly a term denoting 'life' in the sense of what happens to man after death. It is 'used of life in the blessed period of final consummation'.[47] With this meaning must also be

[47] Arndt and Gingrich, *A Greek-English Lexicon of the New Testament*, p. 341.

considered the question whether the phrase has any implication
of the life of that blessed period already begun now. Our conclusion from a study of the synoptic records seems to limit the
phrase to a future meaning; it is mainly in the Johannine literature that the idea is clearly expressed that eternal life begins in
this present life.

Although the phrase 'eternal life' is found in Greek thought[48]
it is to the Jewish use that we turn for help in understanding its
meaning in the New Testament. The phrase comes into use only
at the close of the Old Testament period, when the question of a
different destiny for good and bad was being increasingly considered. Thus Daniel 12[2]: 'Many of those who sleep in the dust
of the earth shall awake, some to everlasting life and some to
shame and everlasting contempt.' In the Apocryphal and
Pseudepigraphical literature there is a very considerable teaching
about eternal life. This is especially interesting and relevant
because it indicates the ideas about eternal life which were current
in the time of Jesus. Along with the assertion that there is to be
eternal life for some, goes the teaching who they are who gain
this wonderful possession. The usual answer is 'the pious', they
that fear the Lord, and so on. A few examples will indicate the
range of conceptions here. Psalms of Solomon (first century B.C.)
3[16]: 'But they that fear the Lord shall rise to life eternal'; 13[9]:
'For the Lord spareth His pious ones . . . the life of the righteous
shall be for ever.' A more personal claim is found in Enoch 37[4]:
'According to the good pleasure of the Lord of Spirits, by whom
the lot of eternal life has been given unto me.' The condition of
repentance is mentioned in Enoch 40[9]: 'the fourth [Presence],
who is set over the repentance unto hope of those who inherit
eternal life, is named Phanuel.'[49] In The Secrets of Enoch, which is
dated in the period A.D. 1–50 there is a description of the Great
Aeon after the Last Judgement, which is exceptional in that it
describes eternal life in terms which imply timelessness: 'All time
shall perish, and the years, and thenceforward there will be
neither months nor days nor hours, they will be stuck together,
and will not be counted' (65[7]).[50] This idea of eternal life is
usually contrasted with the transitory nature of present life, and

---

[48] Dodd, *New Testament Studies*, pp. 16off. Cf. *TWNT*, I.197-8.
[49] This part of Enoch is dated 105-64 B.C. by Charles, *A. & P.*, II.164.
[50] Cullmann recognizes this passage as an exception 'to the general Jewish view of
eternity as endless time'; *Christ and Time*, p. 46, note 16.

'to possess oneself of the future age' was a very popular Jewish expression from the first century A.D. onwards.[51]

In view of the way in which the gospels often use 'life' when there is an implication of 'eternal life', it is instructive to notice this also obtains in the Jewish literature. In some instances of 'life' in the Old Testament (e.g. Deut 30[15, 19], Jer 21[8], Prov 2[19]) 'the meaning does not extend beyond earthly life and well-being'.[52] But in some passages such as Psalm 16[11], the term 'life' seems to contain also an implication of life after death. 'Thou didst show me the path of life; in thy presence is fullness of joy; in thy right hand are pleasures for evermore.'[53] This equation of life with eternal life is clearly expressed in Jewish Pseudepigraphical books. For instance, Psalms of Solomon 9[9]: 'He that does righteousness layeth up life for himself with the Lord.'

The background of this conception of eternal life is the reality of judgement. Eternal life lies on the other side of that final judgement in which all men are to be involved. This precludes any view that eternal life can be a mere continuation of present life. 'In the final judgement it is not the ending or continuation of earthly existence that constitutes the decisive issue; but either, on the one hand, the penalty of an eternal death by fire, the scene of which is Gehenna, which involves permanent exclusion from the theocracy; or on the other hand, appointment to the eternal life which is consummated in the theocracy.'[54] Thus, although there is a close connexion between this present life and the coming future life, especially in the sense that actions and attitudes in this life are determinative of future destiny, yet there is always this idea of discontinuity. To live in the future age is not simply to carry on from this present age; it is successfully to pass the great day of judgement, and to receive the gift of eternal life.

The most important point of contact between these Jewish ideas and the teaching of Jesus is the relevance of the idea of the theocracy or rule of God, in the conception of eternal life. Dalman asserts that 'eternal life' really means the same thing as entrance into the theocracy.[55] This provides us with the key to solving the question of the extent to which Jesus accepted these contemporary ideas, and also how he differed from them. If the centre of the

---

[51] Dalman, *Words*, p. 125.    [52] Ibid. pp. 158-9.
[53] So Dalman, ibid. p. 159; others regard this as a reference to present life only.
[54] Ibid. p. 161.    [55] Ibid.

idea of 'eternal life' is the rule of God, then it is to the latter that we must look for the distinctive views of Jesus on this subject. In this connexion it is important to notice that the gospels do in fact regard 'life', meaning 'eternal life', and 'Kingdom of God' as synonymous. This is clearly indicated if Mark 9[47] ('It is better for you to enter the Kingdom of God with one eye') is compared with Mark 9[43, 45], where the same phraseology is used with 'life' in place of 'Kingdom of God'; compare also Mark 10[17] with 10[23], and Matthew 18[9] with Mark 9[47]. This reinforces the point that our Lord's characteristic teaching about 'eternal life' is connected with his distinctive use of 'the Kingdom of God'. When we recall that our Lord's view of the Kingdom of God is closely concerned with his own person, we can begin to see the intimate relation between the Person of our Lord and the Christian view of eternal life. The Kingdom is not only announced by Jesus; it brings him with it.[56] This can also be expressed in terms of the idea of the New Age, in which the Messiah will rule. 'The Christian *differentia*, as always, lies in the affirmation that it is Jesus who is Messiah.'[57] This insight also further confirms the relation between God the Father and eternal life. Eternal life, or the Kingdom of God, is the gift of God. It is not the natural right of man, but that which is given to man by the only one who can give it—namely God himself.

When we turn to the actual instances of the use of 'life' and 'eternal life' in the gospels, we notice immediately that there is practically no description of what eternal life is, since all the emphasis concentrates upon the conditions for obtaining it. For instance, Matthew 7[14]: 'For the gate is narrow and the way is hard, that leads to life, and those who find it are few.' There is an apparent parallel, which, however, is not remarkably close, in Luke 13[24]: 'Strive to enter in by the narrow door; for many, I tell you, will seek to enter and will not be able.' If we can assume that these two verses are interdependent, there seems little doubt that Luke preserves the more original account. In this case the saying of Jesus is part of his answer to the question, 'Lord, will those who are saved be few?', and the answer emphasizes that while God has opened the door, and it is now possible for man to enter, it must be realized that entry is not easy: 'The entrance is narrow

[56] R. Otto, *Kingdom of God and Son of Man*, p. 103.
[57] C. Ryder Smith, *The Bible Doctrine of the Hereafter*, pp. 224-5.

and it is a case of struggling through rather than strolling in.'[58] This Lucan passage goes on to emphasize the need for immediate action, for the door will not always stand open, and once it is shut entry will be impossible. This discourse seems to be the authentic record of our Lord's answer to a common question, which he answered with more hope than his contemporaries. They were inclined to take a gloomy view of the numbers of the saved and to suggest that there was something quite inscrutable in the choice of those who were to be saved. Jesus, on the contrary, places no limit upon the number of the saved, except men's willingness or unwillingness to accept the conditions. If then, the Lucan version is to be accepted here, does the form of the saying in Matthew add anything to our knowledge of 'life'? Matthew presents the saying in antithesis to the saying about destruction: 'The gate is wide and the way is easy, that leads to destruction, and those who enter by it are many.' (Mt 7$^{13}$). In other words, Matthew's account has become the picture of the two ways; one, which is easy and popular, leading to destruction; the other, which is difficult and unpopular, leading to life. Thus Matthew has 'moralized' the saying by the addition of the reference to the wide way leading to destruction. The fact that the concept of Two Ways is quite common in contemporary literature, both sacred and profane, suggests the strong possibility that the form of Matthew's account is influenced by this contemporary idea.[59] The secondary character of Matthew 7$^{14}$ is also suggested by Dalman's comment that 'the way that leads to life ($\dot{\eta}$ $\delta\delta\delta s$ $\dot{\eta}$ $\dot{a}\pi\acute{a}\gamma o \upsilon \sigma a$ $\epsilon\dot{\iota}s$ $\tau\dot{\eta}\nu$ $\zeta\omega\acute{\eta}\nu$) may be derived from the simple "the way of life" ($\dot{\eta}$ $\delta\delta\delta s$ $\tau\hat{\eta}s$ $\zeta\omega\hat{\eta}s$)'.[60] A further distinction between Matthew and Luke is pointed out by Lagrange. 'It is important to note that the door is not at the end of the road, but at its entrance. This is not a $\theta\acute{\upsilon}\rho a$ giving entry to the festive chambers as in Luke's different logion, but a $\pi\acute{\upsilon}\lambda\eta$ which must be a door at the entrance of a way, as in ancient cities.'[61] Matthew has in fact very considerably changed the significance of Luke's saying, and on this account it seems impossible to regard Matthew 7$^{13-14}$ as part of the authentic sayings of Jesus.

[58] Manson, *The Sayings of Jesus*, p. 125.
[59] Manson (ibid. p. 175) gives an impressive list of the instances in which the figure of Two Ways appears in Jewish and Classical writings.
[60] *Words*, p. 160.
[61] *Évangile selon Saint Matthieu*, p. 150.

N

In so far as we can see in Luke something close to the original, we can conclude that the logion teaches that the way into salvation (or 'life') is difficult. This certainly is a point which we have already noted Jesus did emphasize. Perhaps we can accept Matthew's account as drawing out some of the legitimate implications of Luke's 'narrow door'. The way, says Matthew's account, is 'restricted' (τεθλιμμένη). Lagrange expresses the meaning very forcibly here: '*La voie est τεθλιμμένη, pressée, serrée, comme un col qui passe entre deux rochers ou entre un rocher et le précipice.*'[62] We therefore conclude that Matthew 7[14], although secondary, correctly interprets the idea in Luke 13[24], that the way to 'life' is hard. It is certainly going beyond the reasonable implications of either account to say that God has deliberately restricted the number of those who can enter life. Whatever restriction there is arises out of man's refusal to face the conditions which have to be fulfilled if entry is to be made. God has opened the door; man may go in; but the matter is urgent, as the door may soon be closed. Thus Luke's version has a note of urgency, which is surely preferable to Matthew's which 'takes a very gloomy view of human life and destiny'.[63] The view of Jesus was always serious and compelling in its urgency; but it was never gloomy.

The passage in the synoptic gospels which is most revealing of our Lord's teaching about the way to eternal life is the story of the discussion occasioned by the question: 'Good Teacher, what must I do to inherit eternal life?' (Mk 10[17], Mt 19[16], Lk 18[18]). The details of exposition of this passage are fully treated in the standard commentaries, and there is no need here to consider every detail of the story. We can recognize the priority of the Marcan version over the other two, and note that the story has so many marks of authenticity that it is accepted without question as a reliable account of a real conversation in which Jesus was involved.

The first matter which concerns our special interest is the question asked by the rich man. What did he mean by it? and why did he ask it? There can be no doubt that the question refers to life in the coming age, for as we have seen, this meaning of the phrase was well established in current thought (see above, pp. 183-4).

'Inherit' (κληρονομέω) has two meanings in the LXX and other Jewish literature.

---

[62] *Évangile selon Saint Matthieu*, p. 150.    [63] Manson, *The Sayings of Jesus*, p. 175.

(*a*) To inherit, strictly as heir, e.g. Proverbs 13$^{22}$: 'A good man leaves an inheritance to his children's children.' Tobit 3$^{15}$: 'I am my father's only child and he has no child to be his heir.'

(*b*) To acquire, come into possession of, without any implication of right of possession owing to birth, and so on. Psalm 25$^{13}$: 'He himself shall abide in prosperity, and his children shall possess the land' (*RV*, 'inherit'). Enoch 5$^{7}$: 'But for the elect there shall be light and joy and peace, and they shall inherit the earth.'

The particular phrase 'inherit eternal life' occurs in several instances of which the following may be given as examples. II Enoch 50$^{2}$: 'Now therefore my children, in patience and meekness spend the number of your days, that you inherit endless life.' Dalman interprets the last phrase as 'take possession of the endless life to come'.[64] Cf. Sibylline Oracles, Frag. 3$^{46-9}$: 'But they who honour the true and everlasting God inherit life, through the aeonian time, dwelling in the fertile garden of Paradise, feasting on sweet bread from the starry heaven.'[65]

Dalman's comment on the meaning of inherit is instructive: 'The context must determine whether inheritance is really meant, or whether it is the acquisition of any object to which previously there existed a title, or to which the title was contemporaneous with its acquisition.'[66]

The outcome of this linguistic inquiry is that the rich man was not necessarily assuming that he possessed a title deed to eternal life and wanted to know how to obtain possession of that which was his by right. Rather, we can assume that he used 'inherit' in the more general sense of 'gain possession of'. He was asking how he could obtain eternal life, that is, the life of the coming age.

It is interesting to speculate on the reason which prompted the man to ask Jesus this question. Lagrange suggests that he was prompted to ask about his own possession of eternal life because he had heard Jesus promise the Kingdom to the children,[67] but this is regarded by Taylor as 'slenderly based'.[68] Taylor suggests that he evidently thought there were additional conditions above those prescribed in the Law.[69] Possibly the question implies

---

[64] *Words*, p. 157.
[65] For further refs., see Arndt and Gingrich, *A Greek-English Lexicon of the New Testament*, p. 435.
[66] *Words*, p. 126.　　[67] *Évangile selon Saint Marc*, p. 264.
[68] VTM, p. 425.　　[69] Ibid. p. 426.

dissatisfaction with the replies currently given to this question, which can be inferred from the teaching concerning the life of the coming age, which we have already considered. From these references we can assume that the usual reply to the rich man's question would contain the following items of advice 'Fear the Lord' (Ps Sol 3[16]), 'live piously' (Ps Sol 13[9]), 'repent' (Enoch 40[9]), 'be righteous' (Enoch 58[3]), 'be patient and meek' (II Enoch 50[2]). Less easy to expound would be the passages which say that 'the elect' will be in the light of eternal life (Enoch 58[3]), for if election is seriously accepted, it is never possible to say how one can become one of the elect. Equally without much help to our inquiries would be the statement of Enoch that it was by the good pleasure of God that the gift of eternal life had been granted to him personally (Enoch 37[4]). While these implied directions are sufficiently comprehensive and exacting, it may be that the rich man had no confidence in them because they were indirect; they did not come to him from a living person in whom he had confidence. So when he saw and heard Jesus he may have thought that here was someone whose word on this vital matter he could trust.

The first part of the answer of Jesus is 'Why do you call me good? No one is good but God alone' (Mk 10[18], Lk 18[19]). The version reported by Matthew, 'Why do you ask me about the good?' (19[17]), is generally regarded as an evasion of the doctrinal difficulty of this reply. The value of Matthew's version is in its indication of what the original account of Mark and Luke appeared to mean. Matthew has altered the form of the reply of Jesus because it could too easily be taken to imply some imperfection in our Lord's character. Without agreeing with these commentators who regard it as Jesus' own confession of sinfulness, we can accept the view which sees in the reply an assertion of the difference between the goodness of God and all other goodness.[70] This seems to imply that Jesus began his answer by directing his questioner's thought to the absolute goodness of God. Without denying his own goodness, Jesus is saying that this absolute goodness of God is to be first considered. The question and statement of Jesus is not only an introduction to the answer to the rich man's inquiry: it is the beginning of the answer. The

[70] The various interpretations of this passage are conveniently summarized in VTM, pp. 426-7.

matter of eternal life is only to be understood in the context of thought about God; Jesus means that in order to answer this question, a man must think about God; about His goodness, that is, about the unique character of the divine nature. We have here further evidence for the assertion that thought about the life hereafter must be 'religious thought'. Eternal life is a gift from God and to obtain that gift a man must direct his thoughts to God, who gives the gift according to His mercy and covenanted promise.

The second part of our Lord's reply is a selection of the Ten Commandments. The selection is interesting, especially in the fact that it omits both the commands which Jesus elsewhere said were the greatest—namely 'Hear, O Israel, the Lord our God is one; and thou shalt love the Lord thy God with all thy heart and with all thy soul and with all thy mind and with all thy strength', and 'Thou shalt love thy neighbour as thyself' (Mk 12$^{29-31}$). Matthew's version of Jesus' reply to the rich man includes the second of the greatest commandments, 'Thou shalt love thy neighbour as thyself' (19$^{19}$), but this is generally regarded as additional to the original. Not only is this clause omitted by Mark and Luke, but also it is pointed out that if this had been included, it would have been impossible for the man to have claimed that he had kept all these precepts from his youth. Origen seems to have been the first commentator to remark that if this man had been able to claim that he had kept this law of love to his neighbours he would already have attained perfection.[71]

The commandments Jesus did mention are such that a man might well say that he had observed them all, and therefore he would have to ask: 'What lack I yet?' It appears that Jesus deliberately encouraged the man's confident claim to have observed these laws, to show him that something more than obedience to laws was required in order to inherit eternal life. It is also true that these commands quoted by Jesus are all connected with human relations. 'The questioner's attention is directed to the part of the Decalogue which deals with human relationships.'[72] While this point is no doubt significant in itself, it does not adequately explain the omission of the first precept of the

---

[71] See Lagrange, *Évangile selon Saint Matthieu*, p. 376.
[72] VTM, p. 428.

Decalogue: 'Thou shalt love the Lord, . . .'[73] Furthermore, this first commandment is not mentioned in the subsequent discussion about what was lacking in the man's attitude. We seem forced to conclude that although Jesus placed great emphasis on the commandments, he also taught that something more was required for the inheritance of eternal life, than obedience to commands.

The third part of our Lord's reply shows what this 'something more' is. 'You lack one thing; go sell what you have and give to the poor, and you will have treasure in heaven; and come, follow me' (Mk 10[21] and par.). If our discussion so far has indicated that Jesus dealt with this inquirer in a personal and individual way, this is further confirmed by the words now under consideration. It is generally agreed that this is not a commandment applicable to all and sundry, but a specific challenge to this particular person. His obstacle was his money; but to other people different things stand in the way, for beneath the particular command there lies a general principle which is universally applicable. Furthermore, obedience to the commands of God involves not only prohibitions but also positive actions. Jesus indeed had already referred to one such positive command, 'Honour your father and mother', but the emphasis in this last part of the discussion falls completely on the positive element. We notice too that in effect this is an outworking of the command to love God with all one's powers. As has often been remarked, this man was challenged to put into practice the love of God by placing the will of God before that which he cared most about; namely his money. This is the principle of general application which must not be avoided by too much concern to show that the Christian way does not mean poverty for everyone. It certainly means for everyone the need to place the will of God before every other desire. And it is that which we care for most which has to be placed in a subordinate position to our love of God.

Not even this exacting demand is the total of our Lord's challenge to this man. It is, in fact, in the last few words of his reply that Jesus says the most important thing of all: 'Come, follow me.' It is probably due to the obvious stringency of the demand that the man should sell all, that we tend to minimize the importance of this last invitation. In any case, we readily think of ourselves as followers of Jesus and we cannot easily appreciate

[73] Lagrange, *Évangile selon Saint Matthieu*, p. 375.

what following Jesus would have involved for this man. Nothing less than giving up home, reputation, security, possibly even life itself, was involved in being one of the disciples of Jesus. This was not an easier thing than the voluntary sale of possessions; it was part of that total commitment to God which Jesus demanded, and it would have been very difficult.

But the real significance of the invitation to be a disciple does not lie in the high demands involved. If we pause for a moment, we can see wherein this is the most important part of the whole discussion. Thus far we see Jesus confronting his questioner with a rigorous standard. He had already to some degree accepted the discipline and difficulty of obedience to the law. His question shows that he was not satisfied; he had no certainty that even with his good record in the things Jesus mentioned, he was sure to inherit eternal life. Can we then suppose that he would be so convinced if the conditions were made harder? There is no certainty at all of this. Merely to add greater demands would not give this man the assurance that he so far lacked. Therefore, up to this point the reply of Jesus is tragically incomplete.

From the point of view of the full Christian faith, we have to add that not only is the answer incomplete; it is positively misleading. For one of the basic assertions of the fully developed Christian faith is that we are not saved by obedience to the law, however complete that obedience may be. We are then faced with this dilemma. Is there this fundamental difference between the way to be reconciled to God in this present life, and the way to inherit eternal life? Is one the way of faith in Christ and the other the way of obedience to commands? If this were so, it would seem as if there were a fundamental contradiction at the very centre of the Christian faith.

Thus from the point of view of a satisfactory answer to the rich man, and from the point of view of the Christian faith, the story is grievously incomplete if nothing is said about 'Follow me'; or if this is passed off as a formal saying, included merely to round off the discourse.[74] These words provide the climax and key to the whole discussion. This is the great thing lacking in this man;

[74] The Commentaries generally fail to bring out the significance of this invitation; see VTM, p. 429; McNeile, *The Gospel according to St Matthew*, p. 279; Easton, *The Gospel according to St Luke*, p. 272. Plummer (*I.C.C.*, *The Gospel according to St Luke*, p. 424) takes the invitation more seriously, connecting it with the command to sell all. See also Lagrange (*Saint Matthieu*, p. 376), who discusses the place of '*conseils et commandements*' in perfection.

this also is the factor which transforms this discussion from barren legalism into the way of triumphant faith.

'Faith' of course is not mentioned in this passage, and we must avoid reading into our Lord's words more than they mean. But if we ponder the implications of this invitation, we can see in it the beginning of a relationship of trust in Christ. If this man were to have responded to this invitation it could only have been on the basis of confidence in Jesus. On no other grounds could he conceivably have accepted the invitation, except that he was prepared to throw in his lot with the Lord. If he had done this, he would have joined the company of the disciples, accompanied Jesus on his journeys, and finally come to Jerusalem. There can be no doubt that he would have grown in knowledge of Jesus and his way, stumbling upon the truth as the others did; sometimes proving unbelievably slow to learn, and in the end failing to keep faith with Jesus when he went to the cross. This hard and sometimes disappointing road was the way by which those who followed Jesus came eventually to faith. Likewise, this man was being invited to undertake this great adventure of faith, for to follow Christ is to start out on the way which leads to faith.

The complete answer then, to the question, 'What shall I do to inherit eternal life?' is 'Keep the commandments, and follow me'. As we have seen, even the full list of commandments, faithfully kept, would not have given the inquirer the certainty he desired. There is, indeed, a sense in which the function of commandments is to prove that even when they are faithfully observed they do not lead to eternal life; rather they bring a man to realize that he has a lack which Jesus alone can satisfy. This must not be taken to mean that the commandments have only a negative role in the Christian life. They do, in fact, take a very important place in the life of faith, for part of the proving of faith is in keeping the commandments. 'Follow me' directs the attention of all who seek eternal life to the person of Jesus Christ. In him alone is the way that leads to life; to follow him is to begin to trust in him as Master and eventually to trust in him completely as Saviour.

The question, 'What shall I do to inherit eternal life?' also occurs in Luke 10²⁵. This question, asked by a lawyer, was answered by the questioner at the prompting of Jesus, in the words of the twofold summary of the law: 'Thou shalt love the Lord thy God with all thy heart . . ., and 'Thy neighbour as thyself'.

This same summary of the law in terms of love is also recorded in Mark 12²⁹⁻³¹ (par. Mt 22³⁷⁻⁴⁰), and this has led many scholars to assume that Luke's account of the lawyer's question is of the same incident as Mark's account of the question of one of the scribes about which commandment is first. If this parallel is accepted, the majority of scholars assert that the Marcan account is nearer the original, in which case we have to doubt the veracity of Luke's account, which is thought to have been influenced by the story of the rich man which we have considered above.⁷⁵

But a closer examination of Luke 10²⁵⁻⁸ and Mark 12²⁸⁻³⁴ raises the question whether they are true parallels. In fact the only part they have in common is the summary of the law. In view of the fact that all the other details are different, there seem grounds for Manson's assertion that these are independent accounts of different incidents; the repetition of the summary of the law can well be explained as our Lord's method of teaching an important religious truth.⁷⁶ It is certainly conceivable that Jesus should repeat some of his teaching on different occasions and it is possible that in his reply to Jesus the lawyer deliberately framed the summary of the law in the form in which he knew Jesus taught it. In that case there was common ground between the two, and the point of the question and our Lord's reply is to consider more carefully what are the practical implications of the rule of love of neighbours. Thus the discourse in Luke 10²⁵⁻⁸ is a fitting introduction to the parable of the Good Samaritan, which gives our Lord's answer to the question: 'Who is my neighbour?'

If this critical judgement which asserts the independence and reliability of Luke's narrative is accepted, there is clearly further evidence here concerning our Lord's teaching about eternal life. This teaching is all the more interesting because it must be considered alongside the answer to the same question posed by the rich man. That the replies are different cannot be denied. As we have seen, the reply to the rich man was a selection of the commandments, leading to the awareness that to keep these commandments leaves a sense of lack, which can only be met by responding to our Lord's 'Follow me'. But the answer of the lawyer, which Jesus approved, embraces the principle underlying the whole law. It is the practice of this principle which engages the interest of Jesus in this second story. Further, there is no reference to following

⁷⁵ VTM, pp. 484-5.          ⁷⁶ *The Sayings of Jesus*, p. 260.

Christ, which we have considered to be a most important factor in the earlier story. The only conclusion we can draw from this is that Jesus gave different answers to the question, according to the particular need and attitude of the questioner.

In the case of the rich man, Jesus emphasized the need to recognize the ineffectiveness of commandments as a way to certainty of eternal life. With the lawyer our Lord's attitude is based on the awareness that his questioner knows the correct answer. He is possibly in no danger of thinking that he has kept all the commandments. His danger is that he makes the theoretical question about the definition of the term 'neighbour' an excuse for not putting into practice what he knows to be true. Jesus does indeed make clear in the story of the Good Samaritan that any attempt to define the meaning of neighbour is wrong; for love is the determinative term in this commandment. It is not a question of firstly deciding who is, and who is not, one's neighbour and then proceeding to love one and ignore the other. Christ's principle is that human need determines neighbourly acts, and he is our neighbour whose need impels us to help him. The reply to the lawyer is fundamentally: 'You know the right answer. What you have to do is to put into practice what you know.'

This is a most important insight into the way to obtain eternal life. That way is a way of practice, of action as well as attitude and thought. Not only must right things be thought, but also right things must be done. It is only a shallow view of faith and works which sees in this any conflict with the way of salvation by faith alone. There is no suggestion in our Lord's reply to the lawyer that he can earn eternal life by acting in a neighbourly way to those in need. We must remember that our Lord's full answer is 'Love God; love your neighbour'. Without the first, the second is certainly impossible, and the attempt to practise it can only lead to self-righteousness. But the principle of love of God not only makes possible love of neighbour; it is in itself a relationship based on faith. To the Christian there is no doubt that Jesus is the sharer of the divine nature, and to love God is indeed to love Christ. That our Lord was reticent about any claim to divine nature is part of the authentic gospel witness. But his reticence is not a denial of the truth of his divinity, but rather a confirmation of it. So to a fully Christian interpretation of this passage there is no contradiction of the principle of faith, which is so prominent in the story of the rich man. As with so many truths of the Christian gospel, the basis is to be found in the teaching of Jesus. The truth is implicit, needing to be drawn out and amplified by Christian thought and experience.

The further point to be noted in regard to this passage is that, like others we have considered, the stress is on the conditions by which eternal life is to be obtained. Nothing at all is said or even implied about the content of that life. The way to heaven is plain; the description of what heaven is like is obscure.

The other occurrence of 'eternal life' which must be discussed here is in Mark 10²⁹⁻³⁰. Subsequent upon the remark of Peter that the disciples had left all to follow Him, Jesus said: 'Truly I say to you, there is no one who has left house or brother or sisters or mother or father or children or lands, for my sake and for the gospel, who will not receive a hundredfold now in this time, houses and brothers and sisters and mothers and children and lands, with persecutions, and in the age to come eternal life.' Both Matthew and Luke record the saying in shorter and simpler forms. Luke includes the statement about eternal life in the coming age, but Matthew merely says he shall inherit eternal life (Mt 19²⁹, Lk 18³⁰).

It will not surprise any sensitive reader of the gospels to hear that many scholars have expressed doubts about the authenticity of this saying. The reiterated details of things lost and things promised in their place does not seem to be in the style we usually discover in our Lord's words. Further, the saying seems to go perilously near to encouraging us to think that we can eat our cake and have it, or that Christians are apparently promised the best of both worlds. That difficulty was felt on this ground is shown by the comments and emendations by some early commentators.⁷⁷ There is the further difficulty which arises on more critical grounds. According to Dalman, it is doubtful if Jesus used the idea of 'the present age' and 'the coming age', and even if he did, these ideas were not prominent in his thought.⁷⁸ But in

---

⁷⁷ E.g. Clement of Alexandria: 'He shall receive a hundred-fold. To what end does he expect to have now in this time fields and riches and houses and brothers, with persecutions? But in the coming age there is eternal life.' (Quoted by VTM, p. 435.)

⁷⁸ *Words*, pp. 147-8. Dalman's arguments, based on the absence of a uniform witness to this phrase, do not seem to me to be entirely convincing. How many other phrases might be equally suspect on the ground that there is no universally common witness to them in all three synoptic gospels?

spite of these and other difficulties, Taylor cautiously affirms that the saying as a whole should be taken as substantially authentic; but with greater doubt on the authenticity of the phrase which is our special interest, namely 'in the world to come eternal life'.[79] Because of the hesitation about this particular phrase, it would be foolhardy to build upon it any definite view of the meaning of the future life in the teaching of Jesus.

Our consideration of the term 'eternal life' leads to the following conclusions:

(1) 'Eternal life' describes life after death; but there is no suggestion that thought about eternal life precludes interest in this present life.

(2) 'Eternal' means that which belongs to the coming age which is inaugurated by the coming of Christ. The teaching of the synoptic gospels is distinctive in that it claims that the coming age has begun in the life and ministry of Jesus of Nazareth. In him the rule of God is now present. 'Eternal' does not mean 'never ending' in the sense of timeless; nor does it imply inactivity.

(3) Eternal life is closely connected with God the Father in the thought of Jesus. It is a gift of God, not a natural possession of man—this implies that eternal life is not necessarily possessed by everyone. There are conditions under which the gift is given.

(4) These conditions are: thought about God, obedience to His commandments, discipleship of Christ, leading to faith, and the practice of the love of God in love of one's neighbour.

(5) The conditions are not assumed to be easy; they make great demands upon men. These demands are not the same in detail for everyone, but they always involve the requirement of placing the will of God before our own desires and possessions.

### III. BLESSED

In popular modern speech the future life is described as a life of 'bliss' or 'the 'blessed life'. This terminology has some foundation in the language of the synoptic gospels. There are two Greek words which in various forms are rendered 'blessed' in the English versions. One of these, εὐλογητός, does not directly concern us here, as it is never used to describe the state of man, either in the

[79] VTM, p. 435.

present or the future. The cognate participle εὐλογημένος is used in Luke 1⁴² in the greeting of Elizabeth addressed to Mary and in Matthew 25³⁴ to describe the happy destiny of those whom the King placed on his right hand. Otherwise the participle and the verb εὐλογεῖν are used either to describe Jesus (Mt 21⁹, 23³⁹, Mk 11⁹, Lk 13³⁵), or to indicate his attitude and words, in blessing the loaves at the feeding of the five thousand (Mk 6⁴¹ and par.); as part of the symbolic act at the Last Supper 'Jesus took bread and blessed and broke' (Mk 14²², Mt 26²⁶); in what appears to have been a eucharistic meal the same action is reported in Luke 24³⁰. Also we read that Jesus blessed his disciples, as he departed from them into heaven (Lk 24⁵⁰⁻¹).

Of greater importance to our present study is the word μακάριος, which is rendered 'blessed'; although in ordinary non-religious usage this word approximates more closely to our 'fortunate' or 'happy'.⁸⁰ If more regard is given to the Aramaic phrase behind this word, it is probably to be taken as an interjection—'Oh, the happiness of'.⁸¹ Clearly the most significant occurrences of this phrase, with possible application to the future state, are in the Beatitudes (Mt 5³⁻¹², Lk 6²⁰⁻³).

Before we consider these passages in detail, it is well to pose the question with which we are faced. This is—'Does "blessed" apply to this life, to the future life, or is there a sense in which it applies to both?' While these words have often proved true in practical everyday experience, for those who have practised these principles of Jesus have found great happiness in so doing, there is an unmistakable future element in many of these promises.

Four Beatitudes are recorded by both Matthew and Luke, those referring to 'the poor' (Mt 5³, Lk 6²⁰), 'those who hunger' (Mt 5⁶, Lk 6²¹), 'those who weep' (Mt 5⁴, Lk 6²¹), and those who are hated (Mt 5¹¹, Lk 6²²). There are significant differences in the two presentations, which suggest that Luke's version is more original. For instance, Luke presents these words as directly addressed to those who hear, while Matthew puts them in the third person. Again, Luke's form is more simple and direct; he speaks of 'the poor', to which Matthew adds, apparently feeling the need for explanation, 'in spirit'. Those whom Luke describes

⁸⁰ Moulton and Milligan (*The Vocabulary of the Greek Testament*, p. 386) quote examples from the papyri.
⁸¹ Ibid. p. 386, McNeile, *The Gospel according to St Matthew*, p. 50.

as 'the hungry' Matthew refers to as 'those who hunger and thirst after righteousness'. Luke says: 'Happy are those who weep now, for they shall laugh.' Matthew presents this saying in a more rounded form with a reference to those who mourn being comforted. In each case Matthew seems to have drawn out the implication of our Lord's words, and applied them specifically to religious situations. Luke's version is direct and challenging and no doubt means what Matthew takes it to mean.

The other Beatitudes which are found only in Matthew appear to present our Lord's teaching in terms of Old Testament and current Jewish ideas. 'Blessed are the meek' (Mt 5⁵) expresses the same thought as Psalm 37¹¹. 'Blessed are the merciful' (Mt 5⁷) not only confirms our Lord's teaching about forgiveness being dependent on a forgiving attitude but is paralleled in Jewish teaching (e.g. Ecclus 28²⁻⁵). Manson's comment on this is 'Such difference as there is between Jesus and Judaism is a difference of emphasis'.[82] 'Blessed are the pure in heart' (Mt 5⁸) reflects the thought of Psalm 24³⁻⁴, and 'Blessed are the peacemakers' can be compared with similar teaching in Jewish literature, especially *Pirke Aboth* (1¹²).[83] Lest this comment appears to detract from the originality of the teaching of Jesus, it ought to be noted that *Pirke Aboth* is a collection of sayings dated from the third century B.C. to the third century A.D. There is, therefore, no proof that Jesus depended on this work; the dependence could be the other way. It is also worth noting that although the work has had a great effect upon Jewish piety, it lacks the dynamic quality which has been evidenced in the Christian teaching on this subject.[84] For our present purpose it seems best to limit our consideration to the four Beatitudes which appear in both Luke and Matthew, as the other Matthean Beatitudes do not seem to be distinctively and exclusively the teaching of Jesus.

One further point about the Lucan version should be noted. Alongside the four 'blessings' are four 'woes' (Lk 6²⁴⁻⁶). Although these verses are suspected by some scholars of being secondary, it is reasonable to hold that the first three might well be genuine, with the fourth in parallel to the Beatitude about the hatred of men, added later to complete the series.[85] The importance of

[82] *The Sayings of Jesus*, p. 150.
[83] Other references in Montefiore, *Rabbinic Literature and Gospel Teachings*, pp. 27ff.
[84] See Herford, *A. & P.*, II.688-9.
[85] Manson, *The Sayings of Jesus*, p. 49.

these woes is that they add considerably to the eschatological impression of the Lucan account. Along with the Beatitudes the Woes twice use the significant 'now', which points the contrast between the present and future. In the same category we notice the future tenses of the verbs—'you shall be satisfied', 'you shall laugh', 'you shall hunger', 'you shall mourn and weep'. This future aspect of the promised blessings is not weakened by 'yours is the Kingdom of God' (Lk 6²⁰, Mt 5³) for, as McNeile points out, in view of the absence of any connecting particle in Aramaic, the present tense cannot be pressed here.[86]

We have then in these sayings, a description of the future state of the disciples. They will possess the rule of God, they will be filled, as with good food at a feast, they will laugh, they will have a great reward in heaven. If the Woes are accepted as genuine, this happy state of the disciples is contrasted with the unhappy condition of those who have had all good things in this life and will be in want in the future. This is not just an expression of the idea that fairness demands recompense. We must remember that in the Bible as 'the poor' often signify 'the pious', so 'the rich' often signify 'the wicked'. Equally, those who weep are those who are persecuted for the sake of the Son of Man, and those who laugh are their persecutors, the opponents of Christ. Those who are evil spoken of, and become unpopular, are those who take the side of Christ in a world which inevitably opposes him. And those of whom all men speak well are those whose lives and actions are approved by the crowd just because they do popular things. In all this it is necessary to notice that it is not anyone who is poor or sad, in need, or unpopular, for any reason whatsoever, who is promised these joys. To be poor is not necessarily to be pious, any more than to be rich is necessarily to be wicked. There are some who are sad, not because they have stood up for the truth, but because they have been selfish. Some are unpopular for the reason that they have proved unreliable, self-seeking, vain and so on. These words of our Lord do not promise a happy future to all who are now miserable, but certainly that promise is made to those whose need arises because of their loyalty to the Son of Man. And it must be added that there is nothing exclusive about these promises. A man may be sad or in need or unpopular, for less than the most worthy reasons.

[86] *The Gospel according to St Matthew*, p. 50.

But in his misery he can, indeed is more likely to, turn to Christ, identify himself with his way, become his disciple, and then indeed his sorrow is turned to gladness.

There remains the question whether there is also a present meaning involved in these words of blessing. The answer must surely be that those who are promised these blessings in the future are already happy in the anticipation of them. Both the implication of the language and the total picture of the disciples confirms this. As we have seen μακάριος means 'Oh the happiness of—'. This cannot mean only in the future. Those who accept the yoke of the Kingdom are now 'happy', in a sense which goes deeper than the temporary sorrows and difficulties of this life. It is not only in anticipation of future bliss, that a believer is happy. He is happy in the realization of his fellowship here and now with Christ. In other words, it is not true to say that the Christian 'trades' present happiness for the promise of future bliss. The truth is rather in the words of Charles Wesley:

> *Happy, while on earth we breathe,*
> *Mightier bliss ordained to know.*[87]

[87] *Hymns for the People called Methodists* (1779), 58³.

# CHAPTER NINE

# TWO SPECIALLY SIGNIFICANT PASSAGES

## I. THE SADDUCEES' QUESTION

ONE of the incidents in the gospels which requires special consideration is the Sadducees' question about the nature of the resurrection (Mt 22$^{23-33}$, Mk 12$^{18-27}$, Lk 20$^{27-40}$). Although this is the second in a group of three questions put to Jesus—by the Pharisees (Tribute to Caesar); by the Sadducees; and by one of the scribes (which is the greatest commandment)— it is not impossible to believe that this incident did take place on a day of theological questioning, and that the answer to one group prompted the next question.[1] Taylor asserts that 'the story preserves genuine tradition of the most primitive kind'.[2] The difference between the three accounts of the Sadducees' question are not very great, and apart from the additional material in Luke 20$^{35-7}$, do not call for detailed consideration in our present study.

The first question to be faced is concerned with the beliefs of the Sadducees. It is well known that this section of Jewish leaders were in active opposition to the Pharisees on this particular question of the resurrection. The Sadducees, although more influential than their numbers might lead us to expect, were at this time losing the struggle with the Pharisees. The rarity of reference to the Sadducees compared with the frequent appearance of the Pharisees in the gospels is in itself evidence of the relative positions of the two parties in the religious life of the time of Jesus. Two aspects of the life of the Sadducees which have been emphasized by recent study is that they were all well-to-do, and they had very little popular following.[3] One consequence of their attitude of opposition to the ruling party of the Pharisees, and their diminishing influence, might well have been to make

---

[1] McNeile, *The Gospel according to St Matthew*, p. 320.
[2] VTM, p. 480.
[3] Moore, *Judaism*, I.70. For reference to the waning influence of the Sadducees, see Branscomb, *Jesus and the Law of Moses*, pp. 11-19.

them exaggerate and even overstate their opinions. Thus it is suggested by some interpreters that although they did not believe in the resurrection, they did believe in immortality, or at least something more than the vague shadowy existence of Sheol.[4] However reasonable it may be conjecture that this must have been so, there is insufficient evidence to assert it. The positive evidence from Josephus and the New Testament is quite strongly in favour of the view that the Sadducees were completely sceptical about anything more than the shadowy existence of the old conception of Sheol.[5] The view of Lightley, that the 'Fragments of a Zadokite Work' show that the Sadducees had advanced to a belief in immortality, is seriously weakened by Charles's opinion that this work shows very considerable variations from common Sadducean views, especially regarding the future life.[6] Therefore it seems best to conclude that underlying the question which the Sadducees put to Jesus was not only disbelief in resurrection, but scepticism about any significant life after death. This view is considerably strengthened by the fact that in his reply Jesus deals with the whole question of future life, and not with a particular expression of it.

There is no doubt that the Sadducees aimed at discrediting the doctrine of the future life held by Jesus in common with the Pharisees, by the method of ridicule. 'The intention is to show that belief in the resurrection leads to an absurdity.'[7] The situation they describe is meant to illustrate a possible outworking of the Deuteronomic law about Levirate marriage (Deut 25[5-6]), which mainly provides for the continuation of a man's family name in the event of his early death. In the supposed situation described by the Sadducees, the fact that the succession of husbands had no offspring, is not strictly relevant to the difficulty, but is included in order to place this unusual course of events within the framework of the Law of Moses. It is a reminder that the Sadducees were almost fanatical in their insistence on the absolute superiority of the Pentateuch. They are, therefore, describing a state of affairs which, however unusual, was certainly

[4] So J. W. Lightley, *Jewish Sects and Parties in Time of Jesus*, pp. 95-6.

[5] Josephus, *History of the Jewish War*, II.8[14]: 'The Sadducees take away belief in the immortality of the soul and in punishments and rewards in Hades.' Cf. *Antiquities*, XVIII.1[3, 4]: 'The doctrine of the Sadducees is that souls die with bodies.' See Acts 23[8].

[6] Lightley, *Jewish Sects and Parties in Time of Jesus*, p. 95; *A. & P.*, II.790-1.

[7] VTM, p. 482.

in accordance with the Law of Moses. The end of their story, which is the question they posed, is framed in a distinctly Semitic form, further suggesting a genuine historical record. 'In the resurrection, when they arise, whose wife will she be?' (Mk 12²³).[8]

The answer of Jesus falls into two parts. The first shows that the Sadducees had misunderstood the scriptures on which they placed so much reliance. The result of this error is that not appreciating the power of God, they had wrongly limited the possibilities of the future life to the known conditions of the present. The second part of our Lord's reply shows that on the basis of the authority they claimed to accept, the Sadducees ought to have seen that there is ground for concluding that there is a future life. The most important point here is that Jesus bases his conviction of future life on the nature of God. We must now consider these two parts of our Lord's reply in detail.

The first part of Jesus' answer contains an implied rebuke to these men who claimed to be so faithful to the scriptures. Like some today, their acquaintance with the letter of the scripture, and ability to quote from it, was not allied to an appreciation of its meaning. In this way they 'knew' the scriptures, yet were far from understanding them. Especially their acquaintance with the books of Moses had not produced in them much appreciation of the power of God. Not realizing that power, they had assumed that to rise again must mean a continuation of the same conditions which now operated in human affairs. The interesting and important feature of this discussion is the comparison that is possible between the teaching of Jesus and that of the rabbis on this issue. There is a similarity between these words of Jesus and those credited to Abba Arika in the early part of the third century A.D.: 'In the world to come there is neither eating nor drinking, no marital relations, no business affairs, no envy, hatred, nor quarrelling; but the righteous sit with their garlands on their heads, enjoying the splendid light of the Divine Presence (Shekinah) as it is said; And they beheld God and they ate and drank (Ex 24¹¹).'[9] While the theme of this statement is closely in agreement with the words of Jesus, it is not thought by scholars

---

[8] RV and RSV omit 'When they arise', but as Taylor shows (VTM, p. 482), the MS evidence is not conclusively in favour of omitting this clause, and 'it is in accord with Mark's style, and is probably original'.

[9] Quoted by Abrahams, Studies in Pharisaism and the Gospels, I.168.

that there is any direct dependence in either direction.[10] It must be allowed by Christian commentators that on this issue Jesus may have said no more than the rabbis.

Yet there remains a significant difference of emphasis, which arises out of our Lord's reference to the 'power of God'. The rabbinical statement refers to the divine Presence, as one of the blessings to be enjoyed in the future bliss. Jesus insists that the basis for believing in this new sort of life is the power of God. There also seems to be a different attitude to the matter of authority, which must always be a most significant question in this regard. 'How do you know that there is a future life, and that in it conditions are radically different from this life?' To that most vital question the rabbis tend to give an answer based on the authority of their sources. Indeed, a good deal of the division of opinion in Jewish thought on this matter arose out of the quotation of conflicting authorities.[11] With Jesus, this is not to be decided by quoting different authorities, but by taking the power of God fully into account. This is closely connected with the way in which Jesus directed the conversation with the rich man who asked about eternal life, to the reality and significance of God.[12] Both incidents show that in the thought of Jesus assurance about the future life arises from the nature of God, not from any other 'authority'; nor firstly from a consideration of human hopes and needs.

On the basis of this reminder of the power of God, Jesus goes on to say something which is closely in agreement with rabbinical teaching. This should occasion no surprise, nor give rise to doubts about the authenticity of this passage. As might be expected, the statement of Jesus contains far less detail than the teaching of the rabbis, but the thought is the same.

This is one of the few passages in which Jesus gives any hint about conditions in the future life. As an explanation of the fact that in the hereafter there are no marital relations, Jesus says 'they are as angels in heaven'. Belief in and speculation about angels is a comparatively late development in Judaism, and there is no need here to go into the many ideas which came to be expressed in connexion with the activities of angels. It is sufficient

---

[10] 'In either direction' because although the words are credited to a third-century writer, it is believed that the ideas involved are much older. Cf. Abrahams, ibid.

[11] Abrahams, loc. cit.          [12] See above, p. 190f.

to note that in Jewish thought, angels were active, personal beings, closely connected with God, often being regarded primarily as divine messengers.[13] Beneath the obvious mythological context of these words 'they are as the angels in heaven', there is the assertion of a life which is fully personal and active, and not any longer limited by the inevitable restrictions of physical bodies. This is the most important feature of the assertion that in the future life there will be no marriage. This may be partly explained on the basis of the fact that angels live for ever and therefore there is no need to arrange for the propagation of the species. But of greater significance is the implication that the limitations in human relations will be removed. This means that in the future life, the closest relationship which here is only possible between two people joined together in marriage, will be possible among all who share this blessed life. Life in heaven is not to be regarded as taking away the joys and blessings of those intimate relationships of earth. What is to be taken away is the limitation which on earth inevitably attaches to close relationship. Admittedly, such a state is in the nature of the case beyond our understanding, for we cannot see how a relationship can be intimate and at the same time shared with an unlimited number of people. Yet this must be the prospect before those who, as Luke's version puts it, 'are accounted worthy to attain to that age and to the resurrection from the dead' (Lk 20[35]).

The second part of the reply of Jesus concerns the fact of a future life, rather than the manner of it, which has been treated in the preceding section. This seems, on the face of it, to be the wrong order, for normally the fact must first be established, then the manner and details can be discussed. The order in which the subject is treated in the gospels is no doubt due to the way Jesus met his questioners and critics on the ground they chose, and then proceeded to give his own distinctive teaching.

It has to be admitted that to a modern method of reasoning and exegesis, this 'proof' is not very satisfying. Quoting from the account of the call of Moses in Exodus 3, our Lord seems to argue thus. 'God described Himself as the God of Abraham, the God of Isaac, the God of Jacob. Now God cannot be the God of the dead, but of the living. Therefore, Abraham, Isaac and Jacob must still be alive, for God is their God.' This does not appear to

[13] For details of contemporary Jewish teaching see Moore, *Judaism*, I.401-13.

have been the plain sense of the passage in Exodus, which emphasizes that the One who called to Moses from the midst of the
Burning Bush was the One who used to be worshipped by these
patriarchs. Thus the only meaning which necessarily attaches to
the term 'The God of Abraham', is 'The God whom Abraham
worshipped'. There is no suggestion in Exodus that these phrases
even imply that the patriarchs are still alive. Indeed, according
to all the evidence, both Moses and those who compiled these
accounts which are credited to him, believed that Abraham,
Isaac and Jacob had gone down into Sheol.

It may be admitted that this is an argument which might well
have been used by the contemporaries of Jesus,[14] and it is possible
that in accommodating himself to the thought of his questioners,
Jesus here employed a rabbinical argument. If this is so, we seem
forced to say that while the argument is unconvincing, its conclusion must be accepted on the authority of the One who
expressed it. The other way of looking at the matter, which may
be more satisfactory, is to consider more carefully the premisses
of the argument outlined above.

Especially the statement 'God cannot be God of the dead' needs
careful consideration. This is not a logical proposition to be
subjected to the verification principle of logical analysis. In a
sense which is far more significant than any truth revealed to
logical argument, this may represent the conviction Jesus had
about God. Perhaps we could put it in other terms by saying that
Jesus could not think of God and of 'dead' people at the same
time. The two terms are virtually contradictory according to the
knowledge of God possessed by Jesus. In other words, this assertion is not based on a peculiar significance attached to the genitive
in the phrase 'of God'; but on the direct knowledge of God
which was the most wonderful reality to our Lord.

It is clear from an examination of the parallel accounts in the
three gospels, that Mark is the most original; but this must not
lead us to neglect the interpretation implied in the variations of
Matthew and Luke. In this quotation from Exodus, Matthew
includes εἰμί, which is omitted by Mark from the LXX reference.
This has the effect of emphasizing ἐγώ εἰμι ('I am'), which may

---

[14] VTM (p. 484) cites as examples rabbinical interpretations of Deuteronomy
11[9] and Numbers 18[28]; cf. Strack-Billerbeck, I.892, for examples of the way
rabbinical thought based belief in life after death on the most unexpected texts—
e.g. Psalm 16[3].

be a specific divine title in the Old Testament. By including the full LXX text Matthew has centred greater interest upon the Being of God. Thus the quotation appears to emphasize the reality of God before it treats the question of the continued existence of the patriarchs. It is the God who is I AM, who is not the God of the dead but of the living. Luke's variation at this point is an additional explanatory phrase at the end of the comment that God is not God of the dead but of the living—'for all live to him' (Lk 20[38]). Easton conjectures[15] that this phrase may show the influence of 4 Maccabees 7[19] and 16[25], but of greater interest than its source is its significance. If our discussion of the meaning of the quotation is on the right lines, we can say that by this additional phrase Luke correctly draws out the implications of the Marcan version. The emphasis, as we have seen, falls upon the nature of God. It is especially as the living God that God cannot be thought of along with the dead, and one necessary aspect of the meaning of the nature of God as the living God is that He is the life-giving God. Possibly 'live' is used here in a wider sense than physical existence. The inference is that God gives 'life' as well as physical existence to men, and it is in relation with God that men truly live. If this is so we are very close to the fundamental Christian basis for belief in future life. It is ultimately because man knows fellowship with God that the Christian believes in future life. It seems allowable to say that at least the germ of this notion can be found in this passage.

On the surface this whole discussion with the Sadducees appears to have a possible universalistic inference. That is, if the hope of life depends on the power of God, and those who have died cannot be thought of as merely 'dead' because God is not God of the dead, there seems to be an implication that all will rise again. But to make this a basis for true universalism, we have to go farther and say that all will eventually come to a blessed future life. This is difficult indeed to assert, especially when account is taken of our Lord's teaching about judgement and about the fate of the lost.[16] It seems better, therefore, to agree with the view of Taylor that 'Jesus is thinking only of the resurrection of the righteous'.[17] The emphasis in the passage is on the continuity of life of the patriarchs who were regarded as righteous men *par excellence*.[18]

---

[15] *The Gospel according to St Luke*, p. 303.    [16] See above, pp. 137-55.    [17] VTM, p. 483.
[18] Note Strack-Billerbeck (I.892) in which the rabbinical author quoted refers to Isaak as righteous ('*mit Isaak, dem Gerechten*').

The other point that is sometimes raised is that in his answer to the Sadducees Jesus did not demonstrate the fact of resurrection but only the fact of immortality. The answer to this difficulty is that in the thought of Jesus and his contemporaries, the two concepts of immortality and resurrection were synonymous. This is assuming that the typically Greek content of the idea of immortality as a quality inherent in the human soul, was not influential among the Jews. We can say resurrection and immortality meant the same thing to Jesus and his contemporaries, providing we recognize that the Jewish view of immortality is not to be equated with the Greek view.[19] In view of this fundamental difference of approach between Jew and Greek, it is better to use the term Resurrection for the Christian hope of the future, leaving the term Immortality to describe that view which sees in the nature of man the hope of man's future destiny.

## II.    THE PARABLE OF THE RICH MAN AND LAZARUS

(Lk 16[19-31]). This story, which appears only in Luke, has several features of particular interest to our subject. It contains the most vivid and colourful account of the after life that is to be found in the teaching of Jesus, in which the situation of both the rich man and Lazarus is described in some detail (16[23-6]). These verses also introduce the idea of the future life as a redressing of that unbalance between virtue and happiness which is one of the most persistent features of human life. Then the second part of the parable refers to the possibility of the need for more tangible proof of the reality of life after death. It is clear from these facts that this parable deserves careful attention in our attempt to understand the teaching of Jesus on the future life.

There is no need for us to enter into a discussion of all the details of this story, as this is fully provided in all the standard commentaries on the third gospel. All the modern discussions refer to the fact that a story of the fate of a rich man and a poor man was current in Egyptian and Jewish circles at the time of our Lord, and that it is likely that this traditional story is the basis for our Lord's parable.[20] The conclusion drawn from the evidence

---

[19] Oscar Cullmann clearly distinguishes the Greek and Jewish views in his '*Immortality of the Soul or Resurrection of the Dead?*'—see esp. pp. 25ff.

[20] J. M. Creed, *The Gospel according to St Luke*, p. 209f. gives a good summary of these Egyptian and Jewish stories as they have been documented by Gressmann.

of these similar stories is not to question the authenticity of the parable's origin in the words of Jesus, but rather to place the emphasis on the latter part of the story. For it is in the application of the story that we have the distinctive teaching of Jesus.

The application in $16^{26-31}$ appears to be specially directed firstly to discouraging the idea of possible movements between the two worlds in the after life. So $16^{26}$: 'Besides all this, between us and you a great chasm has been fixed, in order that those who would pass from here to you may not be able, and none may cross from there to us.' This emphasizes the idea that the division among men made at death, on the basis of their earthly life, is an unchangeable and final division. This incidentally removes any possibility that 'Abraham's bosom' is a description of an intermediate state. This phrase probably indicates a position of close fellowship with the patriarch; it is not a reference to a state which is not really permanent, nor to a part of Hades reserved for the righteous.[21]

The second emphasis which is apparent in our Lord's use of the traditional material is that no external or undeniable proof of the fact of life after death can be found or expected. Thus $16^{31}$: 'If they do not hear Moses and the prophets, neither will they be convinced if some one should rise from the dead.' We shall return to this very significant point later in this discussion. Meanwhile we can notice that the way in which the traditional story is used bears the stamp of authenticity, and there seems justification for asserting that the whole parable is substantially from our Lord himself.

In a most interesting and enlightening discussion of this passage,[22] Manson persuasively argues that the parable is addressed to the Sadducees. He points out that Luke $16^{14-15}$, although ostensibly related to the Pharisees, is much more applicable to the Sadducees,[23] and suggests that this parable, although not described as directed to anyone in particular, is very appropriate as a warning to the Sadducees. As we have already noted, these were the aristocratic class, of whom it might well be said that they lived luxuriously ($16^{19}$). Furthermore, they were not renowned for their concern for the poor, and in particular,

---

[21] So Manson, *The Sayings of Jesus*, p. 299. Cf. Jeremias, *The Parables of Jesus*, p. 130: 'The gulf expresses the irrevocability of God's judgement; hence Jesus knows no doctrine of purgatory'.

[22] *The Sayings of Jesus*, pp. 296-301.     [23] Ibid. pp. 295-6.

believed in living entirely in the present, having no hope of future blessing, nor fear of future condemnation. Thus it is especially appropriate that a Sadducee, having had the most out of life and expecting only a vague existence in Sheol, should be confronted with the reality of his own punishment and the visible felicity of the poor man ($16^{23}$). Also of special significance to the Sadducean position is the assertion at the end of the story that the proof of the fact of future life is found in Moses and the prophets, for these were the very authority accepted by the Sadducees. If we accept this view about the immediate objective of the parable, we can see more clearly the living, historical situation which is its setting. This makes it more feasible to examine the questions which the parable prompts.

The first of these is concerned with the idea of the future life as a setting right of the wrong balance of this life. This idea seems to be plainly stated in $16^{25}$: 'Son, remember that you in your lifetime received your good things, and Lazarus in like manner evil things; but now he is comforted here and you are in anguish.' As we have seen, this is the theme of the traditional story which Jesus appears to be using. For this reason it may be questioned whether we can regard these words as indicating the special position of our Lord. The answer must surely be that Jesus would not have employed this story, from which the idea of redressing the balance cannot be separated, unless he were in general agreement with that idea. Furthermore, this idea of the future life providing a reversal of the conditions of this life is several times expressed in the teaching of Jesus.

Firstly there is the saying: 'Many who are first will be last, and the last first.' This logion is found in different contexts in the synoptic gospels. In Mark $10^{31}$ (par. Mt $19^{30}$) it appears at the end of the words of Jesus in answer to Peter's question about the position of the disciples who had left all to follow him. In this context the saying seems to be 'an appendage derived from a primitive collection'.[24] The saying appears again in Matthew $20^{16}$, at the conclusion of the Parable of the Labourers in the Vineyard. Here it must be regarded as loosely attached, as it seems to arise directly out of the instruction of the owner of the vineyard that payment should begin with the labourer who was hired last; which is not a point of great significance in the

24 VTM, p. 433.

parable.[25] In Luke the saying comes at the end of the Parable of the Door that was shut (13[30]). The conclusion from this evidence is that this saying, which from internal evidence is regarded as 'early', belongs to the genuine teaching of our Lord, although the precise circumstances in which it was spoken cannot be determined. There is little doubt that it had an eschatological meaning for Jesus,[26] and it bears witness to our Lord's teaching that in the future the positions of the present will be reversed.

Another group of sayings which appear to teach the same lesson about a change of fortune in the future life, are the Beatitudes, especially in the Lucan version. We have already pointed out the clearly eschatological emphasis of Luke's version of the Beatitudes.[27] The inclusion of the parallel Woes in Luke 6[24-6] seems to give more emphasis to the idea that in the future the conditions of this life will be reversed. Not only will the poor be recompensed with possession of the rule of God; the rich have already received their consolation so certainly that they may be said to have signed the receipt for it.[28] Again, not only will the hungry be satisfied, but those who are full now will be hungry. The same reversal of conditions is applied to weeping and laughing, and to the favour and hatred of men. In view of these close parallels between the Beatitudes and the Woes, and the absence of the Woes from Matthew, it is not surprising that doubt has been expressed about their authenticity.[29] But it is admitted by those who reject these verses that they 'contain nothing positively inconsistent with Christ's teaching'.[30] If, as we suggest, this idea of a reversal of fortune is in fact found in the teaching of Jesus, this objection cannot be regarded as so weighty.

It is possible that the same idea is present in the saying recorded in Matthew 11[28-30]. Those who labour and are heavy laden are promised rest in the yoke of Jesus, which is easy, and in the carrying of his burden, which is light. The authenticity of this

[25] Jeremias, *The Parables of Jesus*, p. 26.
[26] Ibid. p. 153.
[27] See above, pp. 200-1.
[28] Arndt and Gingrich (*A Greek-English Lexicon of the New Testament*, p. 84): ἀπέχω means 'receive a sum in full and give a receipt for it'. Moulton and Milligan (*The Vocabulary of the Greek Testament*, pp. 57-8) have an interesting collection of samples of this use of ἀπέχω in the papyri.
[29] Easton, *The Gospel according to St Luke*, p. 86: 'The creation of these woes by the earliest church is highly probable—the Beatitudes have only to be reversed.'
[30] Ibid.

saying is also questioned on the ground of close parallels in Ecclesiasticus 51²³⁻⁷; but Manson points out that the contrast between the yoke of Jesus and the yoke of the law is more significant than the similarity between the saying of Jesus and that of Ben Sirach.[31] In addition to the question of authenticity, there is a difference of opinion among scholars whether this promise applies to the present or to the future.[32] While it is very widely recognized that these words express a promise which is amply fulfilled in this present life, there is perhaps a suggestion of a future reward in the idea of 'I will give you rest'. However, the usage of ἀναπαύω and ἀνάπαυσις (verb and noun meaning 'rest') hardly supports this future interpretation.[33] There seems no doubt that these words refer to our Lord's promise to give in this present life rest and refreshment.[34] We therefore conclude that this saying is not an illustration of the principle of recompense in the future life.

Returning to the passage in the story of the rich man and Lazarus which expresses the idea of recompense, a few observations may be made.

In the first place, it is not suggested anywhere in the teaching of Jesus that in the future all earthly positions will be reversed. The promise is always particular in its application. Here it is the poor man, whose name implies his piety,[35] who was reposing in Abraham's bosom. Equally, the rich man is not to be thought of as being miserable in the future just because he had had good things in this life. It was because he had lived in such ease and had neglected his plain duty to one who was near at hand and needing help, that the rich man is condemned to misery in the

---

[31] *The Sayings of Jesus*, p. 186.

[32] Manson (ibid.) takes it with a present meaning: 'In this way of discipleship men find rest unto their souls.' On the other hand Jeremias (*The Parables of Jesus*, p. 154) includes Matthew 11²⁸ among the promises connected with the consummation.

[33] ἀναπαύω means rest from labour, either in sleep (Mt 26⁴⁵, Mk 14⁴¹), or in retreat from the crowds (Mk 6³¹). In Luke 12¹⁹ it obviously has a present implication. ἀνάπαυσις means resting-place in Matthew 12⁴³ and Luke 11²⁴. The use of the words in the remainder of the New Testament supports this 'present' implication.

[34] Moulton and Milligan (*The Vocabulary of the Greek Testament*, pp. 36-7) give interesting examples from the papyri of the late third century A.D., which show that Christians soon began to think of death as leading to 'rest'. These are thus early examples of 'R.I.P.'

[35] Lazarus is the Greek form of Lazar, a shortened form of Eliazar, which means 'he whom God helps'—Manson, *The Sayings of Jesus*, p. 299. Creed (*The Gospel according to St Luke*, p. 211) discusses the possible connexion between this name and Lazarus of Bethany, whose raising from the dead is recorded in John 11¹⁻⁴⁴.

future. There is thus no ground for asserting that the view of the future expressed by Jesus always means that misery here produces happiness hereafter, and happiness here produces misery in the future. The decisive factor is goodness, in the widest meaning of the term.

Secondly, if this is a story addressed to the Sadducees, it implies a severe condemnation of the attitude which cares only about present comforts and happiness on a selfish basis. The scepticism of the Sadducees about the future life led them to disregard their plain responsibility to those whom they could have helped. We have to admit that there is a certain consistency in this attitude, for if this life is all there is, and there is no reward or benefit beyond this life, it is difficult to find a sound reason for doing good to others. Even if virtue is its own reward, the sceptic might well calculate that he will gain more happiness in a consistently self-regarding attitude than in trying to help other people. The scepticism and the hard-hearted attitude of the Sadducees are therefore closely connected; the one engenders and feeds the other. In our own time it is also true that scepticism about the future life can produce a self-regarding attitude. This is not to say that we ought to live a good life because we shall be rewarded for it and avoid an evil life because otherwise we shall be punished. But we have to recognize that without hope of the future life, one of the foundations of morality has been knocked away. Modern scepticism can hardly be said to have produced a satisfactory alternative to this belief as a basis for morality.

Our third comment on the implication of this aspect of our Lord's teaching is in regard to the human need which the idea of recompense meets. It would be foolish to deny that there is a great problem involved in the suffering of the innocent, and the prosperity of the wicked. Full allowance must, of course, be made for the fact that suffering can be creative of great good. Again, we do well to remember that the prosperity of the wicked is often superficial and temporary. We should take full account of the argument that if in this life virtue were always adequately rewarded and evil unfailingly punished, there would be no possibility of a true morality, for the good life would merely mean the prudent life. Yet when full account is taken of these and other arguments which mitigate to some degree the problem of undeserved suffering, that problem still remains. It is not only a problem of peculiar intensity to certain individuals, but a problem affecting a total view of the universe. Can this be regarded as a moral universe if there is no future recompense for the wrongs inflicted on innocent people? A generation like ours, which has seen the unspeakable horrors of mass extermination of political enemies and the ruthless activity of state police, has this question forced upon it. If there is no future life, or if that life cannot be regarded as in any sense restoring the balance of morality, then indeed we are forced to admit that this is plainly not a moral universe. Again, it must be emphasized that these can never be adequate grounds for belief in a future life, for if this were our only argument we may be forced to admit the possibility that there is no justice or equality at the heart of things. But in this view of the future life, which involves the belief that after death the balance between good and evil is justly made, lies hope for millions who in this life have no hope. We cannot avoid the implication that in this view there is the warning of fearful condemnation for those who fail to practise love of God and of their fellow men.

The other main question which arises out of this parable is concerned with 'proof' of the fact of a future life. We have already noticed that this conversation between Abraham and the rich man is not part of the traditional story which Jesus used. In this account of the conversation we have our Lord's teaching about proofs of the future life. Having been surprised at his own destiny, the rich man is commendably anxious to spare his brothers the torment in which he is placed. But Abraham insists that they have sufficient indication of the future life in Moses and the prophets; let them hear them. Further, if they will not be convinced by this teaching, no external sign, not even resurrection from the dead, will convince them.

There are two aspects of our Lord's teaching in this part of the story:

(1) The basis for belief in life hereafter is found in the law and the prophets.

(2) No other 'proof' will convince, if this teaching will not.

In regard to (1) we need only refer to our earlier discussion of the reply Jesus gave to the Sadducees.[36] It is because Moses and the prophets bear witness to the reality of a living God that belief

---

[36] See above, pp. 207-9.

in life hereafter must be held. The basis of the belief is in the nature of God; those who enter into communion with God will know that He is not God of the dead but of the living. The reference to 'the prophets' along with Moses is simply the traditional way of referring to the scriptures which were the only authority accepted by the Sadducees. This reference, as we have seen, does not infer that either Moses or the prophets believed in a future life. The evidence of the Old Testament is against this. But Jesus meant that those who, like the Sadducees, used these scriptures ought to have realized that they did provide a firm basis for belief in life hereafter. This suggests that in the thought of Jesus, those who were able to see the truth of God, and refused to do so, were held responsible for their blindness. Nowadays, it is often supposed that whether or not a man believes in life after death, is purely his own affair. On the other hand, Jesus is very critical of those who, like the rich man, had evidence upon which to base their belief, and simply refused to accept it. The blame attaching to this is, of course, all the greater because disbelief in a future life leads to indifference to the needs of others. Yet it must be admitted that actions do inevitably follow beliefs, and it is dangerous to suppose that we can reject the belief and yet remain free of the selfishness of this rich man. If it seems unreasonable to suppose that a man's disbelief has an effect on his eternal destiny it is perhaps not unreasonable to say that men will be judged on the basis of their activity. In that case, as the activity arises directly out of the belief, a man's belief is seen to be closely related to his destiny. This rich man had been perfectly consistent in his view of life. He had thought that this life is all there is, and therefore one must get the most out of it. Beggars lying at one's door must not get in the way of full enjoyment. But he thought and acted in this way because he did not believe in a real future life; certainly in his conception of the shadowy existence of Sheol, there was no place for inconvenient moral distinctions. But in so far as all these actions and attitudes arose out of his avoidable unbelief, he is accounted responsible for that unbelief. The plain inference is that his brothers will be equally responsible if they continue in his way, for there is ample reason for believing in a future life and for acting on that belief, in the teaching of Moses and the prophets.

(2) In answer to the plea of the rich man that although they

have not been convinced by Moses and the prophets, his brothers would be convinced if someone rose from the dead, Abraham asserts that not even this would 'prove' the reality of the future life. Quite apart from the special significance of this reference to resurrection, we have to recognize here a statement of profound religious significance. In all matters of faith, of which the reality of life hereafter is a good example, there can be no undeniable external proof which clinches the argument beyond all question. However striking or inexplicable any phenomenon may be, men can always find a way of denying its authority if they choose. This teaching of Jesus which is expressed through the imaginary figure of Abraham, is in entire agreement with our Lord's attitude to a request for a sign to validate his ministry (Mk 8$^{11-12}$; cf. Lk 11$^{29-30}$, par. Mt 12$^{38-40}$). The request was refused, for the only sign to be given was, according to the Lucan account, 'the sign of Jonah', which is the preaching of repentance.[37] We can see in our Lord's refusal of a sign his recognition that however remarkable it may be, a 'sign' will not bring anyone to real conviction. There seems to be a necessary element of effort and risk involved in arriving at a deep conviction. The Sadducees were being urged to take this way, and not to suppose that there could be any short cut to a conviction on this matter of faith. Jesus refused a sign because it would not have proved convincing. In the story he teaches that the way to faith is the hard and sometimes slow way by which all worth-while convictions are formed.

There is also in this part of the story a possible reference to our Lord's own resurrection, or to the raising of a man also called Lazarus (Jn 11$^{1-44}$). It is possible that Lazarus in this story is a name deriving from the Johannine account of the raising from the dead of the brother of Martha and Mary. It is remarkable that this parable is the only one in which a proper name is given, and although Lazarus was a common name, the double occurrence is difficult to account for as purely incidental. If there is some relation between this parable and the story of the raising of

[37] Matthew 12$^{38-40}$ interprets the sign of Jonah as a reference to our Lord's coming resurrection. In favour of this being a genuine prediction is the fact that for a prophecy after the event, it is somewhat inaccurate. Jonah was three days and nights in the whale; Jesus was part of three days and two nights in the tomb. But this may have been regarded as an unimportant detail, and it seems best to regard Matthew's version as a gloss, and Luke as nearer the original. Cf. Manson, *The Sayings of Jesus*, pp. 89ff; VTM, pp. 362-3.

Lazarus, it seems likely that the story of the raising of Lazarus, being current at the time of the compilation of the gospel of Luke, has produced these references to the name and to rising again.[38]

A more significant possibility is that Jesus is here referring to his own resurrection. Somewhat in favour of this is the occurrence of ἀναστῇ (Lk 16[31]),[39] for this verb is frequently used in connexion with our Lord's resurrection.[40] It cannot be argued against this view that Jesus was unlikely to have referred to his resurrection beforehand, for there is a strong tradition in the gospels which asserts that our Lord foretold not only his coming suffering and death, but also his triumph.[41] If then Jesus is referring to his own coming victory over death in the words 'not even if one rose from the dead', we have a further insight into his attitude to his resurrection. He apparently was not only facing the certainty of rejection which would end in death on the Cross; also he realized that even his triumph over death would not convince everyone of the reality of life hereafter. This indeed proved to be true to the facts, for while our Lord's rising again was a tremendous new fact proclaimed by the Church, there must have been many who knew it was true, yet refused to accept its implication of resurrection for themselves. Although the early Church did indeed emphasize Christ's resurrection,[42] it did not present this primarily as proof of a future life; the resurrection is the evidence of the power of God and the Messiahship of Christ. This conviction of faith in the future life arises in the mysterious way in which convictions do arise. Especially it arises for a Christian as part of his whole knowledge of and fellowship with Christ. The resurrection of Christ is therefore connected with man's hope of future life, through the acceptance of the gospel, which is declared on the basis of Christ's victory over death. We do not see in Christ's resurrection a proof that man is capable of being raised again. Rather we see in it the signal exhibition of the power of God, which does indeed bring men out of their sins into fellowship

---

[38] So Creed, *The Gospel according to St Luke*, p. 211.

[39] There is a variant reading of ἀπέλθῃ (*syr-sin; lat-vt*), but this is regarded by Creed as less likely than ἀναστῇ—ibid. p. 214.

[40] E.g. Mark 8[31], 9[9-10], 10[34], 16[9], Luke 18[33], 24[7], Acts 17[3].

[41] VTM on Mark 8[31] discusses the implications of these predictions.

[42] See Dodd, *Apostolic Preaching and its Developments*, especially the chart at the end. References to future life are in the form of an emphasis on coming judgement. See Acts 10[42], 1 Thessalonians 1[10].

P

with himself. It is this fellowship which is the basis of the Christian hope of a blessed future life.

We can gather together the main implications of the accounts of the Sadducees' question and the Parable of the Rich Man and Lazarus, as follows:

(1) In both passages there is an emphasis upon the nature of God. In answer to the Sadducees, Jesus makes it clear that because God is God of the living, there must be a future life. In the story of the rich man and Lazarus Jesus teaches that belief in the future life must be found in the words and commands of God contained in the Scriptures. If this evidence fails to convince, neither will any remarkable event, even of men coming back from the dead, convince some people.

(2) The details of the future life are more clearly described in these two passages than anywhere else in the synoptic accounts of the teaching of Jesus. In reply to the Sadducees Jesus indicates that circumstances in the life hereafter are not the same as in this life. Especially, the limitations which inevitably attach to this life, must not be supposed to apply in the future life. In the story of Lazarus, the state of the rich man, who is in torment, and Lazarus, who is in Abraham's bosom, is clearly pictured. Yet we must remember that these descriptions of future happiness and misery are necessarily presented in mythological form. This should also remind us that even in these passages we have no more than hints and suggestions about the details of the life hereafter. Although these passages tell us more than most other records of the words of Jesus, their teaching must be recognized as very sketchy and not in any way detailed.

(3) The story of Lazarus raises the issue of recompense in the future life. Again, we have only hints, not definite teaching. But along with the other words of Jesus which point in the same direction, we have in this story some ground for asserting that in the teaching of Jesus the future life will provide a balancing between good and evil, which is necessary if this world is to be regarded as governed by a righteous God.

# CHAPTER TEN

# CONCLUSION

IN the preceding chapters we have considered all the main terms and passages which are significant in the teaching of the gospels about the future life. It will be helpful if now we sum up the positive conclusions of these necessarily detailed studies in order to see what total picture is presented of this vital part of Christian belief. Having first set out our main conclusions, we must then notice what elements of the teaching of the rest of the New Testament are not included in our summary. When we have considered the significance of any such omissions, we shall finally sum up the positive doctrine of the future life which can be based upon the teaching of Jesus recorded in the synoptic gospels.

First, to summarize the conclusions of our study. In Chapter One we have asserted that the problems of historicity are not insuperable. When full account is taken of the work of form-criticism, the demythologizing interpretation, and typology, we can still assert the possibility of discovering with reasonable accuracy what Jesus said on our chosen subject. This assertion of historicity is vital to the true life of Christian faith, and the exegete of the gospels is bound to state his views on the matter. We claim that we are not seeking an impossibility when we look for the answer to the question: 'What did Jesus teach about the future life?' Also in this first chapter we have considered the relation between the individual and the community in the teaching of Jesus, and concluded that providing we do not assume an exclusively individual approach, we can hope to find an answer to the question: 'What did Jesus say about the future of the individual?' Because the Christian faith is never a purely individual relation between God and man, but also involves man's relationship with his fellows, we have had to beware of thinking only of personal destiny in our investigation. What happens to an individual in life and after death, is closely connected with the destiny of the community.

In Chapter Two we have considered the use of the term 'heaven', and have noticed that there are many rich implications in this word. Although 'heaven' is not used in the synoptic gospels to describe human destiny, the word and its cognates imply the sovereignty of God, and remind us of the exalted conception of God in the teaching of Jesus. We have noticed that some uses of this word are inevitably associated with a view of the universe which is now completely out of date. But we have also attempted to show that this out-moded cosmology does not invalidate the teaching of Jesus. Especially when the term heaven is used in eschatological and apocalyptic passages, the conviction of the divine sovereignty shines through the obscurities of the mythological and figurative terminology. It is also to be noted that these expressions of divine majesty and power are closely linked with the person of our Lord. Jesus not only spoke of the wonders of the powers of God, but claimed that these heavenly powers were now operating in himself.

Chapter Three is a discussion of the term 'heavenly Father,' which we maintain should be considered a genuine title used by our Lord, and which reveals important truths related to our study. In the teaching of Jesus, God the heavenly Father is the exalted, transcendent One, who is above the turmoil and temporalities of this life. It is true that the gospels do not speak of the destiny of the departed as 'heaven'; but as our study proceeds we find that the ground for belief in the future life is man's relationship with God. Because God is our heavenly Father, we can think of our destiny in terms of communion with One whose power extends beyond this earthly sphere. Because God is our heavenly Father we can with confidence believe that 'whenever' or 'whatever' the future life is, it is within the power and love of our heavenly Father. Furthermore, because the heavenly One is our Father, we can be sure that beyond this life, as well as in it, we shall know the love of God, who always treats us as beloved children. In this is involved both loving care and the requirements of obedience to our heavenly Father's will, so that the Christian conception can never lapse into easy sentimentality.

We have also seen that this conception of God as heavenly Father is often closely related to our responsibilities to our fellows. This again points out a significant direction taken by Christian thought about the future. The future is intimately related to the present; life hereafter is closely related to life here and now, for the doing of the will of our Father in heaven means acting in a right way toward our fellows on earth. Thus even in the consideration of the title of 'heavenly Father' we find powerful indications concerning the nature and conditions of life hereafter.

In Chapter Four we have completed our study of the term 'heaven', by considering the phrase 'the kingdom of heaven'. We have concluded that this may well be our Lord's own description of the rule of God. Its significance to our study is that it appears to emphasize the other-worldly, supramundane aspect of the future rule of God, which is to be the background and context of the individual's future destiny. This title introduces the concept of the wider aspect of the sovereignty of God, and when it is linked with that which we have already indicated as the significance of 'heaven' and 'heavenly Father', it presents a clearer picture of the rule of God over the present and the future. The phrase 'kingdom of heaven' reminds us that in our thought about the reign of God we must consider not only the question of time, but also that of quality and sphere. There is an undeniable element of the reality beyond this present life expressed in all these terms which use the word heaven.

Chapter Five, which is a study of the meaning of death in the gospels, produces some interesting conclusions relative to our study. The view of death which is almost universal in the gospels is of its physical nature; there is no development of the concept of spiritual death. Far from minimizing the importance of death, this approach leads to a realistic appreciation of physical death. Especially in the attitude of our Lord to the death of others, we find an awareness of the serious nature of death. This, however, does not mean that Jesus apparently thought that those who died were in a dangerous or tragic situation. In this connexion Jesus says nothing about the state of the dead; his concern is for the people who are bereaved. Yet in helping the sorrowing parents, Jesus reveals his mastery over death. There are no suggestions that the resurrection of Christ is a means to this victory, but this can be explained by the fact that apart from predictions of it, and confused accounts of the resurrection appearances, nothing more is said in the synoptic gospels about our Lord's resurrection.

The attitude of Jesus in face of his own death on the Cross agrees with the realism of the other references to death. Jesus faced physical death and experienced it in a particularly brutal form.  We ought not to hesitate to say that Jesus was afraid of death, for this arises out of our Lord's sensitive awareness of the full meaning of human life, and the horrors of death, which is God's last enemy.  According to the gospel records the death which our Lord tasted for every man was physical death.  The death faced by Jesus was a more horrible and painful form of the death we must face.  Our Lord's attitude to it, and eventual triumph over it, are of the utmost importance to Christian believers.  The Christian gospel does not encourage us to minimize or ignore the inevitable fact of death, nor to be surprised if we find ourselves afraid of it.  We are certainly not to be morbid about it, but we cannot face the opportunities of life unless we have a healthy and realistic view of death.

In Chapter Six we have considered the teaching of Jesus about future judgement.  Although there are many words of our Lord which seem to refer to a coming judgement, some of these are found on closer examination to be related to the present crisis which has arisen because in Jesus the rule of God has begun. Further, even when specific references are made to coming judgement, these are frequently seen to apply to particular groups of people such as the scribes or the Pharisees.  These words of condemnation cannot be applied to all without any distinction whatsoever.

Yet it would be wrong to say that there is no teaching in the gospels about a coming judgement. Jesus plainly taught his disciples that they must expect to be judged, and that the criterion to be applied will be the way in which they had confessed him before men, and expressed in their dealings with their fellows the mercy and forgiveness which had been shown to them by God.  To those who have had no opportunity of responding to the offer of God's love in Christ, the standard of judgement will be the attitude shown to the poor and needy.  When Jesus spoke of coming judgement, his main concern was to encourage his hearers to take steps to avoid the condemnation which they might bring upon themselves.  There is a reality of divine condemnation, but the chief purpose in speaking of it is to show people how it can be avoided.  This always involves attention to the responsibilities of living in society, and it always links present duties with future destiny.  Jesus said very little about the nature and conditions of the divine condemnation, but its chief feature is separation from God.

Chapter Seven is a consideration of the fate of the lost, which is an undeniable part of the teaching of Jesus. The two chief terms used in this connexion are 'Hades' and 'Gehenna'. 'Hades' is used in the sense in which the meaning of Sheol developed in later Jewish thought, and is closely associated with death. We have tentatively suggested that the chief emphasis is upon the idea of extinction, rather than everlasting punishment. The same conclusion is suggested by our consideration of the uses of 'Gehenna'. In connexion with the idea of fire, we find the two notions of the sovereignty of God, and destruction; and it is natural to put these two together and suppose that the sovereignty of God can be expressed in the extinction of life just as much as in its origin.

In considering both 'Hades' and 'Gehenna', we have noticed that there is no suggestion that the destiny of the lost is due to the inscrutable decree of God. Jesus made it plain that man has the opportunity of responding to the offer of the love of God, but he can refuse that offer. This means that if he is lost man's destiny depends on his own choice.

Also arising out of this view that God offers to man the gift of eternal life is the implication that if a man refuses the gift, he has no life in himself and must perish. This concept of the destiny of the lost does not imply an easier or more acceptable view of eternal destiny. Even if we say that the concept of eternal punishment is a figurative way of speaking of final annihilation, the latter is harder, not easier. The greatest tragedy that can happen to a living soul capable of eternal bliss is that he should, through his refusal of divine help, cease to be. Compared with this, the idea of punishment leading eventually to restoration would be much more acceptable. But there is no trace in the teaching of Jesus of the idea of remedial punishment.

Chapter Eight is in many ways the most important part of this study because in it we have considered, in its most direct form, the teaching about the future life. Under the terms of the Kingdom, regarded as a gift and as that which can be entered, and eternal life, we have considered the positive teaching of the gospels about the life hereafter. The conclusions of this consideration can best be set out as follows:

(1) The future life is a certainty which is unquestionably accepted by Jesus.

(2) The present life is closely linked with the future. There is no support in the teaching of Jesus for the idea that an emphasis on the future life inevitably leads to neglect of the present. This is particularly clear when the conditions for entry into, or reception of, the Kingdom of God are considered.

(3) These conditions can be summed up as genuine obedience to God, expressed in discipleship and faith in Christ, and worked out in love of our neighbours. There is great stress in the teaching of Jesus upon the necessity for sincere obedience, in deed as well as word, and this obedience must be given to Christ as the one sent by God. The same point is put negatively in the form of warnings against causing oneself or others to stumble.

(4) Although the chief emphasis is on the criteria by which possession of the gift of eternal life will be obtained, we find several indications of the nature of the future life. It is a life in community and a life of activity, in which the responsibility of the saved to judge the world is especially mentioned. The most important fact is presented in a somewhat oblique fashion, by reference to the idea of the coming age which has been inaugurated by the life and ministry of Jesus. Those who respond to the offer of the gospel, those who accept Christ's yoke and enter into faith in him, are those who become sons of the coming age. This is the most distinctive feature of the teaching of the gospels, for it emphasizes the supreme significance of Jesus Christ in his own teaching about the future life.

(5) It is clear from the teaching of Jesus that the future life is not regarded as the inevitable possession of everyone. Throughout our Lord's teaching there is a continual emphasis upon the urgent need to meet the conditions which God requires for entry into eternal life. There may be faint signs of one aspect of universalism in the possibility that in the end even disobedient Jewish leaders may enter the rule of God. But there is nothing in the gospels to suggest that this is inevitable. The teaching of Jesus clearly envisages the possibility that some will remain outside. But our Lord's chief energies were directed to persuading his hearers to fulfil the conditions laid upon them so that they may have God's gift of eternal life.

Chapter Nine, in which we have considered the specially

important passages dealing with the Sadducees' question, and the Parable of the Rich Man and Lazarus, contains some conclusions which confirm what has already been asserted from other points of view, and also some conclusions which are novel.

The conclusion to which witness is borne in almost every part of our study is that belief in the future life depends on belief in God. To the Sadducees Jesus said God is not a God of the dead, but of the living; in the story of the rich man and Lazarus, it is made clear that the basis for this belief is in the Scriptures which contain the word of God. There is no doubt that this is a vital element in our Lord's thought. Man's future destiny does not depend on himself, his needs or qualities, but upon God. Again and again, when Jesus was discussing the future life, he turned the attention of his hearers to thought about God the Father. This is why Jesus so fully confirmed the traditional belief in the resurrection; it expressed his conviction that in communion with God, men could indeed rise to everlasting life.

The second conclusion in this chapter is a confirmation and clarification of the description of the state of the saved and the lost. Lazarus is described as enjoying a blessed life in Abraham's bosom, while the rich man is in a state of misery. We must take account of the figurative terms used in these descriptions of a happy and tragic destiny; but they express a truth. Those who inherit the life hereafter can look forward to an inexpressibly happy state. It is typical of the gospel narratives that they do not give detailed accounts of this happy state; but the hints and suggestions support the belief that God has prepared wonderful things for those who inherit eternal life.

In the account of the answer Jesus made to the Sadducees' question is also the suggestion that the life hereafter is richer than this life because it is freed from the limitations which necessarily belong to bodily existence. This is not expressed in the form of unrealistic predictions of the conquest of the material, but in the form of enriched and extended human relations. The life of heaven is not depersonalized; it is a personal life of far richer significance than this life can ever be. In this, as in the former view of the blessedness of the future life, it must be remembered that we have only suggestions and hints in the teaching of Jesus. It is contrary to the evidence of the synoptic gospels to describe the life hereafter in much detail; we are left to walk by faith, yet by a faith inspired and upheld by the glimpses of the future life which we can find in these stories. It is in agreement with this that we can also say there are no detailed descriptions of the state of the lost in the teaching of Jesus. To be lost is clearly a tragic and unwelcome destiny to fall into; but beyond this, very little can be inferred about the state of the lost.

The third conclusion reached in this chapter introduces a new element into the teaching. This is the idea that the future life entails a setting right of the injustices of this life. This teaching which we have asserted is found in the story of the Rich Man and Lazarus, is also supported by other words of Jesus. In this story this is not the only important truth that is expressed; nor are we encouraged to suppose that all sufferings, deprivations and hardships will be recompensed with good, and that all prosperity, comfort and happiness will be recompensed with evil. Moral and spiritual issues must be brought into consideration. But it would be wrong to ignore this part of our Lord's teaching. It can be granted that the idea of future compensation for wrongs suffered in this life is open to serious misunderstanding. Chief among its dangers are the toleration of wrongs inflicted on others because those who suffer them will be rewarded in the future; and undue attention to future rewards, which may divert our own interest from the responsibilities and duties of this life. But if this idea of future recompense is seen in the setting of the total teaching of Jesus, these dangers are avoided. No follower of Jesus could ever seriously think that the certainty of future reward for the oppressed can be an excuse for inactivity on their behalf by those who are able to help them. We have also noticed more than once in this summary that in the thought of Jesus the present life, with its privileges and responsibilities, is intimately connected with the future life. Jesus taught men to love and serve God here and now, and also to expect greater joys in the future. It is not an overstatement to say that according to his teaching, those who do not find God here, have little hope of finding him hereafter. There is the further consideration in regard to this idea of recompense, that it does provide some help in the difficult problem of divine providence and the inequalities and sufferings experienced by many undeserving people. We must admit that the conception of future recompense is never a complete answer to the problems of the suffering of the righteous, but it is difficult to see how the idea can be left out of any serious attempt to grapple with this matter. There is, therefore, good use to be made of the idea of future recompense, provided it is not overstated or over-elaborated.

This, then, is the picture presented by our study of the teaching of Jesus about the future life. The picture contains no elements which need cause any surprise to anyone conversant with the general outline of Christian teaching on this subject. In fact, the very simplicity and lack of complicated developments are significant factors in this presentation of the belief of our Lord. The elements of simplicity and directness point to an original view which has been developed by later thought in the New Testament and in subsequent Christian history. In the outlines of the doctrine which we have discovered in the words of Jesus, we have the marks of a primitive tradition. These assertions which we have summed up are based upon a tradition which is prior to theological speculation. This is not to infer that such theological speculation is necessarily wrong; in fact much of the developed thought of the New Testament on this subject is an inevitable outworking of the basic facts given in the teaching of Jesus. Nevertheless, it is of the greatest importance to notice that we can claim to have discovered a primitive tradition about the future life, which can reasonably be credited to Jesus himself.

There are two particular emphases in the later New Testament teaching which are not present in the synoptic account of the teaching of Jesus, which are particularly important in this connexion. These are the Pauline teaching of the resurrection of Christ as the basis for Christian certainty of future life; and the Johannine emphasis upon Eternal Life as a present possession, obtained through faith. There can be no doubt that these assertions are two dominant themes of the thought of the Christians of the New Testament period, whenever the question of the future life is raised. If it were true, as some scholars are never tired of asserting, that the Church read back its own ideas into the mind of Christ, these features of New Testament thought ought to appear in the teaching of Jesus.

When we look again at the picture of that teaching which has emerged from our study of the gospels, we find that neither of the above emphases is at all prominent. In particular, the idea of basing the hope of future life on the resurrection of Christ is not mentioned at all in the synoptic gospels. As we have seen, there is no attempt to expound the significance of the resurrection of Jesus in relation to hope of the future life. This must be regarded as important evidence of the independence and authenticity of the gospel records. The situation regarding the Johannine teaching about Eternal Life is substantially the same, although this idea is present in the synoptic accounts. There is, however, no doubt that if the Fourth gospel is compared with the synoptic gospels, one is immediately forced to notice the different emphasis given to Eternal Life. In the Fourth gospel it is repeatedly mentioned; in the synoptics the term is used quite sparingly. These facts have implications for the historical trustworthiness of both the synoptics and John. On the one hand, if we can assume that the Fourth gospel expresses ideas which were current in some communities in the Church, we notice that the term 'eternal life' is not an invention of this gospel, nor of the Church in the area in which the gospel originated. The term is found in the authentic teaching of Jesus, which means that in this respect at any rate, there is a noticeable relation of dependence between the Fourth gospel and the synoptics. This must have the effect of increasing our respect for the historical basis of John. On the other hand, the great difference of emphasis between the synoptics and John argues for the independence of the former. There is no discernible attempt to modify the teaching of Jesus on eternal life to approximate more closely to the Johannine emphasis.

Thus on the basis of these studies, we can add further evidence in support of the independence and trustworthiness of the synoptic accounts. In its basic simplicity and lack of elaboration the synoptic record of the teaching of Jesus on the future life stands forth as the view of one who was utterly convinced on the issue.

We do well to heed the warning implied in the absence of detail in this picture. While the implications of the rest of the New Testament are firmly based on the teaching of Jesus, it is significant that nowhere in the New Testament do we find detailed descriptions of the future state. The simplicity of the picture presented in our Lord's teaching is not only due to a primitive stage, at which complicated developments are not to be expected. It is even more due to the inherent nature of the subject. The absence of detailed description is a warning against our wanting too many details. It is a sound Christian judgement which asserts together the absolute certainty of life hereafter and the inadvisability of describing that life in too much detail. We can claim to have shown the reality of the teaching of Jesus on this subject. It is not true to say, as is sometimes asserted, that we can learn practically nothing about the future life from the teachings of Jesus. We have shown that there is a surprisingly large amount of material available. But again it must be emphasized that this material bears witness to the undeniable reality of life hereafter; it does not say very much about the details of that life.

The subject we have been considering in this study is clearly of vital interest to every living person. There is no one to whom these matters have no significance, for all men are mortal, and the question of what happens after death is important to all. Furthermore it is true to say that this subject has a great fascination for a large number of people. The questions which can be asked are numberless; some of them, such as 'Where are people after they die?' or 'Do the dead know what is going on in the earthly scene that they have lately vacated?', cannot be answered. We cannot properly ask such questions because we cannot know enough about the future life to make the question sensible. But the fact that some questions are beyond understanding, does not mean that all are; some questions seem inevitable, and must be faced in whatever way the subject of the future life is being considered.

When these legitimate questions are considered, they appear to be reducible to three. These are questions which we are bound to say men have a right to ask, and to which some answer must be given in such a study as this. Therefore, to conclude our study, we propose to attempt to answer three basic questions about the future life, to which any ordinary person is entitled to expect an answer. These questions are:

(1) Is there a future life?
(2) How is it obtained?
(3) What is it like?

It must be emphasized that in the answers which conclude this study, the basis of reply is the teaching of Jesus recorded in the first three gospels. This is not an attempt to present the full Christian teaching on these questions, but only to make what appears to be a reasonable reply based on the teaching of Jesus. That this teaching is absolutely fundamental to the Christian position cannot be denied. There can indeed be no more important issue in this, or any other doctrine, than 'What did Jesus say about it?' On this issue a Christian must never be over-dogmatic, but equally he must not be silent.

First, then, it is asked: 'According to the teaching of Jesus, is there a life beyond the grave?' As we have considered the various aspects of the matter presented in gospel teaching, it has become increasingly obvious that one can reply to this question: 'Of course there is a future life!' The certainty of it shines from almost every page of the gospels. Yet it may be questioned whether this is an adequate reply; certainly, to make it convincing, more must be said. Especially, we seem under a necessity to say *why* Jesus so firmly believed in a future life, for we shall not be convinced on the matter merely because Jesus said so. Why did he say so?

The answer to this subsidiary question has two parts. In the first place, Jesus believed in a future life because he was born at a time when this belief had at last emerged as a general possession of spiritually minded people. This is a fact not to be lightly passed over, for at no other stage in the development of human thought was there a more developed or deeply religious conviction on this matter than among the Jews of the time of Christ. The Jewish faith had only gradually emerged from the mists of belief in the shadowy unreality of existence in Sheol. Soon after the days of Jesus, the Jewish faith became increasingly grotesque and nationalist in its vindictiveness. It is no small thing to be able to say that Jesus accepted the contemporary belief in a future life, for this is, apart from the Christian belief, the most fully developed of all men's groping after the truth of this mystery.

In the second place, it is to be recognized that Jesus was no mere imitator of other people's opinions. Some contemporary opinions he plainly rejected. Why did he retain this one? The answer can only be that belief in a future life is completely in accord with our Lord's whole view of life. This is not something added to his faith, which might be regarded as detachable from the rest. At this point it is necessary to notice the connexion between our Lord's faith in God the Father, and his belief in the future life. The two convictions are not only equally clear and inseparable from the total view of life held by Jesus; belief in the future life arises out of belief in God. This was the emphasis repeatedly made by Jesus; when you are unsure about future life, think about God. This was, of course, the way in which this belief had developed among our Lord's contemporaries. They believed in a resurrection because they believed in God. Our Lord's belief in a future life is immeasurably firmer than that of his contemporaries, because his belief in, and knowledge of God was so much more significant.

Thus, belief in the life hereafter, being to Jesus a necessary implication of belief in God, cannot be detached from a total view of our Lord. If you accept the teaching of Jesus, you must of necessity accept this part of it. It is undeniable that this is an authoritative position, for it does not finally rest on argument. But in this matter argument and reason have repeatedly demonstrated their inability to reach a certain conclusion. We are therefore forced back upon this dogmatic position. Jesus believed in a future life. This belief was an integral part of his total life, thought and action. Especially he knew a communion with God which made this belief a certainty. On the authority of one who above all others knew God, we are bound to say that the very basis of faith in God demands and confirms this belief.

The second question which men have a right to ask is: 'According to the teaching of Jesus, how is future life obtained?' Perhaps the question should first be clarified, in so far as it assumes there must be some conditions to be fulfilled if life hereafter is to be gained. This assumes that not everyone will inevitably attain to future life. But in this assumption the question is certainly right, for according to the teaching of Jesus, not everyone will enter into eternal life. We must here leave aside the question about what happens to those who fail to enter into eternal life. This is indeed an important and necessary question, but in our present discussion it cannot be given a prominent place.

We assume then, that there are conditions to be met, if we are to obtain everlasting life. These conditions are related to God, to Christ, and to our fellow men. It is noticeable that they are very close indeed to the conditions under which we can be reconciled to God in the present life. Thus we are to live in dependence upon God, as obedient children of our heavenly Father. We must become disciples of the Lord Jesus Christ and begin in discipleship the life of full Christian faith. This life of faith must be expressed in right relations with our fellow men. The way is not easy, and Jesus never suggested that all will find it in the end. But the way is possible to all, for all are capable of responding to the call of Christ and living by faith in him. We notice the very important place given to our Lord himself in this teaching. He not only points the way; he himself is the way. For the stringent demands of these conditions of entry into the life hereafter can only be met by dependence on Christ. Not only for the present, but also for the future, Jesus points to himself as the only means by which men can come to God, and in communion with God find fullness of life in the present and in the future.

A further aspect of these conditions of obtaining eternal life which receives continual emphasis, is the responsibility in this present life, which must be met. There is absolutely no foundation whatever in the teaching of Jesus for the idea that concern about the future life is a legitimate excuse for neglect of the duties and opportunities of the present. Nothing could be farther from the position stated by our Lord than the old criticism that Christianity teaches men to neglect their present duties in order to obtain everlasting happiness. The position is the complete opposite; unless we practise the love of God and faith in Christ in new, loving, understanding relationships with our fellows, we shall not enter into life.

It will be remembered that in our exposition of the story of the Great Assize, we came to the conclusion that this represents our Lord's view of the destiny of those who have had no chance of responding to his offer of the grace of God. For such the standard which will determine their inheritance of eternal life is their treatment of the poor and needy. It is necessary here to reaffirm that this does not mean a lower or easier standard; nor does it reduce the high demand of Christ's teaching. In any case, if we have heard of Christ and have had an opportunity of accepting his offer of forgiveness, we shall be judged by our acceptance or rejection of him. And to those to whom this standard does apply it does not present an easy alternative, but a very rigorous standard of behaviour and charity.

This aspect of the teaching of Jesus which emphasizes the conditions to be fulfilled in order to obtain everlasting life, cannot be stressed too much. If there is one aspect of the matter which is supremely important, it is that Jesus urges upon all men the absolute necessity of meeting the conditions required to obtain future blessedness. All too often this subject is discussed in a theoretical manner; it is something to argue over; something to question and wonder about. But to Jesus this was not so. To him the subject of the future life demands more than discussion and speculation. It demands action; the action of faith and love, of service to God and man. Here our Lord's teaching must jolt us out of our theoretical remoteness. The most important question of all is not 'What can I think about eternal life?' but 'What must I do to inherit eternal life?'

The last of these three basic questions is: 'What is heaven like?' It must be recognized that this is a sphere of thought in which unlimited speculation is possible. In view of the dangers of extravagant speculation, it is well firstly to assert the reticence and vagueness of our Lord's teaching on this subject. Especially because the teaching of Jesus is presented in figurative form, as all such teaching must be, we must avoid interpreting the symbols and figures in too realistic a way.

It goes without saying that Jesus taught us to think of the future life as a life of great happiness. This happiness is increased by the activity which is involved; but most of all, it is perfected in the communion between God and men which is the true life of heaven. This is expressed most clearly in the conception that the Kingdom of heaven, which is brought into operation by our Lord, is a state in which believers are brought together in Christ. To belong to the Kingdom of God is to be a son of the coming age, and this inevitably means a close relation with him in whom the coming age has dawned. Equally, the idea that belief in the future life must be based upon belief in God, gives rise to the conviction that life in the future must be life with God.

This aspect of our Lord's teaching leads to the conviction that the future life is in one sense a continuation of this life. The communion with God in Christ which we know here, will be continued and fulfilled in fuller communion hereafter. Yet in another sense the future life is a new beginning, a separation from this life. This arises when we consider our Lord's teaching about the future life as a recompense for the inadequacies and sufferings of this life. For those who have suffered many pains,

Q

disappointments and injuries in this life, it is a great comfort to know that Jesus promised a new beginning for those who have lived in faith and love toward God.

Another aspect of our Lord's teaching which must be remembered is that he assumed that life hereafter is a life in community, a life of fellowship. This means not only that we may hope to be reunited with our own families and friends, but that we shall find our fullest joy in the widest fellowship of the redeemed. How this can be must remain a mystery, for we do not know how close fellowship can be separated from the limitations with which it is inevitably associated in our present experience.

It is good that we should end this study on the note of mystery, for many aspects of the future life remain a mystery beyond our grasp. There are many questions which we shall continue to ask, to which we can certainly find no answer in the teaching of Jesus. For a fully developed Christian view we have to take into account the teaching of the rest of the New Testament, and subsequent Christian thought. Yet however fully the doctrine of the future life may be developed, there always remains the central core of the teaching of our Lord. This teaching reminds us of the mystery lying beyond our understanding. But more than this, it assures us that there is absolute certainty of life hereafter for all who believe in Christ and serve their fellow men in the life of faith. We have it on the authority of one who is for Christians the living Word of God; we have this assurance, that is, on the basis of faith. But this is not a second-rate or temporary basis; it is indeed the only possible ground a Christian can have or desire. In this, as in all our relationships with God, we stand only by faith. Faith reaches out to Christ, and in him we apprehend the truth of life and death. Thus in him, though many things are not plain, all that matters is firm and secure.

# BIBLIOGRAPHY

I. Abrahams, *Studies in Pharisaism and the Gospels* (two series), (Cambridge, 1917 & 1924).

W. F. Arndt & F. W. Gingrich, *A Greek-English Lexicon of the New Testament and Other Early Christian Literature* (Cambridge and Chicago, 1957).

C. K. Barrett, *The Holy Spirit and the Gospel Tradition* (London, 1947).

H. W. Bartsch, *Kerygma and Myth* (E.T. R. H. Fuller), (London, 1953).

*The Book of Offices of the Methodist Church* (London, 1936).

B. H. Branscomb, *Jesus and the Law of Moses* (London, 1930).

F. Brown, S. R. Driver, & C. A. Briggs, *A Hebrew and English Lexicon of the Old Testament* (Oxford, 1906).

R. H. Charles, *The Apocrypha and Pseudepigrapha of the Old Testament* (2 vols), (Oxford, 1913). (Cited as *A. & P.*)

J. M. Creed, *The Gospel according to St Luke* (London, 1930).

O. Cullmann, *Christ and Time* (E.T. F. V. Filson), (London, 1951).

O. Cullmann, *Immortality of the Soul or Resurrection of the Dead?* (English edn), (London, 1958).

G. Dalman, *The Words of Jesus* (E.T. D. M. Kay), (Edinburgh, 1902). (Cited as *Words*.)

D. Daube, *The New Testament and Rabbinic Judaism* (London, 1956).

J. G. Davies, *He Ascended into Heaven* (London, 1958).

W. D. Davies & D. Daube, *The Background of the New Testament and its Eschatology, Studies in Honour of C. H. Dodd* (Cambridge, 1956).

C. H. Dodd, *The Apostolic Preaching and its Developments* (London, 1936).

C. H. Dodd, *The Coming of Christ* (Cambridge, 1951).

C. H. Dodd, *New Testament Studies* (Manchester, 1953).

C. H. Dodd, *The Parables of the Kingdom* (3rd edn), (London, 1936).

B. S. Easton, *The Gospel according to St Luke* (Edinburgh, 1926).

B. S. Easton, *The Gospel before the Gospels* (London, 1928).

*Encyclopaedia Britannica* (11th edn), (Cambridge, 1910-11).

*The Expository Times* (Edinburgh, 1889-). (Cited as *E.T.*)

R. N. Flew, *Jesus and His Church* (London, 1938).

T. F. Glasson, *The Second Advent* (London, 1945).

C. L. W. Grimm & J. H. Thayer, *A Greek-English Lexicon of the New Testament* (Edinburgh, 1901).

J. Hastings, *A Dictionary of Christ and the Gospels* (2 vols), (Edinburgh, 1906 & 1908).

I. Henderson, *Myth in the New Testament* (London, 1952).

A. Huck, *Synopsis of the First Three Gospels* (9th edn, revised by H. Lietzmann; E.T. F. L. Cross), (Oxford, 1954).

J. Jeremias, *The Eucharistic Words of Jesus* (E.T. A. Ehrhardt), (Oxford, 1955).

J. Jeremias, *The Parables of Jesus* (E.T. S. H. Hooke), (London, 1954).

*The Journal of Theological Studies* (London/Oxford, 1900-). (Cited as *JTS*).

K. E. Kirk, *The Apostolic Ministry* (London, 1946).

G. Kittel, *Theologisches Wörterbuch zum Neuen Testament* (Stuttgart, 1933-). (Cited as *TWNT.*)

W. G. Kümmel, *Promise and Fulfilment* (E.T. D. M. Barton), (London, 1957).

M.-J. Lagrange, *Évangile selon Saint Marc* (Paris, 1929).

M.-J. Lagrange, *Évangile selon Saint Matthieu* (Paris, 1927).

G. W. H. Lampe & K. J. Woollcombe, *Essays on Typology* (London, 1957).

J. W. Lightley, *Jewish Sects and Parties in the Time of Jesus* (London, 1925).

T. W. Manson, *A Companion to the Bible* (Edinburgh, 1946).

T. W. Manson, *The Sayings of Jesus* (London, 1949—reprinted from *The Mission and Message of Jesus*, London, 1937).

T. W. Manson, *The Teaching of Jesus* (Cambridge, 1931).

A. H. McNeile, *The Gospel according to St Matthew* (London, 1938).

*The Methodist Hymn-book* (London, 1933).

J. Moffatt, *The Theology of the Gospels* (London, 1912).

C. G. Montefiore, *Rabbinic Literature and Gospel Teachings* (London, 1930).

C. G. Montefiore & H. Loewe, *A Rabbinic Anthology* (London, 1938).

G. F. Moore, *Judaism in the First Centuries of the Christian Era* (2 vols), (Cambridge, Mass., & London, 1927).

J. H. Moulton & W. F. Howard, *A Grammar of New Testament Greek* (Vol. II), (Edinburgh, 1929).

J. H. Moulton & G. Milligan, *The Vocabulary of the Greek Testament* (London, 1914-29).

R. Otto, *The Kingdom of God and the Son of Man* (E.T. F. V. Filson & B. Lee-Woolf), (London, 1938).

A. S. Peake, *A Commentary on the Bible* (2nd edn), (London, 1937).

A. Plummer, *The Gospel according to St Luke* (*International Critical Commentary*, 4th edn), (Edinburgh, 1901).

A. Richardson, *A Theological Word Book of the Bible* (London, 1950).

Daniel-Rops, *Jesus in His Time* (E.T. R. W. Millar), (London, 1955).

K. L. Schmidt, H. Kleinknecht, K. G. Kuhn, & G. von Rad, '*Basileia*', article from Kittel's *TWNT* (E.T. H. P. Kingdon), (London, 1957). (Cited as *Basileia*.)

C. Ryder Smith, *The Bible Doctrine of the Hereafter* (London, 1958).

H. L. Strack & P. Billerbeck, *Kommentar zum Neuen Testament aus Talmud und Midrasch* (5 vols), (Munich, 1926-8).

V. Taylor, *The Formation of the Gospel Tradition* (London, 1935).

V. Taylor, *The Gospel according to St Mark* (London, 1952). (Cited as VTM.)

V. Taylor, *Jesus and His Sacrifice* (London, 1937).

L. D. Weatherhead, *Psychology, Religion and Healing* (2nd edn), (London, 1952).

# INDEX OF SUBJECTS AND NAMES

Abba Arika, 205
Abraham, 207, 208, 211, 214, 216, 218, 220, 227
Abrahams, I., 103, 205, 206
Accursed, 134f
Age (The), 83, 150f, 180-3, 226.
Agony in the Garden, 48
Angels, 25, 33, 36, 78, 134, 206f
Anna, 71, 178
Annihilation, 77f, 225
Antiochus Epiphanes, 148
Apocalyptic, 22
Aramaic, 13
Ark, 30
Arndt, W. F., 108, 110, 119, 133, 137, 174, 183, 189, 213
Ascension, 14, 29

Baptism, 46
Baptism of Jesus, 22f
Baptism of John, 32
Baptist, John the, 9, 11, 23, 32, 56, 63, 67, 75, 87, 105, 150, 152
Barrett, C. K., 9, 23, 42
Barth, K., 7
Bartsch, H. W., 6
Beatitudes, 199f, 213
Billerbeck, P., see Strack, H. L.
Birds of heaven, 20, 52
Black, M., 81
Blessed, 133f., 198-202
Blessed One, 50
Branscomb, B. H., 203
Briggs, C. A., 19
Brown, F., 19
Bultmann, R., 6, 7, 126, 175

Canaan, 134
Charles, R. H., 23, 24, 73, 84, 109, 125, 135, 146, 147, 148, 159, 184, 200, 204
Childlike trust, 174-6
Clement of Alexandria, 103, 197
Clouds of heaven, 28
Conditions of condemnation, see Standards of judgement
Copernican cosmology, 1, 8, 38
Cosmology, 6, 8, 22, 38, 222
Creed, J. M., 121, 210, 214, 219
Cross, 17, 29
Crucifixion, 14, 93
Cry of dereliction, 99-100
Cullmann, O., 95, 96, 97, 100, 150, 151, 180, 181, 182, 184, 185, 210

Dalman, G., 31, 32, 34, 35, 37, 42, 49, 50, 51, 64, 67, 122, 150, 181, 187, 189, 197
Daniel-Rops, 97, 99
Daube, D., 5
Davies, J. G., 5
Day of judgement, 108f
Dead (the), 74
Death and baptism, 93
Death, figurative sense, 102-6
Death of Jesus, 91-102, 223f
Demythologizing, 1, 221
Dodd, C. H., 17, 25, 26, 60, 63, 65, 72, 113, 114, 116, 117, 130, 131, 152, 178, 179, 184, 219
Doddridge, P., 142
Driver, S. R., 19

Earth, 21, 37
Easton, B. S., 2, 20, 30, 37, 87, 157, 160, 193, 209, 213
Eleazar, 148
Eliazar, 214
Elijah, 21, 29, 73, 74
Elizabeth, 199
*Encyclopaedia Britannica*, 69
Enoch, 73
Enoch, First book of, 152, and see scriptural index
Entry into the kingdom of heaven, 169-77, 226, 233f
Esau, 134
Eschatology, 22, 72, 158
Eternal fire, 134, 150f
Eternal life, 15, 178-98, 229f
Eternity, 182f
Eucharist, 20, 168-9, see also Last Supper
Existentialism, 7
*Expository Times*, 4
Ezra, Fourth book of (2 Esdras), 74, and see scriptural index

Faith, 194
Farrer, A., 4
Fire, 144, 150-4, 225
Flew, R. N., 9, 33, 64
Forgiveness, 41, 54, 107, 128f
Form criticism, 1f, 3, 221
Fourth gospel, 15, 29
Fuller, R. H., 6

Gamaliel, 42
Gates of Hades, 141-3

Gehenna, 143-50, 225
Gethsemane, 94, 98f
Gingrich, F. W., see Arndt, W. F.
Gift of the kingdom, 159-69
Glasson, T. F., 165
Glory, 46
God and man, 53f
Grave, 78f, 83
Gressmann, 210
Grieve, A. J., 88
Grimm, C. L. W., 95

Hades, 137-43, 225
Ham, 134
Hastings, J., 70
Heaven, 8, 16-39, 135, 222
Heavenly Father, 38, 40-55, 222
Hell, 8, 135, 137, 143-50
Henderson, I., 7
Herford, T., 200
Herod the Great, 70, 75
Herod the Tetrarch, 75
Hezekiah, 141
Historicity, 1-6, 221
Holmes, S., 159
Holy Spirit, 2, 23, 41f, 52, 60
Howard, W. F., 73
Huck, A., 62, 130

Isaac, 207, 208
Immortality, 210
Individual and community, 1, 9-15, 157, 221
Intermediate state, 211

Jacob, 103, 134, 207, 208
Jairus, 80, 85, 86, 87, 88, 90, 178
Jairus' daughter, 80-7
James, 29, 46, 86, 94
Japheth, 134
Jeremias, J., 11, 62, 63, 70, 113, 114, 115, 116, 117, 118, 119, 120, 121, 122, 123, 124, 125, 126, 127, 128, 129, 130, 131, 132, 151, 152, 160, 173, 174, 211, 213, 214
Job, Book of, 76
Johanan ben Zakkai, 79
John the Evangelist, 167, 184, 229, 230
John bar Zebedee, 29, 46, 86, 94
Jonah, 94, 218
Joseph, 103
Josephus, 76, 204
Joshua ben Levi, 28
Journal of Theological Studies, 67
Joy in heaven, 36
Judas, 165
Judge, 130
Judgement, 165f, 185, 224 (see also Last Judgement)

Keble, J., 21
Kingdom of God, 9f, 16, 56-68
Kingdom of heaven, 16, 38, 56-68, 156, 177, 223
Kirk, K. E., 4
Kittel, G., 123, 180, 181, 184
Kuhn, K. G., 156, 157
Kümmel, W. G., 17, 60, 61, 72, 73, 74, 130, 131, 158, 159, 165, 166, 167, 169, 172

Lagrange, M-J., 187, 188, 189, 191, 192, 193
Lampe, G. W. H., 4, 5, 6
Last Judgement, 110, 113, 126f, 131
Last Supper, 11, 47f, 164, 167-9
Lawyer's question, 194-7
Lazar, 214
Lazarus (in the parable), 110, 138, 210, 214, 218, 220, 227, 228
Lazarus of Bethany, 167, 214, 218, 219
Lightley, J. W., 204
Lightning, 30
Loewe, H., 86
Lord's Prayer, 22, 40f, 48
Lost coin, 13f
Lost sheep, 13f
Lost son, 13f, 37

Maccabees, Fourth book of, 148-9, and see scriptural index
Malkuth shamayim, 64, 156
Malkutha dishmaya, 64
Manson, T. W., 3, 20, 22, 35, 43, 44, 45, 47, 48, 103, 104, 110, 130, 131, 138, 160, 165, 166, 172, 187, 188, 195, 200, 211, 214, 218
Martha, 167, 218
Mary of Bethany, 218
Mary the mother of Jesus, 72, 183, 199
Massacre of the Innocents, 70
McNeile, A. H., 21, 22, 61, 62, 63, 67, 70, 79, 108, 109, 139, 142, 145, 172, 174, 181, 193, 199, 201, 203
Melchizedek, 4
Messianic Age, 77, 87, 105, 122, 130, 142, 157, 186
Messianic banquet, 125, 165, 167
Methodist Book of Offices, 137
Methodist Hymn-book, 21, 37, 95, 142
Milligan, G., 108, 109, 137, 199, 213, 214
Miracles
   Centurion's servant, 81, 90
   Deaf mute, 19
   Epileptic lad, 90
   Jairus' daughter, 80-7
   Loaves, 19
   Paralytic, 12
   Son of the widow of Nain, 87-90

Miracles—*cont.*
Syro-Phoenician's daughter, 81
Woman with an issue of blood, 8of
*Mishpat,* 109
Mitchell, P. C., 69
Moffatt, J., 40
Montefiore, C. G., 43, 86, 200
Moore, G. F., 22, 28, 35, 55, 79, 203, 207
Moses, 147, 170, 205, 207, 208, 212, 216, 217, 218
Moulton, J. H., 73, 108, 109, 137, 199, 213, 214
Mythology, 1, 6-8

Names written in heaven, 35f
Nathan, 42
Nestlé, E., 62
New Israel, 9
*Nunc Dimittis,* 71f

Origen, 191
Otto, R., 65, 66, 186

Parables
Door that was shut, 213
Drag net, 10, 60, 111, 151
Good Samaritan, 195f
Great Supper, 75, 111, 124-6
Guest without a wedding garment, 125
Hid Treasure, 60
Importunate widow, 127f
Labourers in the vineyard, 60, 111, 126f, 212
Merchant seeking goodly pearls, 60
Pharisee and tax collector, 20, 62
Prodigal son, 37, 75, 105
Rich fool, 117f
Rich man and Lazarus, 210-20
Servant given authority, 118f
Sheep and Goats (The Great Assize), 123, 130-5, 234
Talents (Pounds), 10, 111, 121-3
Two sons, 173
Unforgiving servant, 60, 110f, 128-30
Unfruitful fig tree, 76, 111, 119f
Unjust steward, 120f
Unrighteous servant, 110
Ten virgins, 60, 111, 123
Wheat and Tares, 10, 60, 111, 151
Wicked Husbandmen, 63, 75, 110, 114-16, 169
Waiting servants, 116f
Parables of judgement, 110-36
Paradise, 147
Parousia, 46, 117, 123, 164
Passion of Christ, 92
Passover, 11
Peake, A. S., 88
Perish, 76ff

Persecution, 153, 161
Pharaoh, 103
Philip, 103
Pilate, 76, 93, 101, 130
Plummer, A., 20, 72, 87, 88, 161, 193
Pollock, T. B., 95
Prayer, 19f
Punishment, 110
Punishment, eternal, 135, 225

Rankin, O. S., 43
Realized eschatology, 17, 66, 114
Recompense, 212-16, 220, 228f
Repentance, 76, 184, 218
Resurrection, 203-10, 218, 227
Resurrection of Christ, 14, 22, 29, 219, 223, 229f
Rich young ruler, 12, 176f, 188-94
Richardson, A., 43
Robinson, H. W., 22

Sadducees' question, 203-10
Samuel, 5
Sanhedrin, 34, 115
Sasse, H., 180
Satan, 30, 61
St Paul, 2, 106, 143, 147, 165, 167, 168, 229
Saul, 83
Schmidt, K. L., 3, 127
Schniewind, J., 6, 7
Schweitzer, A., 74
Sermon on the Mount, 13, 44, 48
Seventy, 34f
Shem, 134
*Sheol,* 83, 137-43, 204, 208
Signs in heaven, 25f
Simeon, 70, 71, 72
Simeon ben Eleazar, 42
Simeon ben Yokhai, 42
Simon Peter, 12, 14, 33, 34, 43, 44, 54, 86, 92, 94, 128, 134, 142, 164, 179, 197, 212
Sky, 18, 19-21, 38
Sleep (describing death), 82-4, 89
Smith, C. Ryder, 18, 75, 82, 83, 109, 110, 115, 134, 142, 147, 152, 186
Socrates, 96
Solomon, 84
Solomon, Wisdom of, 135, 138, 139, and see scriptural index
Son of Man, 4, 25f, 28-30, 72, 77, 92, 117f, 127, 130f, 201
*Sōph^erîm Tractate,* 156
Sovereignty of God, 24, 26, 64, 79, 225
Standards of Judgement, 113, 116, 120, 129-33, 136, 139-41, 146
Strack, H. L., 73, 156, 208, 209
Streeter, B. H., 67

Taste death, 72f

Taylor, Vincent, 2, 3, 10, 20, 21, 23, 24, 25, 26, 28, 33, 41, 46, 47, 62, 74, 77, 80, 81, 82, 84, 86, 90, 92, 94, 95, 99, 101, 108, 133, 144, 151, 157, 164, 165, 167, 171, 175, 178, 189, 190, 191, 193, 195, 197, 198, 203, 204, 205, 208, 209, 212, 218, 219

Ten Commandments, 191f

Tetragrammaton, 43

Thayer, J. H., 95

Theudas, 21

Thornton, L. S., 4

Torment, 110

Tower of Siloam, 76

Transfiguration, 29, 73, 92

Treasure in heaven, 31f, 162f

Two ways, 187

Typology, 4-6, 221

Universalism, 209, 226

Universe, Hebrew idea of, 18

Weatherhead, L. D., 82

Weddings and funerals, 69

Weiss, J., 97

Wellhausen, J., 108

Wesley, C., 37, 202

Widow's mite, 12

Widow of Nain, 74, 105

Will of God, 52f

Woes, 200f, 213

Wood, H. G., 14

Wrath of God, 129

Zadokite Fragments, 204

# SCRIPTURAL INDEX

## OLD TESTAMENT

*Genesis*
$1^{14}$...18
$1^{15}$...18
$1^{17}$...18
$1^{20}$...18
$6^{17}$...18
$7^{11}$...18
$8^{2}$...18
$9^{20-7}$...134
$11^{4}$...18
$19^{24}$...153
$27^{28}$...18
$27^{29}$...134
$50^{5}$...103

*Exodus*
3...207
$3^{2}$...153
$14^{22}$...133
$14^{29}$...133
$20^{18}$...153
$20^{22}$...19
$24^{11}$...205
$32^{32}$...35

*Numbers*
$18^{28}$...208
$19^{11-22}$...78

*Deuteronomy*
$6^{4}$...156
$8^{3}$...178
$11^{9}$...208
$25^{5-6}$...204
$26^{15}$...19
$30^{15}$...185
$30^{19}$...185

*Joshua*
$10^{11}$...19

*Judges*
$5^{20}$...18

*1 Samuel*
$2^{10}$...19
$28^{3}$...83

*1 Kings*
$2^{19}$...133
$8^{30}$...19
$17^{1}$...21
$17^{17-24}$...88
$18^{38}$...29
$18^{45}$...18

*2 Kings*
$4^{32-7}$...88
$7^{2}$...18

*Ezra*
$1^{2}$...19

*Job*
$26^{13}$...18
$38^{17}$...142

*Psalms*
$8^{3}$...18
$16^{3}$...208
$16^{11}$...185
$18^{9}$...19
$24^{3-4}$...200
$25^{13}$...189
$37^{11}$...200
$42^{2}$...94
$42^{5}$...94
$43^{5}$...94
$78^{23-4}$...19
$104^{4}$...154
$110^{1}$...28, 133
$122^{4-5}$...166
$139^{8}$...137

*Proverbs*
$2^{19}$...185
$13^{22}$...189

*Isaiah*
$5^{7}$...63
$9^{1-2}$...102
$13^{9-10}$...26
$14^{10}$...138
$14^{13-15}$...138
$38^{10}$...142
$64^{1}$...19, 23
$66^{1}$...19
$66^{24}$...143, 144, 151

*Jeremiah*
$5^{29}$...110
$8^{13}$...120
$21^{8}$...185
$24^{4-6}$...110
$51^{15}$...18

*Ezekiel*
$1^{1}$...24
$13^{9}$...36
$32^{17-32}$...138

*Daniel*
$7^{13}$...28
$7^{18}$...159
$7^{22}$...159
$9^{26}$...110
$12^{1}$...35
$12^{2}$...184

*Hosea*
$9^{7}$...110
$9^{10}$...120
$13^{14}$...143

*Jonah*
$4^{9}$...94

*Micah*
$7^{1}$...120

*Zechariah*
$9^{9}$...28

## APOCRYPHA AND PSEUDEPIGRAPHA[1]

*3 Maccabees*
$5^{51}$...141

*Tobit*
$3^{15}$...189
$14^5$...180

*Sirach (Ecclesiasticus)*
$28^{2-5}$...200
$37^2$...94
$45^{19}$...154
$47^{23}$...84
$51^{23-7}$...214

*Wisdom of Solomon*
$1^{14}$...159
$5^{16}$...159
$12^3$...134
$12^{11}$...134
$13^9$...180
$16^{13}$...141
$18^4$...180

*Prayer of Manasses*
9...20

*Martyrdom of Isaiah*
$2^2$...30
$2^7$...30

*1 Enoch*
$5^7$...189
$25^4$...110
$27^1$...148
$27^{2-3}$...147
$37^4$...184, 190
$40^9$...184, 190
$58^3$...190
$65^7$...184
$100^5$...83

*Testament of Levi*
$18^6$...24

*Testament of Judah*
$24^2$...24

*Sibylline Oracles*
$3^{46-9}$...189

*Assumption of Moses*
$10^{10}$...146
$12^4$...180

*2 Enoch*
$50^2$...189, 190

*2 Baruch*
$22^1$...23, 24

$54^{21}$...180
$59^5$...147
$59^{10}$...147
$69^4$...180

*4 Ezra (2 Esdras)*
$6^{25}$...180
$6^{26}$...73
$7^{31-2}$...84
$7^{36}$...147, 153
$7^{38-44}$...109
$7^{102-5}$...109

*Psalms of Solomon*
$1^5$...21
$3^{16}$...184, 190
$9^9$...185
$13^9$...184, 190
$16^{1-2}$...141

*4 Maccabees*
$7^{19}$...209
$12^{11-12}$...153
$16^{25}$...209

*Pirke Aboth*
$1^{5a}$...147
$1^{12}$...200
$5^{24}$...147

## NEW TESTAMENT

*St Matthew*
$2^{13}$...77
$2^{16-18}$...70
$3^2$...56
$3^{10}$...152
$3^{12}$...150
$3^{16}$...23
$4^4$...81, 178
$4^{16}$...102
$4^{17}$...56
$4^{19}$...11
$5^1$...13
$5^2$...13
$5^3$...57, 199, 201
$5^{3-12}$...199
$5^5$...200
$5^7$...131, 200

$5^8$...200
$5^{10}$...59
$5^{12}$...31
$5^{16}$...40, 52
$5^{18}$...22
$5^{19}$...59
$5^{20}$...59, 170
$5^{21}$...108, 170
$5^{22}$...108, 144, 145, 150, 170
$5^{23}$...170
$5^{24}$...170
$5^{27}$...170
$5^{28}$...170
$5^{29}$...77, 144, 171
$5^{30}$...144, 171
$5^{31}$...71
$5^{34}$...22, 31

$5^{45}$...40, 52
$5^{48}$...40
$6^1$...13, 40, 53
$6^2$...13
$6^3$...13
$6^5$...13
$6^6$...13
$6^9$...40, 52
$6^{10}$...17, 22
$6^{12}$...128
$6^{14}$...40, 41, 54, 131
$6^{15}$...131, 132
$6^{20}$...31, 32
$6^{26}$...20, 40, 52
$6^{32}$...40, 52
$7^1$...107
$7^2$...107

[1] The works indexed here are listed in the order in which they are found in R. H. Charles, *A. & P.*

*St Matthew—cont.*

$7^{7-11}$...41
$7^{11}$...40, 52
$7^{13}$...187
$7^{14}$...186, 187, 188
$7^{19}$...151, 152
$7^{21}$...40, 48, 52, 131, 132, 172, 173
$7^{22}$...131, 172
$7^{23}$...172
$7^{24-7}$...172
$8^{5-13}$...81
$8^{11}$...58
$8^{12}$...118
$8^{20}$...20
$8^{22}$...103
$8^{25}$...77
$9^4$...82
$9^{11}$...125
$9^{18}$...80, 178
$9^{19}$...80
$9^{23}$...86
$9^{23-6}$...80
$10^{2-4}$...11
$10^6$...77
$10^7$...59
$10^8$...104
$10^{15}$...108
$10^{16}$...161
$10^{20}$...48
$10^{28}$...98, 144
$10^{29}$...48
$10^{32}$...40, 48, 54, 131
$10^{33}$...40, 48, 132
$10^{39}$...77
$10^{42}$...77
$11^5$...105
$11^{11}$...10, 57
$11^{12}$...59
$11^{16}$...70
$11^{19}$...125
$11^{22}$...108
$11^{23}$...21, 138, 139
$11^{24}$...108
$11^{25}$...22
$11^{27}$...48
$11^{28}$...214
$11^{28-30}$...213
$12^{14}$...77
$12^{18-20}$...109
$12^{26}$...61
$12^{28}$...60, 62
$12^{32}$...109, 182
$12^{36}$...13, 108, 109
$12^{37}$...13
$12^{38-40}$...218
$12^{41}$...109
$12^{42}$...109
$12^{43}$...214
$12^{50}$...40, 45, 48, 53

$13^{11}$...57
$13^{22}$...181
$13^{24}$...60
$13^{24-30}$...10
$13^{30}$...111
$13^{31}$...57
$13^{33}$...57
$13^{39}$...180
$13^{40}$...180
$13^{42}$...118, 151
$13^{43}$...44
$13^{44}$...60
$13^{45}$...60
$13^{47}$...10, 60
$13^{48}$...10, 111
$13^{49}$...180
$13^{50}$...118, 151
$13^{52}$...59
$14^{22}$...174
$15^{13}$...40, 48, 53
$15^{22-8}$...81
$15^{23}$...71
$15^{24}$...77
$16^3$...21
$16^{16}$...179
$16^{17}$...40, 48, 53
$16^{18}$...138, 141, 142
$16^{19}$...33, 59
$16^{21}$...142
$16^{25}$...77
$16^{28}$...72
$18^1$...56
$18^{1-5}$...174
$18^3$...59, 175
$18^4$...59
$18^6$...172
$18^{6-9}$...171
$18^8$...150, 151, 171
$18^{8-10}$...144
$18^9$...144, 150, 171, 186
$18^{10}$...40, 48, 78
$18^{14}$...40, 48, 53, 77
$18^{18}$...33
$18^{19}$...40, 48, 54
$18^{23}$...60
$18^{23-35}$...128
$18^{27}$...71
$18^{34}$...110, 111, 129
$18^{35}$...40, 48, 54
$19^{13-15}$..175
$19^{14}$...57
$19^{16}$...188
$19^{17}$...190
$19^{19}$...191
$19^{21}$...31, 32
$19^{23}$...57, 176
$19^{24}$...62
$19^{27}$...164
$19^{28}$...164
$19^{29}$...197

$19^{30}$...126, 212
$20^1$...60
$20^{1-16}$...124, 126
$20^{14}$...111, 126
$20^{16}$...126, 212
$20^{21}$...46, 133
$20^{23}$...45, 46, 133
$21^9$...199
$21^{19}$...183
$21^{25}$...32
$21^{28-31}$...173
$21^{31}$...62, 125, 172, 174
$21^{32}$...63
$21^{33-43}$...63, 114
$21^{35}$...115
$21^{39}$...75
$21^{41}$...77, 110, 115
$21^{43}$...63, 159, 169
$22^1$...125
$22^{1-14}$...124
$22^2$...125
$22^6$...75
$22^7$...111
$22^{11-14}$...125
$22^{13}$...118
$22^{23-33}$...203
$22^{37-40}$...195
$22^{44}$...133
$23^{3-32}$...146
$23^9$...40, 48, 53
$23^{13}$...59
$23^{15}$...144, 145
$23^{22}$...31
$23^{23}$...109
$23^{27}$...78
$23^{33}$...144, 146
$23^{34}$...75
$23^{37}$...75
$23^{39}$...199
$24$...24, 123
$24^3$...180
$24^9$...75
$24^{27}$...30
$24^{29-31}$...25
$24^{44}$...118
$24^{45-51}$...118
$24^{51}$...111, 118, 119
$25^1$...60
$25^{1-13}$...123
$25^{10}$...124
$25^{11}$...111, 124
$25^{12}$...111
$25^{14-30}$...10, 121
$25^{21}$...122
$25^{23}$...122
$25^{26}$...111
$25^{28}$...111
$25^{30}$...111, 118, 122
$25^{31-46}$...130
$25^{32}$...131

*St Matthew—cont.*
$25^{34}$...10, 130, 133, 199
$25^{40}$...131
$25^{41}$...112, 133, 150, 151
$25^{45}$...131
$25^{46}$...110, 112, 135
$26^{17-19}$...11
$26^{26}$...199
$26^{29}$...10, 44, 45, 47, 48, 159, 166
$26^{38}$...94
$26^{39}$...48
$26^{42}$...48
$26^{45}$...214
$26^{52}$...77
$26^{53}$...48
$26^{63}$..81, 179
$26^{64}$...27, 50
$27^{34}$...73, 99
$27^{38}$...133
$27^{45-50}$...99
$27^{50}$...99, 101
$27^{63}$...179
$28^{18}$...22
$28^{20}$...180

*St Mark*
$1^{10}$...23
$1^{15}$...10, 16, 56, 60
$1^{16-18}$...9
$1^{17}$...11
$1^{24}$...77
$1^{29-31}$...12
$2^{1-12}$...12
$3^{13-19}$...11
$3^{29}$...183
$3^{35}$...45, 53
$4^{11}$...57
$4^{19}$...181
$4^{30}$...57
$4^{30-2}$...10, 20
$4^{31}$...57
$4^{38}$...77
$5^{21-4}$...80
$5^{23}$...178
$5^{25-34}$...12
$5^{35}$...81
$5^{35-43}$...80
$5^{36}$...82
$5^{38}$...82
$5^{39}$...86
$5^{40}$...84
$6^{14-29}$...75
$6^{31}$..214
$6^{41}$...19, 199
$7^{24-30}$...81
$7^{34}$...19
$8^{11}$...21, 218
$8^{12}$...218
$8^{27-33}$...92

$8^{31}$...219
$8^{35}$...77
$9^{1}$...17, 72
$9^{2-8}$...73
$9^{9}$...92, 219
$9^{10}$...219
$9^{14-29}$...90
$9^{22}$...77
$9^{26}$...74, 90
$9^{30-2}$..92
$9^{35}$...126
$9^{37}$...175
$9^{41}$...77
$9^{42}$...144, 172
$9^{42-8}$...171
$9^{43}$...144, 151, 171, 186
$9^{43-8}$..144
$9^{45}$...144, 171, 186
$9^{47}$...144, 171, 186
$10^{13-16}$...175
$10^{14}$...57, 175
$10^{15}$...13, 175
$10^{17}$...186, 188
$10^{17-31}$...33
$10^{18}$...190
$10^{21}$...31, 32, 33, 192
$10^{23}$...176, 186
$10^{24}$...57, 176
$10^{25}$...62, 176
$10^{27}$...177
$10^{28}$...164
$10^{29}$...197
$10^{30}$...182, 197
$10^{31}$...126, 212
$10^{32}$...92, 173
$10^{32-4}$...92
$10^{34}$...219
$10^{35-45}$...14
$10^{37}$...46, 133
$10^{38}$...93
$10^{39}$...46, 93
$10^{40}$...46, 133
$10^{45}$...93
$11^{9}$...199
$11^{10}$...157
$11^{14}$...183
$11^{21}$...134
$11^{24}$...41
$11^{25}$...40, 41, 54
$11^{28-30}$...33
$11^{30}$...32, 33
$12^{1-11}$...63, 114
$12^{8}$...115
$12^{9}$...77, 110, 115
$12^{12}$...115
$12^{18-27}$...203
$12^{23}$...205
$12^{27}$...81, 179
$12^{28-34}$...195
$12^{29-31}$...191, 195

$12^{40}$...108
$12^{41-4}$...12
13...24
$13^{13}$...131
$13^{24-7}$...25
$13^{31}$...22
$13^{33-7}$...116
$14^{1}$...93
$14^{3-8}$...12
$14^{12-6}$...11
$14^{18}$...11
$14^{22}$...199
$14^{25}$...17, 44, 47, 166
$14^{29}$...14
$14^{34}$...94
$14^{41}$...214
$14^{44}$...93
$14^{45}$...93
$14^{61}$...50
$14^{62}$...27, 133
$15^{2}$...130
$15^{33-7}$...99
$15^{34}$...97, 99
$15^{37}$...99, 101
$15^{39}$...101
$15^{44}$...101
$16^{9}$...219
$16^{11}$...81

*St Luke*
$1^{32}$...183
$1^{33}$...157, 183
$1^{42}$...199
$1^{54}$...183
$1^{55}$...183
$1^{70}$...182
$1^{79}$...102
$2^{13}$...18
$2^{25-35}$...70
$2^{29}$...71
$2^{34}$...73
$2^{35}$...73
$2^{36}$...81, 178
$2^{36-8}$...71
$3^{17}$...150
$3^{21}$...23
$4^{4}$...178
$4^{25}$...21
$5^{37}$...77
$6^{14-16}$...11
$6^{20}$...57, 199, 201
$6^{20-3}$...199
$6^{24-6}$...200, 213
$6^{28}$...134
$6^{35}$...50, 52
$6^{37}$...71, 107
$6^{38}$...107
$6^{46}$...172
$6^{47-9}$...172
$7^{2-10}$...81, 90

*St Luke—cont.*
7$^{11-17}$...87
7$^{12}$...141
7$^{14}$...88
7$^{15}$...74, 88
7$^{22}$...87, 105
7$^{28}$...57
7$^{29}$...63
7$^{32}$...70
8$^5$...20
8$^{21}$...53
8$^{24}$...77
8$^{40-2}$...80
8$^{49-56}$...80
9$^2$...59
9$^{24}$...77
9$^{27}$...72
9$^{28-36}$...29
9$^{47}$...82
9$^{48}$...175
9$^{54}$...29
9$^{60}$...103
10$^1$...34
10$^3$...161
10$^{15}$...21, 138
10$^{17}$...30, 35
10$^{18}$...30
10$^{20}$...34
10$^{25}$...194
10$^{25-8}$...195
10$^{28}$...81, 179
11$^2$...17
11$^4$...128
11$^{13}$...40, 41, 52
11$^{20}$...60
11$^{24}$...214
11$^{29}$...218
11$^{30}$...218
11$^{42}$...109
11$^{44}$...78
12$^4$...98, 144
12$^5$...144
12$^8$...54
12$^{13-15}$...118
12$^{13-21}$...32
12$^{16-21}$...117
12$^{19}$...214
12$^{21}$...163
12$^{22-30}$...160
12$^{22-34}$...161
12$^{24}$...52
12$^{30}$...52
12$^{32}$...159, 160
12$^{33}$...31, 32, 160, 161, 162, 163
12$^{35-8}$...116
12$^{37}$...116, 117
12$^{40}$...118
12$^{41}$...119
12$^{41-8}$...118

12$^{46}$...110, 118, 119
12$^{47}$...119
12$^{48}$...119
12$^{50}$...97
12$^{56}$...21
13$^{1-5}$...76
13$^3$...77, 78
13$^5$...77, 78
13$^{6-9}$...76, 119
13$^7$...111
13$^{12}$...71
13$^{20}$...57
13$^{24}$...186, 188
13$^{28}$...58, 118
13$^{30}$...126, 213
13$^{33}$...77
13$^{35}$...199
14$^{15}$...157
14$^{16-24}$...124
14$^{21}$...111
14$^{24}$...73
15...13, 77
15$^7$...36
15$^{10}$...36
15$^{11-32}$...37
15$^{13}$...81, 178
15$^{24}$...75, 105, 179
15$^{30}$...62
15$^{32}$...75, 105, 179
16$^{1-13}$...120
16$^8$...120, 181, 182
16$^9$...121
16$^{10}$...121
16$^{11}$...121
16$^{14}$...211
16$^{15}$...211
16$^{16}$...59
16$^{17}$...22
16$^{19}$...211
16$^{19-31}$...210
16$^{23}$...138, 110, 212
16$^{24}$...151
16$^{25}$...212
16$^{26-31}$...211
16$^{28}$...110
16$^{31}$...211, 219
17$^{24}$...30
17$^{26}$...30
17$^{27}$...77
17$^{28}$...30
17$^{29}$...77, 153
18$^1$...128
18$^{1-8}$...109, 124, 127
18$^8$...127, 128
18$^{9-14}$...20, 62
18$^{15-17}$...175
18$^{16}$...57
18$^{18}$...12, 188
18$^{19}$...190
18$^{22}$...31, 32

18$^{24}$...57, 176
18$^{25}$...62
18$^{30}$...182, 197
18$^{33}$...219
19$^{1-10}$...12
19$^{10}$...29, 77
19$^{11-27}$...121
19$^{17}$...122
19$^{19}$...122
19$^{22}$...111
19$^{24}$...111, 122
19$^{47}$...77
20$^4$...32
20$^{9-18}$...63, 114
20$^{16}$...77, 110, 115
20$^{27-40}$...203
20$^{34}$...181, 182
20$^{35}$...207
20$^{38}$...209
20$^{47}$...108
21...24
21$^{16}$...75
21$^{22}$...109, 110
21$^{25-8}$...25
22$^{7-13}$...11
22$^{18}$...17, 166
22$^{19}$...168
22$^{28}$...161
22$^{28-30}$...159, 163
22$^{69}$...27
23$^{40}$...108
23$^{42}$...157
23$^{46}$...99, 101
24$^5$...179
24$^7$...219
24$^{20}$...108
24$^{21}$...14
24$^{23}$...179
24$^{30}$...199
24$^{50}$...199
24$^{51}$...199

*St John*
3$^5$...56
8$^{52}$...72
9$^{32}$...182
11$^{1-44}$...214, 218
11$^{25-7}$...167
18$^{37}$...130

*Acts*
2$^{27}$...142
2$^{31}$...142
2$^{32}$...14
2$^{34}$...133
3$^{10}$...141
7$^{55-6}$...133
9$^{24}$...141
10$^{42}$...219
12$^{10}$...141

*Acts—cont.*
$16^{13}$...141
$17^3$...219
$23^8$...204
$26^{19}$...18

*Romans*
$9^{16}$...50
$12^{14}$...134
$14^7$...75

*1 Corinthians*
$6^2$...165
$11^{23-6}$...168
15...167
$15^{55}$...143

*2 Corinthians*
$11^2$...123

*Galatians*
$1^4$...182
$4^4$...182

*Ephesians*
$3^9$...182
$5^{31-2}$...123

*Colossians*
$1^{26}$...182

*1 Thessalonians*
$1^{10}$...219

*1 Timothy*
$6^{17}$...182

*2 Timothy*
$4^{10}$...182

*Hebrews*
$1^{13}$...133
$2^9$...72
$6^5$...73
7...4
$13^{12}$...141

*James*
$3^6$...143

*1 Peter*
$1^{15}$...50

*Revelation*
$3^5$...35
$13^8$...35
$17^8$...35
$20^{12-15}$...35

# INDEX OF GREEK WORDS

ἀναπαύω, 214
αἰών, 150, 180–3
ἀπολλύμεθα, 77
ἀπολύω, 71
αὐλητής, 86

βάσανος, βασανισταί, 110, 129
βασιλεία, 160

γέεννα, 143
γῆ, 21

δεσπότης, 71
διχοτομήσει, 119
δοῦλος, 71
δυνάμεις, 139

ἐγώ εἰμι 208f
ἐκδικεῖν, ἐκδίκησις, 109
ἐξέπνευσεν, 101
ἔσχατα, 22
ἔφθασεν, 60
ἕως θανάτου, 94–7

ζάω, 81, 178f
ζωή, 171, 178f
ζωὴ αἰώνιος, 178–88

Θεός, 50
θύρα, 187

κατακρίνειν, κατάκρισις, 110
καταράομαι, 134
κατεγέλων 86
κληρονομέω, 188f
κόλασις, 110
κρίμα, 108
κρίνειν, 107
κρίσις, 108f
κριτής, 127
κύριος, 88, 120, 122

μακάριος, 199
μεθ'ὑμῶν, 166

νεκρός, 74

οὐρανός, etc., 18–21

παλινγενεσία, 164
πάντα τὰ ἔθνη, 131
παρακούσας, 82
προάγω, 173f
πύλη, 187

σκάνδαλα, 170–2